Korea Yearbook

Korea Yearbook

Volume 2

Politics, Economy and Society

2008

Edited by

Rüdiger Frank
James E. Hoare
Patrick Köllner
Susan Pares

TUTA SUB AEGIDE PALLAS · 1683 ·

BRILL

LEIDEN • BOSTON
2009

This book is printed on acid-free paper.

ISSN 1875-0273
ISBN 978 90 04 16979 1

PRINTED IN THE NETHERLANDS

CONTENTS

PREFACE

Another year of major developments in Korea has passed since the publication of the first volume of this yearbook. A new president has been elected in Seoul, South Korea's North Korea policy has changed, progress has been made on the denuclearisation issue, and news about a looming new famine in North Korea has caught worldwide attention. The *Korea Yearbook 2008* aims at improving understanding of these and other issues. It offers the reader both a series of broad survey articles which provide overviews of developments in South and North Korea in the period between April 2007 and late March 2008, together with chronologies, and refereed articles that provide in-depth analysis of specific topics. The fact that the book is published by a leading European publishing house and edited by scholars residing in Austria, Germany and the United Kingdom emphasises the energy and dedication of the Korean Studies community in Europe. It provides an important balance and addition to other publications on related topics that mostly originate in the United States.

We hope that this book series will establish itself as a reference tool for students and researchers who need a continuous source of information on contemporary Korean affairs. Needless to say, the value of this publication will grow with the number of its editions. This is the second volume of the yearbook *Korea: Politics, Economy and Society*, and the third (2009) volume is already under preparation. Developments on the Korean peninsula during the coming months promise to be interesting and should stimulate a flow of comment and analysis. Scholars from all over the world are invited to submit contributions to the refereed section. We are particularly interested in current papers dealing with North Korea and inter-Korean affairs as well as papers which analyse Korean affairs from a comparative perspective; for more information, please contact the editors at www.brill.nl/koyb.

The editors are supported by two associate editors, Charles Armstrong in the United States and Sung-hoon Park in the Republic of Korea. The editors would like to thank the dedicated staff at Brill, in particular Albert Hoffstädt and Patricia Radder, who have supported this publication with enthusiasm from its inception to the final printing process. Special thanks go to Siegrid Woelk at GIGA who did a fine job (again) by making the yearbook look the way it does. A final word on transcription and the rendering of Korean names: in the *Korea Yearbook* we basically follow the conventions of the McCune-Reischauer system. The only exceptions regard international renderings of well-known geographical units and Korean words (Pyongyang, Seoul, won) and also individuals (e.g. Syngman Rhee, Park Chung-hee, Kim Dae-jung, Kim Il Sung, Kim Jong Il). Moreover we respect the way Koreans transcribe their personal names, where these transcriptions are known to us.

Rüdiger Frank, James E. Hoare, Patrick Köllner and Susan Pares

Vienna, London, Hamburg, July 2008

CHRONOLOGY OF EVENTS IN THE KOREAN PENINSULA 2007

SOUTH KOREA

04.01.07	Iraqi embassy re-opens in Seoul.
09.01.07	President Roh Moo-hyun proposes amending the constitution to allow future heads of state to serve a 4-year term with the possibility of re-election for a further four years.
10.01.07	Nine South Korean employees of Daewoo Engineering and Construction Co. abducted by Nigerian militants but released unharmed, 13.01.07.
13-15.01.07	President Roh attends ASEAN + 3 conference in the Philippines, meets Chinese and Japanese prime ministers.
15-19.01.07	6th round of negotiations on ROK-US Free Trade Agreement, Seoul.
23.01.07	Seoul Central District Court grants posthumous acquittals to eight critics of Park Chung-hee's regime executed in 1975 under Park's emergency decrees.
23.01.07	South Korean scientists claim success in producing the first cure for diabetes using adult stem cells taken from umbilical cords.
31.01.07	Truth and Reconciliation Commission publishes names of 492 judges who passed sentences under Park Chung-hee's emergency decrees in the mid-1970s.
05.02.07	Government announces plan to reduce gradually the lengths of compulsory military service by 2014.
05.02.07	Chung Mong-koo, chairman of Hyundai Motor Co., sentenced to three years' imprisonment for embezzlement.
06.02.07	Ministry of Foreign Affairs announces it will open a consulate in Sakhalin, end February 2007.

11-14.02.07	7th round of negotiations on ROK-US FTA, Washington DC.
11-16.02.07	President Roh visits Spain and Italy, meets Pope Benedict XVI.
21.02.07	Foreign Minister Song announces plans to set up 25 new diplomatic missions during coming two years.
22.02.07	ROK-US agreement on date (17.04.12) for return of wartime operational command from US to ROK. ROK-US Combined Forces Command to be dissolved on same date.
27.02.07	Death of South Korean soldier in Afghanistan, first to die on an overseas assignment since Vietnam War.
07.03.07	Prime Minister Han Myeong-sook resigns.
08.03.07	Government announces draft plan to change current single 5-year presidential term to four years with possibility of one consecutive re-election.
08-12.03.07	8th and final round of negotiations on ROK-US FTA, still without conclusion, Seoul.
19-21.03.07	Further informal negotiations on ROK-US FTA, Washington DC.
24-29.03.07	President Roh visits Saudi Arabia, Kuwait and Qatar.
26-30.03.07	Further negotiations on ROK-US FTA, Seoul, between ROK Minister of Trade and US Deputy Trade Representative, with deadline extended to 02.04.07.
02.04.07	ROK and US conclude FTA. Agreement signed 30.06.07, Washington DC.
02.04.07	National Assembly approves Han Duck-soo's nomination as prime minister.
11.04.07	National Assembly opposition to Roh's proposed constitutional revision of the presidential term of office leads Roh to postpone his proposal, 14.04.07.
18.04.07	President Roh sends telegram to President Bush, expressing regret over massacre of 33 people (including gunman) by Cho Seung-hui, a student of Korean origin, at Virginia Tech University, US.
02.05.07	Government decision to confiscate assets of descendants of nine people said to have amassed wealth through co-operation with Japanese colonial authorities between 1910 and 1945.

03.05.07	Three South Koreans among group of 12 employees of Daewoo Engineering and Construction Co. seized by Nigerian insurgents, but released 09.05.07.
07-11.05.07	South Korean and Japanese delegates to 17th general meeting of International Hydrographic Organisation, Monaco, in dispute over naming of East Sea/Sea of Japan.
07-11.05.07	ROK and European Union hold first round of negotiations on Free Trade Agreement, Seoul.
15.05.07	Four South Koreans among 24 fishermen abducted by Somali pirates, who seized their two fishing vessels. Boats and crews released 11.11.07.
19.05.07	Death of first South Korean soldier serving in Iraq.
09-10.06.07	20th anniversary marked of 10 June 1987 demonstrations against Chun Doo-hwan regime.
27.06.07	UNESCO designates Cheju island and its lava tubes a world Natural Heritage site.
30.06-07.07.07	President Roh visits US and Guatemala.
04-19.07.07	350 ROK troops arrive in stages in Lebanon to serve with UNIFIL.
05.07.07	On 20th anniversary of ROK's overseas aid fund, ROK announces increase in its annual aid to developing countries from US$600 million in 2007 to US$1 billion, beginning in 2008.
16-20.07.07	2nd round in ROK-EU negotiations on FTA, Brussels.
19.07.07	Missionary and aid group of 23 South Koreans kidnapped in Afghanistan by Taliban. Two male hostages murdered in July, two women released in mid-August, remaining 19 released 28.08.07 following negotiations.
20.07.07	Ground-breaking ceremony for new administrative city of Sejong in South Ch'ungch'ŏng province.
13.08.07	Government announces it will confiscate land from descendants of further ten alleged collaborationists with Japanese colonial authorities.
23-25.08.07	Government sends relief supplies by land to North Korea, worth US$7.5 million, announces it will further supply cement and heavy equipment worth US$ 36 million. Supplies sent overland, 10.09.07.

25.08-01.09.07	Foreign Minister Song Min-soon visits Saudi Arabia, Qatar, UAE and Russia.
28.08.07	Grand National Party selects Lee Myung-bak as its candidate in 2007 presidential elections.
08-09.09.07	President Roh attends 15th annual summit meeting of APEC leaders, Australia.
10.09.07	Lee Soo-ja, widow of composer Yun Isang, returns to ROK for first time in 40 years, to participate in 2007 Isang Yun festival.
16-24.09.07	Prime Minister Han Duck-soo visits Hungary, Norway, Sweden and France, attends UN meeting on climate change, New York.
17-21.09.07	3rd round in ROK-EU negotiations on FTA, Brussels.
11.10.07	Lim Chai-jin, head of Legal Research and Training Institute, appointed prosecutor-general.
15-19.10.07	4th round in ROK-EU negotiations on FTA, Seoul.
23.10.07	Government proposes to extend deployment of South Korean troops in Iraq by one year to end 2008, but to halve troop numbers to 600. Proposal agreed by National Assembly, 28.12.07.
14-16.11.07	Nong Duc Minh, general secretary of Vietnamese Communist party, visits ROK.
19-22.11.07	President Roh attends 11th ASEAN + 3 meeting in Singapore, meets Chinese and Japanese prime ministers. ROK signs FTA on investment and services with ASEAN, 21.11.07.
19-23.11.07	5th round in ROK-EU negotiations, Brussels.
07.12.07	Spill of 10,500 tons of crude oil from a Hongkong tanker threatens Taean county on west coast of ROK.
14.12.07	The 200 South Korean troops in Afghanistan leave the country.
19.12.07	Lee Myung-bak of Grand National Party wins presidential elections.

North Korea

03.01.07	Death of Paek Nam Sun, foreign minister of the DPRK.
11.01.07	Opening of Pyongyang Law Office announced.
22.01.07	Ban Ki-moon, UN secretary-general, orders audit of UNDP's operation in North Korea, amid charges UNDP is mismanaging expenditure in DPRK.
22.01.07	KCNA announces opening-up of access to cyber education centre at Kim Chaek university to outside organisations, enterprises and 'those at home'.
31.01.07	Government announces intention to participate in APEC-related development construction in Vladivostok if city is chosen for 2012 APEC summit.
16.02.07	Kim Jong Il's 65th birthday celebrated in North Korea.
26.02.07	Government protests to UN secretary-general against Japanese authorities' investigation of Chongryun and arrest of Korean residents in Japan.
01.03.07	UNDP suspends its operations in DPRK.
06-08.03.07	EU troika delegation visits DPRK.
23.03.07	Digital library at Kim Il Sung university opens.
08-11.04.07	Governor Bill Richardson leads US all-party delegation to DPRK.
11.04.07	5th session of 11th Supreme People's Assembly. Kim Yong Il appointed prime minister in place of Pak Pong Ju.
15.04.07	95th birthday of Kim Il Sung commemorated in DPRK.
19.04.07	Vice-Foreign Minister Kim Yong Il visits Indonesia, Myanmar, India, Pakistan and Iran. DPRK and Myanmar agree to restore diplomatic links, 25.04.07.
07-26.05.07	Vice-Foreign Minister Kim Hyong Jun visits Cuba, Venezuela, Brazil and Nicaragua. DPRK restores diplomatic links with Nicaragua, 25.05.07.
16-23.05.07	1st group of Korean-Americans visit DPRK for family reunions.
18.05.07	Pak Ui Chun named as foreign minister of DPRK.
25.05.07	DPRK launches several short-range missiles over East Sea.

01.06.07	UN secretary-general states that external audit of UNDP's operations in North Korea reveals no systematic diversion of UN funds.
07.06.07	DPRK test-fires two short-range missiles off its west coast.
13-14.06.07	National discussion meeting on trade marks, industrial design and place of origin attended by delegation from World Intellectual Property Organisation (WIPO).
14-17.06.07	Festival commemorating 7th anniversary of 15 June 2000 declaration in Pyongyang attended by North and South.
16.06.07	Death of long-term prisoner Ri In Mo.
23-25.06.07	European Parliamentary delegation visits DPRK.
13.07.07	Korean People's Army proposes talks between US and North Korean military establishments, with UN attendance, to discuss peace and security issues on Korean peninsula. US rejects proposal.
14.07.07	North Korea suspends operation of nuclear facilities at Yŏngbyŏn. Visiting IAEA inspection team conducts inspection of Yŏngbyŏn.
20-31.07.07	Kim Yong Nam, chairman of SPA Standing Committee, visits Mongolia, Algeria, Egypt and Ethiopia.
28.07-02.08.07	Foreign Minister Pak Ui Chun visits Philippines to attend ASEAN Regional Forum, meets ROK Foreign Minister Song Min-soon.
04-14.08.07	5th meeting of DPRK-Syria joint economic committee in Syria.
05-18.08.07	Heavy rains cause flooding, leaving hundreds of people dead or missing, 300,000 flood victims and 88,400 houses damaged or destroyed. UN agencies and international aid organisations respond to North Korean appeals for assistance.
14.08.07	Pak Gil Yon, head of the DPRK mission to the UN, meets UN Secretary-General Ban Ki-moon to discuss UN flood aid to the North, the forthcoming inter-Korean summit and the Six Party Talks.
25.08.07	Central Statistics Bureau makes official announcement on flood damage.
25.08.07	North Korea reported to be constructing border fence along section of frontier with China.

31.08-03.09.07	Health Minister Choi Chang Sik participates in WHO regional meetings in Bhutan.
01-04.09.07	Loxley Pacific Co. Ltd. of Thailand visits DPRK.
03-04.09.07	Foreign Minister Pak attends Non-Aligned Movement ministerial talks, Tehran.
04.09.07	DPRK thanks international community for assistance over August floods.
14.09.07	Myanmar and DPRK sign agreement on diplomatic co-operation, Pyongyang.
15-25.09.07	Between these dates, North Korea issues three denials of North Korean-Syrian nuclear co-operation.
18-21.09.07	Typhoon Wipha brings heavy rains to North Korea, causing considerable damage.
20-27.09.07	Syrian delegation from ruling Baath Arab Socialist Party visits DPRK.
24.09-03.10.07	North Korean delegation attends WIPO general assembly, Switzerland.
28.09.07	DPRK announces it has established diplomatic relations with Swaziland, UAE, Dominican Republic and Guatemala during September 2007.
16-18.10.07	Nong Duc Minh, general secretary of Vietnamese Communist party, visits DPRK.
26.10-07.11.07	Prime Minister Kim visits Vietnam, Malaysia, Cambodia and Laos.
29-30.10.07	North Korean cargo ship attacked by Somalian pirates off Mogadishu, receives assistance from US naval destroyer. KCNA issues North Korean statement of gratitude, 08.11.07.
20.11.07	UN Third Committee resolution expressing concern over persistent reports of human rights violations in DPRK. ROK among those abstaining in vote.
06.12.07	Ministry of Foreign Affairs thanks international community for its support in North Korean recovery from summer flood damage.
07-26.12.07	Ceremonies to mark 90th anniversary of birth of Kim Jong Suk, 24.12.07.
19.12.07	DPRK reported to have submitted application to UNESCO to inscribe Kaesŏng's ten major relics in World Cultural Heritage list.

INTER-KOREAN RELATIONS AND SIX PARTY TALKS

16-18.01.07	US and North Korean representatives meet in Berlin.
30-31.01.07	2nd session of US-DPRK talks on US financial sanctions.
31.01-01.02.07	Chun Young-woo, ROK vice-foreign minister and negotiator in Six Party Talks, visits Moscow.
03.02.07	6th person arrested in connection with charges of spying for DPRK, following charges against five others in the ROK in November 2006.
03-05.02.07	US Assistant Secretary of State Christopher Hill visits Seoul for discussions with ROK negotiator in Six Party Talks.
08-13.02.07	3rd session of 5th round of Six Party Talks, Beijing. Agreement on dismantling of North Korean nuclear facilities in return for fuel deliveries and unfreezing of North Korean funds in Banco Delta Asia (BDA). Five working-level groups set up to handle various aspects of negotiations.
27.02-02.03.07	20th inter-Korean ministerial talks, Pyongyang. Joint press statement issued.
05-06.03.07	1st meeting of working group for normalisation of US-DPRK relations, New York.
07-08.03.07	1st meeting of working group for normalisation of Japan-DPRK relations, Hanoi.
13-14.03.07	Dr Mohammad el-Baradei, head of IAEA, visits DPRK at North Korean invitation.
17.03.07	2nd meeting of working group for normalisation of US-DPRK relations.
19-22.03.07	1st session of 6th round of Six Party Talks, Beijing. DPRK leaves early in protest at delayed transfer of North Korean funds.
27-29.03.07	5th session of video reunions between separated families.
05.04.07	Prison sentence passed in ROK on South Korean man convicted of spying for North Korea.
10-13.04.07	8th inter-Korean Red Cross talks, Mt Kŭmgang. Issues include those missing during or after Korean War.

16.04.07	Korean-American man and three other members of a pro-North Korean group sentenced to terms in prison in ROK on charges of spying for DPRK.
18-22.04.07	13th meeting of inter-Korean Committee for Promotion of Economic Co-operation, Pyongyang. Issues 10-point agreement.
09-11.05.07	15th session of family reunions, Mt Kŭmgang.
17.05.07	Test runs of inter-Korean railways on east and west coast routes.
29.05-02.06.07	21st inter-Korean ministerial talks, Seoul.
30.05.07	ROK government announces that it will progressively dismantle barbed-wire fences in coastal and riverside areas and will replace them with a high-tech protection system.
01.06.07	Inner Kŭmgang area opened for first time to South Korean and foreign visitors.
21-22.06.07	Christopher Hill visits DPRK to discuss implementation of initial steps of 13 February agreement.
23.06.07	Confirmation that North Korean funds frozen in BDA have been released via US and Russian banks to North Korean account in a Russian commercial bank.
26-30.06.07	IAEA delegation visits DPRK to discuss shutdown and inspection of nuclear facilities, issues understanding on procedures to be followed.
05-06.07.07	14th meeting of inter-Korean Committee for Promotion of Economic Co-operation, Kaesŏng.
14-31.07.07	Five shipments of heavy fuel oil, totalling 50,000 tons, shipped from South to North Korea.
18-20.07.07	6th round of Six Party Talks resumes in Beijing.
28.07.07	2nd IAEA inspection team arrives in DPRK to relieve first team. Stays until 11.08.07, leaves two team members in DPRK on departure.
06.08.07	North and South Korean border troops exchange fire after North Korean soldiers fire at South Korean frontier post in DMZ.
07-08.08.07	1st working group meeting on economic and energy co-operation, Panmunjŏm.
13-14.08.07	6th session of video reunions between separated families.

16-17.08.07	Working group meeting on denuclearisation of Korean peninsula, Shenyang, China.
20-21.08.07	Working group meeting on peace and security in Northeast Asia, Moscow.
01-02.09.07	US-DPRK meeting, Geneva, discusses second phase of nuclear dismantling.
05-06.09.07	2nd meeting of working group for normalisation of Japan-DPRK relations, Ulan Bator.
10.09.07	Pyongyang University of Science and Technology, first ROK/DPRK joint college, opens in Pyongyang.
11-15.09.07	Expert nuclear disablement team, comprising representatives from US, Russia and China, visits DPRK to inspect Yŏngbyŏn nuclear facilities.
27-30.09.07	2nd session of 6th round of Six Party Talks. Issues agreement, 03.10.07, on measures for second phase of disablement of North Korean nuclear facilities. Seeks progress by end of 2007 in exchange for political and economic incentives.
02-04.10.07	President Roh and Kim Jong Il meet in Pyongyang, issue joint declaration and agreements, 04.10.07.
11-18.10.07	1st US expert group visits North Korea to prepare for nuclear disablement.
17-22.10.07	16th session of family reunions, Mt Kŭmgang.
29-30.10.07	2nd working group meeting on economic and energy co-operation.
14-15.11.07	7th session of video reunions between separated families.
14-16.11.07	Prime ministers of ROK and DPRK meet in Seoul, produce 8-point agreement.
27-29.11.07	2nd inter-Korean talks between defence ministers of ROK and DPRK, Pyongyang.
28-30.11.07	9th inter-Korean Red Cross talks, Mt Kŭmgang.
29.11-01.12.07	Kim Yang Gon, director of KWP United Work Department, visits ROK.
03-05.12.07	Christopher Hill visits DPRK, delivers personal letter to Kim Jong Il from President George W. Bush.
04-06.12.07	1st meeting of joint committee for inter-Korean economic co-operation, Seoul.
05.12.07	Hyundai Asan opens second North Korean tourist project to Kaesŏng.

11.12.07	South Korean freight train inaugurates first regular inter-Korean service across DMZ since Korean War.
12.12.07	3rd working group meeting on economic and energy co-operation.
14.12.07	Shipment of 500 tons of North Korean zinc to the South as first instalment in repayment of South Korean loan for raw materials for North Korean light industries.
17-19.12.07	Chinese Vice-Foreign Minister Wu Dawei, chair of Six Party Talks, inspects nuclear facilities at Yŏngbyŏn.
19-21.12.07	Sung Kim, US State Department official handling Korean affairs, visits DPRK to discuss North Korean declaration on nuclear programmes. North Korea denies existence of a uranium enrichment programme.

Chronologies prepared by Susan Pares from the following sources: Cankor (Canada-Korea Electronic Information Service), *Korea Policy Review, Korea-Rundbrief, Vantage Point,* Yonhap News Agency.

SOUTH KOREA: DOMESTIC POLITICS AND ECONOMY 2007-2008

Patrick Köllner

1 DOMESTIC POLITICS

The year 2007 marked the twentieth anniversary of democratic transition in the Republic of Korea (henceforth ROK or South Korea). There was much to celebrate, or so one would think. After all, democratic rules have become firmly established, several peaceful changes in government have occurred, civilian control over the military is beyond question, and judicial review has become institutionalised. Moreover, South Korea boasts one of the most vibrant civil societies in Pacific Asia. The ROK has not only managed the transfer from conservative to progressive leadership (and back again) without any major political strains, but also weathered a severe financial and economic crisis without relapsing into authoritarianism. The South Korea economy is in relatively good shape and relations with the North—repeated tensions and continuing challenges notwithstanding—have seen unprecedented progress in the past ten years. Certainly, cut-throat ideological confrontation and competition with the North—with all its implications for ROK domestic politics—seem to have become a thing of the past.

Still, South Korea was in no celebratory mood in 2007. While progressives in the ROK considered the country's politics insufficiently liberal and decried existing (and indeed growing) social inequalities, conservatives chafed at the policies and behaviour of the incumbent president, Roh Moo-hyun, and complained that not enough was being done to advance the economy. Perhaps more worryingly, while South Koreans continue to prefer democracy as such to all systemic alternatives, they are also unhappy about the state of existing representational institutions. In particular, politics are still highly personal and political parties have remained under-institutionalised, the Grand National Party (GNP) being the only political party that has been around for more than ten years. Dissatisfaction with the political state of affairs has contributed to a continuing decrease in voter turnout, as witnessed again at the presidential election of December 2007 and the April 2008 parliamentary elections. The following pages will concentrate on domestic political and economic developments between April 2007 and March 2008, but will also throw a glance at the April 2008 National Assembly elections.

1.1 *Media reform: Roh Moo-hyun's final battle*

President Roh Moo-hyun's final year in office was again not an altogether happy one. Roh, who had continued the 'Sunshine Policy' of his predecessor Kim Dae-jung towards the North, managed to arrange a second top-level inter-Korean summit meeting which again took place in Pyongyang.[1] While it remains to be seen whether the October 2007 summit will indeed pave the way to a peace treaty formally ending the Korean War, as was apparently envisaged, and whether the large-scale economic co-operation projects agreed upon will indeed be implemented, Roh's main domestic reform attempt in 2007 can already be judged a failure. As his final domestic project, the president chose media reform. The tone was set in January 2007 when Roh told a Cabinet meeting that 'reporters sat around' press rooms and conspired to write critical stories about his government (*Wall Street Journal Online*, 17 June 2007). Roh considered the numerous press clubs (*kijadan*) inside government agencies élitist institutions whose cartel-like structure not only bred cosy and collusive relations between journalists and government officials, but also led to near-identical reporting by media outlets belonging to the press clubs. Roh charged press clubs with being the 'source of prejudice and collaboration that only does harm and brings no benefit' (*Straits Times Interactive*, 12 October 2007). Access to such press clubs is indeed restricted to registered members who hail mainly from mainstream newspapers, television stations, national (and a few select foreign) news agencies. Less established and smaller media actors, including Internet news sites, are not allowed to join. Roh's criticism of press clubs will be familiar to observers of politics and media in Japan, where similar press clubs

[1] See the article by James Hoare on inter-Korean relations in this yearbook.

exist, and this is no coincidence as South Korea's press-club system traces its roots back to the Japanese colonial period.

In order to instil greater competition and pluralism into media reporting, the government started in May 2007 to close down existing press clubs and to concentrate news conferences in a few new 'open access' facilities outside government agencies. Journalists were also required to carry electronic press passes. These measures were not well received by the established media, which had been at loggerheads with the Roh administration since its inauguration. Some critics were reminded of the repression of journalistic freedom under authoritarian rule in the ROK. The Korea News Editors Association (KNEA) and the three main conservative newspapers (*Dong-A*, *JoongAng*, *Chosun*), which control 70 percent of the print market, argued that the so-called 'measures for developing an advanced media support system' smacked of media control and deprived journalists of access to information. Under the new system the media would be dependent on official press releases and would lose their role as a watchdog on government affairs—or so it was claimed. Numerous journalists protested against the new media policy by boycotting the new facilities and staging sit-ins at the former press clubs. In the face of protests, the government shelved regulations which would have required civil servants and journalists to seek permission before talking to each other but still continued with the closing-down of press clubs until the end of 2007. Yet the new 'advanced media support system' will not outlive the Roh administration as President-elect Lee Myung-bak announced that he would return to the old system. Triumphantly, the KNEA published in March 2008 a 'white paper' on former President Roh's media policy to show, in the words of its chairman, 'who attempted to trample the press underfoot and how journalists fought back' (*Chosun Ilbo*/Internet, 10 March 2008).

1.2 *The 2007 presidential election: contenders and results*

As the ROK's constitution limits incumbent presidents to a single term of five years, all South Korean political parties had to search in 2007 for candidates to fill the country's supreme political office. In the case of the then main opposition party GNP, both Park Geun-hye, former GNP chairwoman and daughter of military dictator Park Chung-hee (president, 1963-79), and Lee Myung-bak, an ex-chief executive officer (CEO) of Hyundai Engineering and Construction and former mayor of Seoul (see Box 1), declared their candidacies in mid-June. From the beginning, the 65-year old Lee Myung-bak enjoyed a lead in opinion polls over his intra-party opponent, with whom he traded barbs until the GNP primary election two months later. The GNP's presidential nominee was chosen not only by party delegates, 11,000 party members and invited non-partisan participants, who together accounted for 80 percent of the total of votes, but also on the basis of a survey among 5,490 citizens, which accounted for the remainder of the votes. While Lee received fewer votes than Park from the former group, his 8.5 percent lead in the survey sufficed to snatch the nomination from Madame Park. The final tally of 49.6 percent for Lee and 48.1 percent for Park showed how close the race between the two conservative contenders became in the end. Park Geun-hye, who is ten years Lee's junior, might well have another shot at the presidency in the future. In any case, she accepted her defeat and did not stand as an independent candidate as the Lee camp had feared.

Box 1 A brief profile of Lee Myung-bak

19 December 1941: Born in Osaka, Japan
1965: Employed by Hyundai Construction
1977-88: President of Hyundai Construction
1978: CEO of Inchon Steel (later merged into Hyundai Steel)
1988-92: CEO of Hyundai Construction
1992-98: Lawmaker for conservative party in the National Assembly
2002-6: Seoul City Mayor

Married, four children (1 son, 3 daughters)
173 cm, 70 kilos, non-smoker
Graduate of Korea University (degree in management)
Languages: English, Japanese

Sources: *Financial Times*, *Nihon Keizai Shimbun*, 20 December 2007.

Lee's main opponent in the December 2007 presidential election hailed from the progressive United New Democratic Party (UNDP, *sic*!) which had only been founded in August as a new party vehicle for former members of the by then largely defunct Uri Party. Uri Party lawmakers had left the governing party in droves in the course of 2007 to distance themselves from the increasingly unpopular President Roh

Moo-hyun. The Uri Party finally disbanded itself and, after a month of primaries, former Uri Party chairman and one-time unification minister Chung Dong-young, 54, was chosen in mid-October by the UNDP as its presidential candidate. Chung had been a TV journalist for 18 years before becoming a member of the National Assembly in 1996. Other 'progressive' candidates included former Kyŏnggi governor Rhee In-je (Democratic Party), former entrepreneur Moon Kook-hyun (Creative Korea Party/CKP), and former labour leader Kwon Young-ghil (Democratic Labor Party).

The field of serious contenders for the presidential office was however only complete in early November when former Supreme Court judge and two-times presidential candidate Lee Hoi-chang, 72, bolted from the GNP (which he had helped to found ten years earlier) and announced a further bid for the Blue House. Lee's candidacy as an independent brought a new dynamic into the presidential campaign. Until Lee Hoi-chang entered the race, his former party colleague Lee Myung-bak enjoyed a more than comfortable lead over the UNDP's Chung—in spite of the fact that the younger Lee had become tainted by a scandal which involved stock price manipulation and embezzlement of funds from BKK, a company that he had founded in 2000. (Lee himself denied all allegations of wrongdoing and was cleared first by state prosecutors and then on 22 February 2008 by a special prosecutor installed by the National Assembly majority.) While Lee Myung-bak emphasised his pragmatic, non-ideological attitude and his credentials as a successful manager and mayor, Lee Hoi-chang stylized himself as the only true conservative candidate who was also willing to take a stern course towards North Korea. Inter alia, the former Supreme Court judge called for a suspension of all aid to the North until the regime in Pyongyang completely dismantled its nuclear programme.

The last-minute split of the conservative camp did not help much to boost the fortunes of the liberal camp and its front-runner Chung Dong-young. As numerous surveys showed, after a decade of progressive rule, and especially after the lacklustre performance of President Roh, Korean voters yearned for change. While Roh's administration had spent much time and energy on a number of morally driven and/or highly contentious issues (relocation of the capital, repeal of the National Security Law, revision of the Private School Law, enactment of a new law governing newspapers, and an inquiry into collaboration under Japanese colonial rule), the government had effectively neglected bread-and-butter issues. During Roh's watch, the economy had only progressed haltingly, the gap between rich and poor had widened, housing prices in the greater Seoul area had skyrocketed, and North Korea had—in spite of the South's continued engagement policy, renamed the 'Policy for Peace and Prosperity'—detonated a nuclear device.

Unlike 2002, foreign policy issues and even the question of relations with North Korea did not play much of a role in the 2007 presidential election campaign. Despite conservative front-runner Lee Myung-bak's possible less-than-clean past business dealings, many voters, disappointed with government policy in the past couple of years, preferred a candidate who promised to devote his energy to reigniting the Korean economy. Regardless of whether they truly believed in Lee's ambitious '747 vision' (annual economic growth rate of 7 percent, per capita income of US$40,000 and the ROK becoming the seventh largest economy in the world by 2012), many South Koreans harboured a clear desire for a 'hands on, can do' president who was unlikely to get bogged down in ideological battles. Even without inspiring much enthusiasm, Lee Myung-bak promised to be just such a man.

The vote on 19 December 2007 did not produce any surprises. Amid the lowest turnout in twenty years (62.9 percent, as compared with 70.8 percent in 2002), Lee Myung-bak scored a landslide win, securing 48.7 percent of the votes, the largest proportion since direct presidential elections were reinstituted in 1987. Chung Dong-young received 26.1 percent and Lee Hoi-chang, who for a time had led Chung in surveys, finished third with 15.1 percent of the vote (Moon Kook-hyun: 5.8 percent, Kwon Young-ghil: 3.0 percent, while five other candidates each received less than 1 percent). Lee managed to win a plurality of votes in 13 out of 16 regions—the exceptions being the two southwestern Chŏlla provinces and the city of Kwangju, indicating again that regionalism in South Korean politics is not yet a thing of the past.

1.3 *Lee Myung-bak's agenda and the parliamentary elections of April 2008*

Lee Myung-bak was elected president of the ROK on the basis of an 'economy first' platform. As part of his 'Global Korea' agenda he promised cuts in corporate tax, further privatisation and deregulation, a greater push for free-trade agreements and other pro-business policies. His most ambitious economic project, however, reflects his past experience as CEO of a major construction company: Lee has pledged to build a canal which, at an estimated cost of US$16 billion, would connect the Han river in the northeast of the country with the Nakdong river in the southwest. The construction of such a canal linking Seoul with Pusan would, among other demands, require tunnelling 15 miles (24.1km) through mountainous terrain in the central area of South Korea. Lee argues that such a canal would substantially lower freight costs and ease traffic problems. The gigantic project, slated to begin in April 2009, is, however, highly contentious. Opponents of the project—and there are many—suggest that the construction of the canal would not only harm the environment but also does not make sense in economic terms as South Korea possesses a number of well-developed ports providing for efficient seaborne transport options. It remains to be seen what the planned feasibility studies for the canal project will say and whether domestic and/or international companies can be found to shoulder the costs of the canal, which is envisaged as a 'build, operate and transfer' project.

Another large-scale project on the agenda of the new president involves the substantial downsizing of the South Korean national bureaucracy. Lee has promised to reduce the 946,000-strong civil service within five years by 300,000 officials. The extent of the envisaged downscaling seems not only overly ambitious but perhaps even threatening to the functioning of the state, as the ratio of public officials to overall population in the ROK is well within OECD norms—in spite of 56,000 new public officials having been added by the government of Roh Moo-hyun. While initial plans of President-elect Lee to close down the Unification Ministry and the Ministry for Gender Equality and Family foundered in the face of massive resistance in the National Assembly, Lee was still able to reduce the number of ministries from 18 to 13 and of government agencies from 56 to 43. The reconfiguration of the ministerial landscape included the merger of the former ministries for education and for science and technology and the absorption of the Ministry of Maritime Affairs and Fisheries into the Ministry of Agriculture. The new administration, led by the 72-year-old Han Seung-soo, a former ROK finance and foreign minister, has also promised to upgrade and remodel the National Intelligence Service, the ROK's spy agency, which was repeatedly hit by scandals under Roh.

President Lee Myung-bak had only lukewarm popular approval when he officially assumed office on 25 February 2008. Newspaper polls found that only 49 percent of South Korean citizens supported the new government—a record low. Preceding South Korean presidents had begun their days in office with much higher support rates (Kim Dae-jung in 1993 with 92.5 percent, Roh Moo-hyun in 1998 with 67 percent), while even Kim Young-sam in 1993 started with a better support rate (50.2 percent). Pollsters explained the tepid reaction to Lee's assuming power with widespread criticism of a number of Lee's pet policy projects, including the inland canal (which according to a *Kyunghyang Shinmun* survey was opposed by 55 percent of polled persons) and plans to boost English-language education in public schools (*Korea Times*/Internet, 3 March 2008).

The comparatively low initial popularity of the new president did not, however, hinder his Grand National Party from making sizeable gains in the National Assembly (NA) elections of 9 April 2008. One reason for this was the sorry state of the opposition parties, in particular the UNDP, which had not managed to free itself from the shadow of former President Roh. The fluidity of South Korea's party system was confirmed again in the run-up to the NA elections. On 10 January 2008, former GNP politician Lee Hoi-chang founded the conservative Liberty Forward Party (LFP), which has its power base in the central Ch'ungch'ŏng area. In the liberal camp, the UNDP, led since January 2008 by Sohn Hak-kyu (also a former GNP politician!), merged with the smaller Democratic Party in mid-February to form the new United Democratic Party (UDP). Also in February, more than 30 supporters of former GNP chairwoman Park Geun-hye broke away from the main conservative party in protest at decisions on the nomination of candidates. Finally, the progressive Democratic Labor Party (DLP) experienced a split in mid-February when a major faction led by former party leader Sim Sang-jeong announced its breakaway after a plan to deprive alleged pro-North Korea party members of their membership had been rejected by a party convention.

The parliamentary elections resulted in a clear victory for the conservative camp. Amid a record low voter turnout of 46 percent (2004: 60.6 percent), the GNP was able to secure a slim absolute majority in the NA by increasing its seats from 112 to 153 (out of 299). The newly established LFP led by Lee Hoi-chang got 18 of its candidates elected but missed its target of 20 seats, which would have given it the right to initiative bills. Fourteen GNP renegades competing under the label of the 'Pro-Park-Geun-hye Alliance' landed seats in parliament. In addition, a majority of the 25 independents who got elected are considered to be supporters of the former GNP chairwoman, who herself was elected on a GNP ticket. The progressive camp, which more or less competed on the basis of an anti-Lee Myung-bak platform, constituted the biggest loser of the parliamentary elections: The UDP, formerly the biggest party in the NA, went down to 81 seats, thus failing to achieve its minimum aim of a third of the NA seats (needed to block constitutional revisions) (see Table 1). Both UDP chairman Sohn Hak-kyu and former presidential candidate Chung Dong-young were beaten in their respective electoral districts by GNP candidates. Although he achieved less than he had hoped for, the GNP victory in the parliamentary elections will enable President Lee to pursue his political agenda with limited resistance. It remains however to be seen how the barely subdued tensions between the supporters of Lee Myung-bak and Park Geun-hye within the GNP and beyond will unfold in the future.

Table 1 Results of the 2008 National Assembly elections

	Direct seats/ electoral districts	Party lists/ proportional representation	Total (before election)
GNP	131	22	153 (112)
UDP	66	15	81 (136)
LFP	14	4	18 (9)
Pro-Park Alliance	6	8	14 (3)
DLP	2	3	5 (6)
CKP	1	2	3 (1)
Independents	25	-	25
Total	245	54	299

Source: National Election Commission, cited in Marc Ziemek, 'Wahlen in Südkorea', Seoul: Konrad Adenauer Foundation Office, April 2008.

2 The Economy

While South Korea has been in recent years among the fastest growing OECD nations, it was overtaken in 2007 by both Russia and India, and now ranks as the world's 13th largest economy (and the fourth biggest in Asia after Japan, China and India). In the five years up to 2007, the ROK economy grew by on average 4.4 percent, with growth peaking at 5 percent in both 2006 and 2007 (see Table 2). In US dollar terms, ROK per capita income in 2007 crossed the US$20,000 mark, according to provisional figures. However, this is still approximately a third lower than the OECD average.

Although domestic demand picked up in the latter half of 2007 against the background of decreasing unemployment and a strong upward trend in the local stock market, South Korea essentially continues to have a two-speed economy. In 2007, as in the years before, growth was mainly driven by exports, which have grown on average annually by 14 percent since the beginning of the new millennium. South Korea's international bestsellers include semiconductors and mobile telephones, whose export value in 2007 stood at US$22.4 billion and US$18.6 billion respectively. On the other hand, the ROK's domestically oriented service sector has not experienced significant productivity growth in the past 15 years. Domestic consumption as such is held back by high levels of debt and other financial burdens households have to cope with. South Korean consumers have yet to fully recover from the burst of the credit card bubble in 2003. Private debt actually increased again in 2007 by 8.4 percent to reach 630.7 trillion won (US$678 billion). This means that the average household in the ROK is indebted to the tune of 38.4 million won (US$41,300). Heavy financial burdens also include spending on education, which reached an all-time high of 12 percent of household expenditures in 2007.

Worries exist about both the short-term prospects of and the longer-term challenges facing the ROK economy. While the latter include the rapid ageing of South Korea's population of 48.5 million and the catching-up of developing nations—according to the Korea Institute of Economics and Trade (KIET), China's technological gap *vis-à-vis* the ROK has narrowed to 3.8 years—short-term risks include the slowdown in the United States and the global economy but also inflationary pressure stemming from high oil and resources prices.

Table 2 ROK basic economic data

	2002	2003	2004	2005	2006	2007
GDP (billion won)	684.3	724.7	779.4	810.5	848.0	901.2
GDP (billion US$)	547	608	681	791	887.5	970
GDP growth (%)	7.0	3.1	4.7	4.2	5.0	5.0
Per capita income (GDP base, in US$)	11,485	12,707	14,161	16,413	18,401	20,045
Exports (billion US$)	162.5	193.8	253.8	284.4	325.5	371.5
Imports (billion US$)	152.1	178.8	224.5	261.2	309.4	356.9
Trade balance (billion US$)	+10.3	+14.5	+29.4	+23.2	+16.1	+14.6
Balance of payments (billion US$)	+5.4	+12.0	+28.2	+15.0	+5.4	+6.0
Gross external debt (billion US$)	141.5	157.6	172.3	187.9	260.1	380.7
International reserves (billion US$)	121.4	155.3	199.1	210.3	238.9	262.2
Inward foreign direct investment (billion US$)	9.1	6.5	12.8	11.6	11.2	10.5
Consumer prices (%)	+2.7	+3.5	+3.6	+2.8	+2.2	+2.5
Producer prices (%)	-0.3	+2.2	+6.1	+2.1	+2.3	+2.7
Unemployed (in thousands)	752	818	860	887	827	783
Unemployment rate (%)	3.3	3.6	3.7	3.7	3.5	3.2

Note: Data for 2007 provisional.

Sources: Bank of Korea, *Monthly Statistical Bulletin*, 3/2008 and earlier editions; Bank of Korea statistics, online: http://ecos.bok.or.kr; Invest Korea, online: www.investkorea.org; *Republic of Korea Economic Bulletin*, March 2008; Korean-German Chamber of Commerce and Industry, 'Wirtschaftsrundbrief', 14/2008.

Negative news abounded in the early months of 2008. First, in January the current account balance—the broadest measure of trade, services and investment—registered a minus of US$2.6 billion, the largest shortfall since January 1997. South Korea's trade balance, which had been in the black for many years, actually posted a deficit of US$5.7 billion in the first quarter of 2008 amid rising prices of crude oil and other raw materials. Second, producer prices increased in February

2008 on a year-on-year basis by 6.8 percent to reach the highest level since November 2004. As a consequence, the spectre of stagflation, i.e. a combination of stagnant economic growth amid high inflation, appeared on the horizon. What is more, amid speculation that housing prices would fall, the number of unsold apartments rose to an 11-year-high of 120,000 units, effectively putting a number of construction companies into financial trouble. The gloomy picture was completed by the downward trend in the stock market: the benchmark KOSPI stock index, which had risen to over 2,000 points in the second half of 2007, fell again by mid-March 2008 to around 1,600 points.

Against the background of the visible economic slowdown, the - Korea Economic Research Institute lowered its growth forecast for 2008 to 4.5 percent, while the incoming government of Lee Myung-bak revised its ambitious 7-percent growth target to 6 percent. To revive the flagging economy, the Lee administration is set to apply well-known neo-liberal recipes. It announced it would lower the corporate tax rate to 22 percent in 2009 and then to 20 percent in 2013. The Cabinet also approved a temporary 10 percent cut in oil tax and the extension of tax concessions for new corporate investments. In addition, the new government has frozen power and public utility rates. It also aims to cut the state budget to the tune of 20 trillion won (US$20.5 billion) to 'enhance the efficiency and competitiveness of government organisations' (Yonhap/Internet, 11 March 2008). While, with respect to government stakes in companies, President Lee is apparently retreating from earlier full-scale privatisation plans, he still intends to restructure wholly owned state corporations such as Korea Development Bank, the utility provider KEPCO, and KORAIL, the national railroad company. The sale of remaining government stakes in private companies such as Hynix Semiconductor and Hyundai Engineering and Construction is also under consideration.

On the external side, the government aims to have the Korea-US Free Trade Agreement, which was agreed upon by Washington and Seoul in June 2007, ratified by the National Assembly as soon as possible and to conclude a similar agreement with the EU. After seven rounds of negotiations between the ROK and the EU it remained, however, unclear whether outstanding hurdles, in particular in the automotive sector, can be overcome for a deal to be signed by the end of 2008. Another priority for the new government will be to revive foreign direct investment (FDI) in the ROK. Such investment has declined since 2004. In 2007, officially registered new FDI amounted to US$10.5 billion (see Table 2).

3 Man-made disasters hit South Korea

In late 2007 and then again in early 2008, South Korea had to face catastrophes. On 7 December 2007, off the coast of Taean county, about 150 kilometres southwest from Seoul, a crane-carrying barge collided with a Hong Kong-registered oil tanker, causing the tanker to leak about 10,900 tonnes of crude oil. The worst oil spill in South Korea's history affected at the core a 20-kilometre shoreline that hosts rich wildlife, oyster and fish farms, and a national park which attracts millions of tourists every year. Toxic remnants of evaporated crude oil were found as far as 130 kilometres away from the disaster site. The region most severely hit by the spill is home to 64,000 residents who are heavily dependent on fishing and seafood farming. The collision occurred when a steel cable linking a tugboat to the barge snapped—the stormy sea then caused the barge to hit the oil tanker which was at anchor. Despite a massive rescue operation, which was hampered by bad weather, an ecological disaster could not be averted. The costs of the clean-up were expected to far surpass the 96 billion won the ROK spent to deal with a 1995 spill on the south coast, when about half as much oil was released. An estimated four or five years are needed to fully remove chemicals used in the rescue operation and other pollutants. In January 2008, Samsung Heavy Industries Corporation, the operator of the crane barge and the tugboats, as well as the Hong Kong-based shipping company owning the oil tanker were indicted over the spill.

Then, on 11 February 2008, South Korea's national treasure No. 1, the 600-year-old Sungnye gate in Seoul—better known as Namdaemun (Great South Gate)—was destroyed by a fire. The gate—a pagoda-style two-storey building on a stone base—had originally been built in 1398. It was rebuilt in 1447 and renovated several times thereafter, but still reputedly contained some 600-year-old timbers. The building, which had survived foreign invasions and the Korean War, had apparently been set on fire by a convicted arsonist who in 2006 had already destroyed part of Chang'gyŏng palace, a World Heritage Site. The South Korean Cultural Heritage Administration said it would take three years and US$21 million to rebuild the gate.

The loss of what was one of the most loved landmarks in a city that has relatively few historic remains led to a brief period of heart-searching about lost values just as the new president prepared to take up office. But South Koreans soon turned back to their everyday concerns and a very different political landscape from that of the last ten years.

NORTH KOREA: DOMESTIC POLITICS AND ECONOMY 2007-2008

Rüdiger Frank

Information about domestic developments in the Democratic People's Republic of Korea (DPRK) is rare. A certain impression of the leadership's thinking is provided by two regular events of programmatic nature that are widely publicised in the North Korean media and are accessible to most North Koreans. The political tone and strategy of the year are set by the New Year joint editorial, usually published by the major newspapers in early January, while the official view on the status of the national economy and other issues is provided by the annual plenary session of the Supreme People's Assembly (SPA) that customarily takes place in spring. This review, covering events from April 2007 to 31 March 2008, provides a comment on the 2007 parliamentary reports followed by the major points of the New Year editorial, while the following sections provide an account of other domestic developments.

1 The annual parliamentary session

The 5th session of the 11th SPA of the North Korean parliament took place on 11 April 2007 in Pyongyang. Standard issues for discussion were the work of the cabinet in the preceding year, the report on the implementation of the state budget 2006, and the new budget for 2007.

The SPA reports about the budget are the closest we have to official macroeconomic data on North Korea. Details tend to vary over the years, so that comparability is not always easy, and absolute numbers have been missing since 2002. However, with some creativity and due caution, interesting conclusions can be drawn. Budgetary revenue, for example, can serve as a rough indicator of economic growth in the DPRK, or at least of the state's estimate thereof. With almost all of the economy in the state's hands, state income is the national income, or in other words, the North Korean gross domestic product. The huge and complex military economy with its own production facilities and export revenue is, however, not included in these numbers.

The 2007 New Year joint editorial had stressed that after the nuclear test of October 2006, the problem of military defence had been settled so that the focus could now be directed at economic construction and the improvement of living standards. This basic approach was reflected in the speeches delivered at the 2007 SPA session. Ro Tu Chol, vice-premier of the Cabinet, reported that budgetary revenue fell short of the planned target and reached 97.5 percent, but still grew 4.4 percent over the previous year; this seems to reflect a certain slowdown of economic growth, since the corresponding number a year before had stood at a huge 16.1 percent (see *Korea Yearbook 2007*, p. 26). Remarkably, local budgetary revenue (*chibang yesan suip*) was well above the planned figure (104.9 percent), leaving room for speculation about a possible drifting apart of local and central economies. It was specifically mentioned that these local units not only covered their own costs with their revenues but also contributed a large amount to the state budget, i.e. generated a profit. This would be particularly interesting as industrial growth in the early period of reform in China also started at the local level.

The target for expenditure was met (99.9 percent as opposed to 104.4 percent a year before), indicating at least that expenditure was growing faster than revenue. In the worst case, this could be seen as a hint of a budgetary deficit. However, since absolute numbers on revenue and expenditure are not available, this is a somewhat speculative analysis based on the general assumption that the plan originally foresaw a balance between revenue and expenditure. The defence budget was 16 percent of total expenditure in 2006 (2005: 15.9 percent), while 40.8 percent (2005: 41.3 percent) of the budget was spent on 'various domains of the national economy'. In accordance with the previous year's emphasis on agriculture, expenditure on this sector grew by 14.5 percent. Power, coal mining, metal industries and transportation were emphasised as pilot sectors that constitute the foundation of the national economy.

It was stressed that the new budget not only aimed at maximising revenue but also at reducing the expenditure for non-productive fields (no details were given) to improve people's living and increase the national defence capability. For 2007, budgetary revenue was expected to grow by 5.9 percent over the previous year; this growth target was significantly smaller than the 7.1 percent announced a year before. The major source of revenue, i.e. profits of state enterprises, was to grow by 6.4 percent (2006: 7.2 percent). A dramatic decrease in the expected productivity of agriculture is reflected in the planned growth rate of revenue from co-operative organisations; this rate was 23.2 percent in 2006 but reached only 4.5 percent in the 2007 budget. Income from utility fees on real estate was to grow by 15.4 percent (2006: 12 percent), and that from social insurance fees by 15.1 percent (2006: 41 percent). A source of revenue that had not been mentioned in the 2006 budget was 'revenue from the depreciation of fixed property' (*kojŏng chaesan kamga sanggakkŭm suip*), which was to grow by 9.6 percent.

The target for expenditure was set at 3.3 percent, only slightly below the previous year's figure of 3.5 percent. The figure for defence expenditure was lowered to 15.8 percent of total, and an unspecified, 'large' amount was to be spent for the development of the economy. Expenditure on agriculture would grow by 8.5 percent (2006: 12. percent). Funds for light industry, not mentioned in 2006, were to grow by 16.8 percent, emphasising the strategic focus on the modernisation of light industry factories. On power, coal and metal industries and on railway transport, the state planned to increase its expenditures by 11.9 percent (2006: 9.6 percent). While in 2006, only a 3 percent increase was earmarked for the development of science and technology, the amount to be spent in 2007 was to grow by 60.3 percent, showing the priority given to technological modernisation.

No mention was made of the new social insurance system for enterprises announced in the previous year's session, or of increased rates of coal and energy production. However, specific growth targets were provided for education (7 percent), public health (9.8 percent) and social insurance and social security (9.4 percent). An interesting new measure highlighting the continuation of the 2002 policy of assigning more responsibility to single production units was the designation of 2 percent of an enterprise's net income (profit) for carrying out 'their own projects for the development of science and technology'. An unspecified amount was set aside for the support of pro-North Korean residents in Japan.

The major thematic issue at the SPA was reflected in a speech by Kwak Pom Gi, vice-premier of the Cabinet. In 2006, this role of speech-maker was played by Choe Thae Bok, secretary of the Central Committee of the Korean Worker's Party, who had primarily stressed information technology (IT); this field has been mentioned only sporadically in 2007. Kwak delivered his report on the work of the DPRK Cabinet in 2006 and its tasks for 2007. The economic situation was described as positive, with growth throughout major sectors. The improvement of the standard of people's living in the 'shortest possible time span' (*ch'oedan kiganane*) was to be achieved emphasising agriculture and light industry. For 2007, among the most crucial tasks were the modernisation of the national economy and solving the 'problem of socialist economic management' (*sahoejuŭi kyŏngje kwalli munje*) in 'our' [the North Korean] way.

Contradicting the budgetary figures, agriculture was emphasised as the mainstay of the economy, on which the state's efforts would be concentrated. Modernisation of light industries received special attention, to strengthen the bases for the production of daily necessities, to increase the variety of consumer goods, and to improve the quality of goods. This reflects the typical problems of a classical socialist economy, where quantity and heavy industries usually receive priority for decades until serious structural disproportions demand a reaction by the government. A newly mentioned strategic issue was the 'satisfactory' solution of the 'housing problem' (*sallimjip munje*), another concern that is typical for socialist economies but has so far not been frequently cited in official North Korean statements. Fields such as power and coal production were touched on only routinely; the former, including alternative energies, took a much more central position in the 2006 report.

The topic of modernisation and upgrading was repeated with regard to transportation, railways in particular, and mining. The last year of the five-year plan for science and technology was announced, along with the prospect of mapping out a new such five-year plan.

Foreign trade and other forms of exchange with international partners were to be expanded, although firmly based on the principle of *chuch'e* (i.e. avoiding unilateral dependence and adjusting everything to the specific conditions of North Korea). Another concern was to diversify foreign trade. Managers were asked to base their work on the principle of profitability, to achieve a balanced development of the economy and to ensure the fullest utilisation of people's creative ingenuity.

2 The 2008 New Year joint editorial

The year 2008 started with the usual New Year joint editorial, published jointly by the country's major print media *Rodong Shinmun* (party), *Chosŏn Inmingun* (military) and *Ch'ŏngnyŏn Chŏnwi* (youth league) and entitled 'Glorify This Year of the 60th Anniversary of the Founding of the DPRK as a Year of Historical Turn Which Will Go Down in the History of the Country'. These annual editorials have, despite their propagandistic tone, achieved the status of programmatic announcements in the absence of other means of learning about the North Korean government's strategic visions.

While in 2007 the nuclear test and its implications were at the centre of the editorial, the 2008 issue was more or less equally concerned with economic construction, ideological struggle, and the October 2007 second inter-Korean summit. Preparations for a mass campaign to mark the 100th birthday of Kim Il Sung in 2012 were announced. Less intensely that before, but still very clearly, the unity of the Korean nation was stressed, combined with the demand that 'fellow countrymen' make proper economic contributions in the spirit of patriotism. Remarkably, the overall tone of the editorial, although still very militant, indicates a certain return to old principles that appeared to have been shaken by the economic reforms since 2002 and their ideological backup. The reasons are unknown and leave room for speculation. This socialist neo-conservativism, if observed correctly, could have been prompted either by external developments such as the new government in South Korea and the mounting problems within the Six Party Talks, or by domestic developments such as the again worsening economic situation and internal discussions about the continuity of political leadership; the most likely explanation is a combination of all these factors.

Chuch'e and *sŏn'gun* (Military First) are equated, and are both linked to Kim Il Sung. This deviates from the former practice of ascribing *sŏn'gun* to Kim Jong Il and presenting it as an update of *chuch'e*, although Kim Jong Il is later strongly praised as a great leader and tactician who perfectly continues the work of his father in the spirit of *sŏn'gun* and who should be followed and protected.

There is a marked return to old formulae, especially an emphasis on socialism. The latter had been pushed into the background in the past years while nationalism was being more actively promoted. The development goal, dubbed *kangsŏng taeguk*, is supplemented by the term 'socialist' and is now again called *sahoejuŭi kangsŏng taeguk* (socialist prosperous and strong great country). The party, which a few years ago appeared to receive less attention because of the rising role of the military, is now at the centre again, and resumes its leadership over the army. The editorial stresses the single-minded unity of soldiers and people 'rallied as one around the Party'.

Continuing the neo-conservative trend, the editorial demands the setting up of an independent production system (*charipchŏgin saengsanch'eje*), relying on domestic sources and technologies. In culture and art, too, independence and domestic forms are praised. The active role of North Korea in promoting peace and security on the Korean peninsula and in Northeast Asia are stressed, the latter being a reference to the Six Party Talks and the agreement of 13 February 2007 with the United States (US). This emphasis also reflects the ambitions of North Korea to be a player in regional politics. The fact that a growing number of states have established diplomatic relations with Pyongyang is interpreted as a success of the Military First Policy.

The most important non-regular commemorative event for 2008 is the 60th anniversary of the foundation of the DPRK in September 1948. The past decades are seen as a time of great change and development, although in a more retrospective way than was usual in previous years. The 'superiority and invincibility' of socialism 'of our own style' are stressed, as well as 'anti-imperialist struggle'. Memories of the Ch'ŏllima movement (the softened North Korean version of the Chinese Great Leap) are evoked, and again the leading role of the party is emphasised.

Ideology is stressed as 'the primary national strength' (*cheil kungnyŏk*), presumably in response to the deteriorating situation after years of destabilisation, uncontrollable interaction with the Chinese, the subsequent spread of South Korean media products, and the increasing number of foreign visitors and contacts. The ideologically hardened mental power (*chŏngsinryŏk*) of soldiers and people is described as being even stronger than nuclear weapons (*haengmugipoda tŏ kanghan*). This is an interesting remark that could be interpreted either as simply trying to emphasise the importance of not losing ground on the ideological front, or as a cautious hint that concessions in the field of nuclear weapons are not too dramatic as long as ideology is safeguarded. This signal is yet too weak to be treated as an indicator of North Korea's willingness to meet Washington's demands on denuclearisation but nevertheless deserves attention. The mental power of the people is connected to the leader, who has to be defended at the risk of the people's own life). Korean-style socialism is stressed as 'the destiny and future' of the North Korean people. The editorial demands the renouncement of individualism and argues that 'no life is more fulfilling than the one devoted to society, collective, country and people'. The 'enemy's reactionary ideological and cultural infiltration' (*sasangmunhwajŏk ch'imt'u*) is addressed directly, described as psychological warfare that will not be tolerated. Socialist morality is to be upheld. These strong words reflect the regime's difficulties in maintaining ideological control and show how successful outside efforts have become in recent years in increasing the North Korea population's awareness of the outside world.

In the section on the military, the building of domestic capacities is again stressed, in particular in the defence industry. The country's economic development is closely connected to the issue of defence. Modernisation is the major theme, combined with the demand to preserve the specific features of North Korea's economic structure. This theme is repeated for external economic relations. The solution for the energy shortage is to be found in the construction of hydroelectric power plants. Mining is mentioned quite often at various occasions, indicating the renewed efforts at utilising the country's abundant natural resources. Joint ventures with Chinese companies are not mentioned, although these play a major role in realising this policy.

In 2007, natural disasters combined with inefficient agriculture, the lack of fertiliser and other inputs, and the reduced inflow of outside resources led outside observers to anticipate another food shortage in North Korea in 2008. The editorial supports this conclusion, stating in dramatic words that 'today there is no more urgent and important task but resolving the issue of people's food.' The solution is sought in new high-yield varieties and potato farming; new ownership and incentive structures in agriculture are not mentioned.

Remarks on the other economic sectors contain no new messages. The role of the Cabinet is again stressed, demanding that all economic activities are strictly organised under its supervision. The party is asked to enhance political awareness, youth should actively participate in the hardest work and the party's vanguard, and unions and other organisations should continue their word as educators of the people so that these play their role in society properly.

In comparison with the 2007 issue, the return to old postures (socialism, party, domestic resources) is the most striking difference.

IT, standing at the core of the 2007 editorial, was not mentioned in 2008; neither was the country's status as a nuclear power. Improving the standard of living is again an issue, but its coverage was less intense in 2008. The Cabinet has been further upgraded from being an 'important' institution to the 'unified command'. The goal of reunification is still a major theme, but the optimistic time-frame of 2007 ('in our generation') has been silently dropped. Insecurity about the future political course of the new government in South Korea was reflected in the absence of any specific attacks against the president or his party, the Grand National Party (GNP); the GNP received much more direct criticism in the 2007 editorial but was not directly mentioned in the 2008 version. To sum up, the 2008 editorial marks a return to traditional political positions. The North Korean leadership is entrenching and preparing for defence.

3 Socialist neo-conservativism in North Korea

Most notable among ideological trends in North Korea in 2007 and early 2008 was what could be called socialist neo-conservativism, although it remains to be seen how long this trend actually lasts or whether it was a short-term pre-emptive reaction to the prospect of a conservative government in South Korea. On 14 September 2007, *Rodong Shinmun* carried an editorial warning against Western attempts at spreading democracy, which were described as attempts at dominating the world, destroying order and preparing for aggression. A few days later, another editorial revived the decades-old slogan of 'Let us produce, study and live like the anti-Japanese guerrillas!' September and October 2007 saw an increase in the intensity of articles in *Rodong Shinmun* that referred to traditional, conservative views of socialism. A number of articles in October stressed the inevitable victory of socialism, its scientific nature, its superiority over capitalism and the fact that socialism's victory is a 'natural law of history'. On 26 September, the theme of a more than a decade-old article by Kim Jong Il on the importance of ideology and ideological work (a belated reaction in 1995 to the Eastern European transformation) was again brought to the public's attention. The article warned that without proper ideological work, revolutionary enthusiasm would cool off and people would turn towards leading an easy life. No illusion about capitalism should be allowed.

The target might have been of a much more precise nature. On 6 October 2007, *Rodong Shinmun* carried a short article in which the term 'corruption' (*pup'aesŏng*) appeared with conspicuous frequency. The article explained the 'true nature of capitalism' as looking nice from the outside, but being rotten on the inside. North Koreans should not be tempted and misled, corrupted and depraved by its appeal. Capitalism, it said, spends huge sums on ideology and tries to turn people into slaves of money. The corrupt bourgeois lifestyle paralyses the sound mentality of the people and reduces them to mental and physical cripples. What can be identified as an anti-corruption drive was supported by the systematical implementation of a double-entry accounting system and a number of measures directed at scaling down the influence of markets on the North Korean economy (see below).

Conservativism in North Korea, too, goes hand in hand with traditionalism. On 29 October, it was emphasised that the *chuch'e* idea means 'believing in people as in heaven'. This is not a new expression, yet nevertheless provides another interesting parallel to Korea's past. During the semi-religious nationalist Tonghak movement of the late 19th century, the principle of 'People are heaven', or more literally 'Man and God are one' (*innaech'ŏn*) had been used widely and today is a key concept of the Ch'ŏndokyo religion that is also practiced in South Korea. Supporting the notion of a partial return to even pre-socialist traditions was the re-introduction of a Confucian holiday on 4 April 2008, when for the first time in North Korean history Chŏngmyŏng (tomb sweeping day) was officially celebrated. This is remarkable because it reflects the readiness of the leadership to openly embrace traditional concepts to support both the nationalist agenda and ideas of filial piety. The latter of course is directly related to the two leaders. In April 2007, *Rodong Shinmun* had carried a short article reminding its readers of Chŏngmyŏng and its old meaning, especially tending to the graves of ancestors.[1] Chusŏk, the Korean equivalent to thanksgiving and the most important holiday in South Korea, was covered by *Rodong Shinmun* on 24 September as a 'folk holiday', continuing the re-integration of traditional customs into ideologically and politically correct life in North Korea. While there were reports that, despite the official condemnation of religions and 'superstition',

[1] The People's Republic of China (PRC), too, introduced Qingming as an official holiday for the first time in 2008, lasting for two days (4-5 April).

memorial services for ancestors were held regularly in the past decades, such official recognition is rare.

The offensive against the West continued, in support of traditional socialist ideas and the attack on new negative trends in North Korean society. On 15 October, an article denounced the imperialists' tendency to demand more and more concessions, hinting at an unwillingness to sacrifice socialist principles for economic aid. On 31 October, a further article stressed the need for self-reliance as the party's strategy for the economy in the 21st century. However, external aid is still not to be sacrificed. In an editorial in November 2007, *Rodong Shinmun* called upon 'all Koreans' to regard it as their sacred duty to support the Military First Policy, since without it Korea would be subjugated by big powers again. Sŏn'gun was also described as guaranteeing the 'dignity and prosperity' of the nation. These remarks are especially interesting against the background of the alleged progress in the Six Party Talks and the inter-Korean summit. North Koreans, used to reading between the lines of official statements, could interpret this as the government's reluctance to give up its nuclear arsenal despite the many peaceful signals in the preceding months, and as a hint that the anticipated aid and assistance coming in from the outside was a reaction to the North Korean possession of these weapons.

In November 2007, there were more signs of efforts aimed not only at consolidating the leading role of the party but also at a more decisive fight against any deviation from conservative socialist orthodoxy. *Rodong Shinmun* emphasised that in order to build socialism, 'it is necessary ... to strengthen the working-class party' and to 'fully ensure the party leadership over the revolution and construction.' The editorial demanded that people 'protect and develop socialist ownership'. This could be interpreted as a crackdown on private economic activities that in the last years have led to the growth of a middle class in North Korea. The sentence 'abandoning the above-said principle means surrender and betrayal' is an open threat that non-compliance will be punished severely. The same article went to great lengths to explain that if there were the slightest compromise with socialist principles, this could lead to the unprincipled introduction of capitalist ownership and methods of managing the economy that had brought about the collapse of socialism in Eastern Europe.

December 2007 saw another large number of programmatic editorials in *Rodong Shinmun*, continuing along the path of socialist neo-conservativism. In an editorial on 5 December 2007, the paper hailed socialism as the 'ideal of mankind' and the only way to achieve independence, freedom and dignity, repeating that the victory of socialism was inevitable and a law of history. One day later, an editorial asked all North Koreans to learn from the 'soldier culture', described as enthusiasm, militant spirit, optimism and emotion. On the same day, another editorial called for preserving the spirit of national independence, asking all Koreans 'in the north, south and overseas' to contribute their share. On 9 December, *Rodong Shinmun* denounced 'Western style democracy' as being a tool to secure the prosperity of only a few while subjugating the masses. If one allowed 'deceptive democracy', one would not be able defend the hard-won revolutionary gains, the sovereignty of the country and the destiny of the nation.

Although reports of this kind are hard to verify, the description by the South Korean conservative newspaper *Donga Ilbo* of a 'major restructuring' of party, government and military organisations ordered by Kim Jong Il since early 2008 fits into this context. All institutions are said to have been ordered to reduce their bureaucracies and the number of senior officials by 30 percent. Neither details nor the original source of the information were made public, however.

It remains to be seen whether such and other messages are meant to prepare the population for another 'arduous march' of food shortages, whether they constitute a pre-emptive reaction to the new South Korean government, an attempt to control the impact of the recent years of reform, or whether they indeed are the expression of a neo-conservative trend in North Korean policy. However, a glance at other events in the political and economic sphere especially since late summer 2007 seems to support the conclusion that the DPRK has at least temporarily reversed, or tried to reverse, a number of official positions and actual economic measures that in the past years had pointed at reformist tendencies on the domestic scene.

4 Other Ideological and Political Trends

Other meetings and events took place in addition to the annual parliamentary session. On 29 July 2007, North Korea held country-wide local council elections, which come every fourth year according to Article 133 of the constitution. The North Korean media reported that by 12:00, 80.05 percent of all voters had cast their ballots. By 18:00, it was announced that all voters except for those staying abroad had participated in the election. On 30 July, the Central Election Guidance Committee for the Election of Deputies to the Provincial (Municipality Directly under Central Authority), City (District) and County People's Assemblies of the DPRK issued its report on the results of the election. According to this report, 99.82 percent of all the voters registered on the list of voters participated in voting and 100 percent of them voted for the candidates. A total of 27,390 officials, workers, farmers and intellectuals were elected deputies. As is usual in most state-socialist systems, voters could only confirm the candidates but not select between alternatives.

More than a decade since the last meeting of this kind, the national meeting of Korean Worker's Party cells took place on 26 October 2007. The delegates were told to uphold the principle of *chuch'e* as developed by Kim Il Sung and systematised by Kim Jong Il. The cells were described as vanguard organisations carrying out the cause of the party with loyalty. The emphasis on the party cells, repeatedly supported by quotations from Kim Il Sung, could be interpreted as attempts at developing a more decentralised leadership structure following the Chinese model, although this would stand in contrast to the Korean tradition of strong centralisation. It also corresponds with the trend of a revival of the party as the centre of political leadership, something that at least in official statements seemed to have made way for the army in recent years.

Another rare event in 2007 was a meeting of 'intellectuals' (*chisikin*) in late November, defined as those holding academic degrees or titles; the last such meeting had taken place 15 years before. As reported in September, their number had grown 25 times and now stood at 2.1 million, with a growth rate of about 1,000 annually since 1970. In what sounded like a warning, on 24 November 2007 *Rodong Shinmun* carried an editorial cautioning that intellectuals can avoid 'degeneration' (*pyŏnjil*) only if they are led and educated by the working-class party. Four days later, a lengthy article was full of praise and appreciation, referring to 'uninterrupted heroic accomplishments', describing intellectuals as 'soldiers and disciples of Kim Jong Il', whose trust in intellectuals is 'undisputed'.

Other themes covered by the official North Korean media such as the South Korean presidential election, other relations between the two Koreas and foreign affairs, are dealt with elsewhere.

According to reports by the Seoul-based Citizens' Alliance for North Korean Human Rights, since 2002 the North Korean authorities have treated those caught in attempts to leave the country illegally less severely. This claim was, however, challenged by reports later in 2007 that the position of the government has again hardened. The issuance of travel permits between counties in North Korea and to China has become much more restrictive than it used to be in the years following the 1995-97 famine.

5 Economic trends

5.1 *Infrastructure and social overhead capital*

Infrastructure modernisation continued to be a priority of North Korean economic policy. In May 2007, the first test-run of trains on the restored tracks along the west (Kyŏngŭi line) and the east coast (Tonghae line) between the two Koreas at last took place. The meaning was more symbolic, but it also reflected the North's desire to show signs of goodwill after the 13 February 2007 agreement. Although construction had been completed in 2005, earlier test- runs had been called off repeatedly by North Korea for 'technical reasons'. In December 2007, the first regular cargo service across the DMZ started. Co-operation between North Korea and Russia on the modernisation of railways continued. Russian estimates of a railway rehabilitation project (around US$2-7 billion) suggest that this will be a major effort, but progress so far has been slow. After a *Rodong Shinmun* note in November 2007 on the visit by the Russian Railway Company, North Korean Central Television reported in March 2008 that Russia and North Korea had agreed to start work soon on repairing the railway linking the Russian Far East city of Kazan to the DPRK's northern port of Rajin. In June 2007, it was reported that the DPRK had agreed with Russia to allow foreign ships to enter and leave the port of Rajin in the northeast; a similar measure had been agreed in 1991, but the concession was taken back in 1994 because of the nuclear crisis and a lack of interest. Soaring economic growth in China and Russia in the intervening period could, however, lead to better results this time.

In early October 2007, it was reported that North Korea is planning to develop its seaport of Nampo into a logistics hub. The complex is to extend over 9.7 million sq m and is to include a scrap metal processing site. China and Canada are to invest in the development of the logistics centre, while Canada and Japan are to finance the building of the processing site.

On 3 September 2007, the 22nd meeting of the board of directors of the North-East Asia Telephone and Telecommunications Co. Ltd. was held in Pyongyang. In January 2008, CHEO Technology, a subsidiary of Orascom Telecom, the fourth-largest Arab telephone operator based in Egypt, announced that it had won the first commercial licence to provide mobile telephone services in the DPRK. The North Korean state-owned Korea Post and Telecommunications Corporation holds a 25-percent share in CHEO Technology. Reports suggested that the existing ban on mobile telephone use would be lifted in April 2008.

Efforts at human resource development added to the impression of a concerted effort at improving the country's social overhead capital. According to a Radio Free Asia report, about 6,000 North Koreans who took the TOEFL test of English proficiency between September 2005 and December 2006 fared better on average than Japanese and only a few points below South Koreans. This indicates that for those who do have access to English education, the quality is quite high, and raises hopes that modernisation of the North Korean economy and society, once the political environment was right, would not be hindered by the state of human resources.

Corresponding with the overall line of development as announced in the New Year joint editorial, the Pyongyang University of Science and Technology (PUST) has been set up, staffed and financially supported at least partly by international contributors. It is modelled after the Yanbian University of Science and Technology in China. The language of instruction is English. The president of PUST is a Korean-American and a former head of a US university. The plan is to have 600 graduate and 2,000 undergraduate students by 2012. Also involved is the president of Pohang University of Science and Technology in South Korea. In April 2008, North Korea announced a new five-year plan for the development of science and technology to last until 2012.

5.2 *Agriculture, food production and related issues*

These have traditionally taken centre stage both for external observers of North Korea as well as in domestic policy. In June 2007, visitors reported that the food situation in North Korea was not as bad as they would have expected from the figures issued by international aid agencies. In fact, cash crops were planted in response to decreasing demand for staple foodstuffs and to both interest in and opportunity for increasing farmer's incomes through individual activities. It was reported that the price of rice in euros was remaining relatively stable as compared to 2006, and had even dropped slightly to reach 80 cents per kg. Public distribution was still working in Pyongyang; the little notebooks in which the records are usually kept were observed to be within reach of the sales personnel. However, dark clouds appeared, literally, with regard to food in August 2007 and then again in September. Heavy rains and subsequent floods hit North Korea, taking hundreds of lives and destroying between 11-16 percent of the country's corn and rice crops. Over 100,000 people lost their homes, and the World Food Programme estimated that about 960,000 people were in need of help following flooding. About 580 km of roads, 490 bridges and 1,200 public buildings were damaged or destroyed, and as many as 171,000 animals were lost. According to South Korean estimates, the North Korean harvest in 2007, at about 4 million tons of rice and rice equivalent as opposed to roughly 4.5 million tons in 2006, was much lower than expected because of natural disasters. In March 2008, the official news agency KCNA started issuing reports about food difficulties. According to reports from the PRC Customs Bureau, North Korean food imports from China in 2007 rose significantly (over 100 percent in the case of rice) over the previous year. With imports growing, rising food prices on the global market have had a negative effect on the DPRK, although higher export prices for minerals may have offset some of the losses.

According to an almanac released by KCNA in 2007, the country's population has grown by about 200,000 annually since 1996 and reached 23,612,000 in 2004, which is about one million higher that the 2004 US CIA estimate. Interestingly, North Korea in the past used to underreport its population numbers; with renewed interest in food aid, this policy might have changed.

Because of floods and malnutrition, diseases such as tuberculosis have continued to spread. The magnitude of natural disasters in the country became visible in the World Disasters Report 2007, released by the International Federation of Red Cross and Red Crescent Societies. The DPRK was described as having suffered over 458,000 deaths in natural disasters between 1997 and 2006, some 38 percent of the approximately 1.2 million related deaths reported in 220 countries across the world during that period.

5.3 *Other economic issues*

On other economic issues, information from North Korea was as usual scarce and often anecdotal. Nevertheless, one can gain an overall impression of the country's economy and of a number of trends that not been covered in other sections of this overview. There were reports that in the aftermath of the 2002 reforms, the collection of real estate usage fees had begun in some areas and was to be expanded to the whole country. This would be the equivalent of a real estate tax and would mark another attempt at modernising the North Korean system of economic management. This ties in with the parliamentary session on the national budget, discussed above, where it was stated that income from utility fees on real estate was to grow by 15.4 percent (2006: 12 percent) and that local budgetary revenue showed strong growth.

Reports based on testimonies by defectors and North Koreans crossing the border to China indicated that in 2007 a widening income gap persisted, leading to a further segregation within society and amounting to a threat to stability and legitimacy of the socialist regime. Even a real estate boom in the capital was reported, where political connections and money were said to have helped in overcoming strict legal ownership rules. The existence since 2002 of an officially monetised economy supports the credibility of reports that defection was possible against bribe money, and that corruption has been spreading further.

The North Korean leadership in 2007 did not end its attempts to improve its economic performance by new means, such as internet sales. For example, an 'e-shop' section was added to the DPRK's official business information site (www.dprk-economy.com). The 3rd Pyongyang Autumn International Trade Fair was held 24-27 September 2007 under the auspices of the European Business Association in Pyongyang. And despite the neo-conservative trend in ideology, an official North Korean scholarly publication (*Economic Studies*) argued quite pragmatically in January 2008 that the DPRK's trade structure should be reframed in order to match the demands of the capitalist market, that goods were better processed at home before export rather than being shipped right away as raw materials, that international demand should be taken into consideration, and that market niches should be identified and utilised. However, by the end of 2007, North Korean market activity had reportedly been reduced significantly, although it had not stopped. The most controversial measure was the reported regulation on a minimum age for trading women, which could be interpreted as another desperate and politically risky attempt at bringing back the workforce to their state jobs. Previous measures towards that goal had included a higher food ration for those with regular employment.

In 2003, in a unique move, bonds had been issued to take liquidity off the market and to improve the state's fiscal situation. These bonds were special in that they offered no interest but rather the chance to win larger amounts of money. The promise was indeed kept; in January 2008, the winners of the 6th draw in the lottery on the ten-year People's Life Bonds were announced on Korean Central TV.

In November 2007, it was reported that a South Korean entrepreneur planned to open a fried chicken delivery service in Pyongyang. The somewhat unusual nature of the plan aside, it was interesting to see how he tried to argue in line with nationalist sentiments. He explained to the North Korean authorities that this product would come to their country eventually, and rather than letting Kentucky Fried Chicken take over the North Korean market, this privilege should be granted to a Korean.

6 Administrative and Personnel Changes

An unusual third item on the agenda of the April 2007 SPA session was the replacement of the prime minister. Pak Pong Ju was relieved of the premiership, and Kim Yong Il was elected as the new premier of the Cabinet of the DPRK. Kim Yong Chun was elected as vice-chairman of the National Defence Committee. No explanations for these personnel changes were provided. However, Japanese sources suggested Pak Pong Ju had been 'fired' for promoting an incentive-based capitalistic wage system.

With the reconfirmed central function of the Cabinet for economic policy, the new premier Kim Yong Il's post is a key one for North Korea's economic development. The official North Korean media reported that Kim was born on 2 May 1944, served in the Korean People's Army, and then graduated from the University of Marine Transport as a navigation officer. After spending three years as a three-revolution team member, he worked as instructor and deputy director of a general bureau in the Ministry of Land and Marine Transport for 14 years. He had been Minister of Land and Marine Transport since 1994, in which position he was responsible for a major economic modernisation project near Nampo. He has also worked on maritime communications and transportation agreements with China, Pakistan and Syria, travelling to Syria as head of an economic delegation in May 2005.

In late November 2007, Chang Song Taek (61) was appointed the country's chief internal security supervisor. Outside observers had watched Chang keenly because of his marriage to Kim Jong Il's sister in 1972. His resulting close relationship with Kim Jong Il had led to speculation that Chang might be a possible successor. Chang, seen as reform-minded, had also been associated with plans to develop the city of Sinŭiju into a special economic zone, and led an economic delegation to Seoul in 2002, visiting Samsung Electronics, Hyundai Motor and Posco Steel. He has also made several visits to China, leading a delegation of the North Korean Chamber of Commerce to Shanghai. He had been absent from public affairs for about one year from 2004 until the end of 2005, triggering speculations about a failed coup or an anticipated threat to Kim Jong Il.

Veteran diplomat Pak Ui Chun took the post of foreign minister, left vacant by the death of Paek Nam Sun at the beginning of 2007.

In May 2007, rumours were floating that Kim Jong Il had to undergo heart surgery. While speculations about his health have occurred repeatedly in the past and are usually hard to validate, they remind us that the most crucial non-economic factor for domestic stability in North Korea, continuous leadership, remains largely unresolved. This will be the case until a successor to the leader or, most likely in the context of the overdue 7th Party Congress, some form of collective leadership has been proclaimed and endorsed by Kim Jong Il.

RELATIONS BETWEEN THE TWO KOREAS 2007-2008

James E. Hoare

If 2006-07 was a period when relations between the two Koreas moved from hostility to a return to engagement, 2007-08 followed the reverse path. The government of the Republic of Korea (ROK—South Korea) under President Roh Moo-hyun pursued with considerable success a determined policy of engagement once the freeze in relations that followed the post-2006 nuclear test was lifted. Exchanges reached unprecedented levels in 2007. The transport links between the two parts of the peninsula were beginning to be restored, and a second North-South summit, initially planned for August but postponed because of flooding in the North, was held in Pyongyang in October. But at the same time, Roh's popularity and that of his party plunged lower and lower, and conservative voices became stronger and stronger. Well before the ROK presidential election in December 2007, it was clear that ROK policies towards the DPRK would be in more critical hands from 2008. The Democratic People's Republic of Korea (DPRK—North Korea) held its fire during the election period and well after, but the final days of the period under review saw it making harsh criticisms of the new government under Lee Myung-bak. The outlook might improve if the nuclear issue is settled, but for the present, North-South relations seem destined for a rough passage.

1 THE RESUMPTION OF CONTACTS

1.1 *Humanitarian aid*

After the February 2007 breakthrough in the Six Party Talks,[1] North-South relations gradually entered a new and more positive phase that lasted until the change of ROK president in February 2008. Talks re-

[1] See *Korea Yearbook 2007*, pp. 44-5, 56.

sumed on a variety of issues, although at first, while the atmosphere was positive, there was little substantive development. Agreement in principle on the resumption of ROK aid, distinct from the fuel oil promised in the February 2007 agreement, was reached in April, after stormy exchanges at economic co-operation talks, with the leader of the DPRK delegation walking out at one point. However, when the DPRK failed to meet a deadline on the nuclear issue, on the grounds that the United States (US) had not released blocked DPRK funds, the ROK held back the aid to bring pressure on the DPRK. But with the long-delayed first cross-border test runs on the railways linking the ROK with the Kaesŏng industrial zone and the Mt Kŭmgang tourist complex in May,[2] there began to be progress in the North-South political and economic dialogue. Once the issue of the blocked funds was resolved, and the nuclear talks seemed back on track, ROK rice and fertiliser deliveries to the DPRK finally resumed in the summer. In a separate move, the ROK also began to send heavy fuel oil to the DPRK in July under the terms of the February 2007 agreement, after the International Atomic Energy Agency (IAEA) had resumed contact with the DPRK over its nuclear facilities. A further tranche of aid, including construction materials and heavy equipment, was sent in August, following heavy flooding and widespread devastation in the North.

1.2 *Trade*

Trade between the two halves of Korea continued to grow; by the end of 2007, cross-border trade was up 33 percent, and totalled US$1.79 billion, compared to $1.35 billion in 2006. The ROK remained in 2007 the DPRK's second largest trade partner after the People's Republic of China. DPRK sales of marine products and minerals showed a large increase. One consequence of the growing trade was a steady increase in the number of South Koreans travelling to the DPRK. Excluding tourist visitors to Mt Kŭmgang, over 102,000 South Koreans went to the North in the first nine months of 2007, an in-

[2] Agreement was reached during the June 2000 inter-Korean summit on the reconnection of the railways across the Demilitarized Zone (DMZ), cut since the Korean War (1950-53), but implementation was delayed because of problems over security and other issues. The tracks were reconnected in 2003, and an agreement for a test run was reached in 2006 but was cancelled at the last minute by the DPRK.

crease of over 30 percent over the same period in 2006. While this figure included government officials and representatives of non-governmental organisations, the majority, almost 70,000, were engaged in one or another form of business. By contrast, only 730 North Koreans visited the South during the same period.

1.3 *Kaesŏng and other industrial zones*

The Kaesŏng industrial zone, situated just across the DMZ, played an important part in the increase in trade, and much effort went into its continued development. Over the year, trade involving Kaesŏng rose by 48 percent. According to a report by the Kaesŏng Industrial District Management Committee, since the beginning of operation in 2005, the total value of goods manufactured in the Kaesŏng Industrial Complex surpassed US$300 million in February 2008. Production rose from US$15 million in 2005 to US$74 million in 2006 and to US$185 million in 2007. By October 2007, a total of 45 companies were employing 19,433 DPRK workers and 800 workers from the ROK. In August 2007, following DPRK demands, wages in Kaesŏng were raised for the first time since the zone was opened. The new pay rate increased by 5 percent and now guarantees a minimum wage of US$52.50. North Korea had originally demanded a 15 percent increase. Following the first North-South prime ministerial-level talks for 15 years in November, regular railway freight service commenced in the following month, pushing up hopes of a further expansion of the zone. The railway was seen as a sign of hope for the future, and raised the prospect of reducing inter-Korean freight transportation costs by a large margin. There were also discussions of a commuter service, bringing ROK managers and staff from Munsan to P'anmunjŏm and then on to Kaesŏng. ROK officials also put forward the idea of eventual expansion to link the ROK with the Trans-Siberian rail system. However, soon after the beginning of the freight service, DPRK officials began suggesting that the frequency of trains be reduced since the volume of traffic did not justify the number of trains, a move that did not augur well for the future of the project. In a further development, a trial 'factory-apartment', a complex including small factory units, recreational facilities, dining halls and apartment blocks built by the ROK-government-owned Korea Industrial Complex Corporation was completed in October. This was along the lines of similar complexes in South

Korea, and seemed to be of most interest to ROK textile companies eager to move to an area with cheaper labour costs. It was followed by an agreement in principle in December to build workers' apartments in the zone. In March 2008, the special zone saw the first ground-breaking ceremony for a foreign company, Prettl, a German firm making auto parts; two Chinese companies had earlier announced their intention to open there but had not done so by April 2008.

The Sinŭiju Special Economic Zone, moribund since the Chinese imprisoned its first designated director, the Netherlands-Chinese businessman Yang Bin, in 2002, showed signs of being revived, on more modest terms than originally envisaged. From August 2007, real estate prices in Sinŭiju started to increase, residents were relocated, and some areas were fenced off. Presumably, this time the North Koreans will take account of Chinese interests and susceptibilities.

1.4 *Other links*

Other links between the two countries continued to develop. In May, the first North Korean ship to dock in the ROK in over 50 years arrived at Pusan as part of a planned regular sailing schedule between that port and the North Korean port of Rajin. Family reunions, which had been suspended after the 2006 nuclear test, resumed, with both face- to-face meetings and contacts via video links taking place at regular intervals. The two Red Cross societies began to discuss the difficult question of those missing since the Korean War, a growing issue in the ROK as Japan continued to press the DPRK on the question of abductees.[3] ROK tourist visits to the DPRK expanded. The Inner Kŭmgang region opened in June 2007, and Hyundai Asan began discussions with the DPRK on a possible US$3 billion project to develop tourism on the east coast north of the Mt Kŭmgang region. In March 2008, the first private vehicles from South Korea were allowed to drive directly to the Kŭmgang area, albeit under very tight control.

In December 2007 there was a further expansion of the tourist exchanges, when Hyundai Asan began day tours to Kaesŏng for both ROK and foreign tourists. It was planned that 300 persons a day would cross six times a week. These tours were not cheap, at 180,000 won (US$190) per person. Before the outbreak of the Korean War in

[3] See the survey article on the foreign relations of the two Koreas in this volume.

1950, Kaesŏng had been in South Korea, and some of the first visitors had lived there until the war. There was much dissatisfaction among them when they found that, as on the Kŭmgang tours, visits were heavily controlled, contact with North Koreans strictly limited, and attempts to visit former homes frustrated. Nevertheless, it was a start and it enabled ordinary South and North Koreans to get some feel for each other, albeit at a distance and in very controlled circumstances. If the poor housing and pinched looks of the citizens of Kaesŏng made an impact on the ROK visitors, the wealth of the latter would not have been lost on those North Koreans who could observe them. Following the October summit (see below), the North Koreans indicated that tourist visits to Mt Paektu on the Sino-DPRK border might be possible, and Hyundai and Korean Workers' Party officials signed an agreement in November to develop this project. However, implementation of the agreement will depend on how the political climate develops under a new president.

Information technology was another positive area. At the end of 2007, the DPRK confirmed that South Korean companies could run computers with Internet access in the Kaesŏng industrial zone, while, in a separate development, there were growing signs of North-South co-operation on computer software technology. The Pyongyang University of Science and Technology, the first joint North-South educational project, which opened in September, and which is due to take in its first students in April 2008, is expected to contribute to this process.[4]

2 The October 2007 summit

Most important of all, however, as proof of improving relations was the second North-South summit. Early in the year, ROK officials began hinting that there might be a second summit, even though the DPRK leader, Kim Jong Il, had failed to make a planned return visit to the ROK following the 2000 visit to Pyongyang by then ROK President Kim Dae-jung. The conservative media and the main opposition Grand National Party (GNP), now riding high in the opinion polls, objected both to the summit and to a related move to cancel military exercises associated with the annual US-ROK Ulchi Lens Focus exer-

---

[4] See also the survey article on DPRK internal developments in this volume.

cise as a means of improving the summit atmosphere—the exercise itself is largely a computer one and in the event was not cancelled. On 8 August, it was announced by the two sides that the visit would take place from 28 to 30 August. Despite the opposition's stance, most South Koreans accepted that a second summit would be a positive development even if they did not have high expectations about its likely outcome—one opinion poll showed 74 percent support for the visit, although around 60 percent thought that there would be little in the way of positive outcome from it. Outside observers were concerned that Kim Jong Il would use a second summit to circumvent the Six Party Talks and the denuclearisation process.

In the event, the DPRK requested a postponement because of the floods, and eventually the summit took place in October. Because of the proximity to the presidential election, the GNP again demanded postponement, but President Roh Moo-hyun refused, and the visit duly went ahead from 2 to 4 October. Roh took his wife and a large business entourage, all of whom crossed the DMZ, Roh and his wife symbolically walking across the demarcation line. Despite some continued criticism, the visit passed off successfully.[5] Kim Jong Il was not as enthusiastic as he had appeared to be in 2000, and commented that the ROK engagement policy appeared to be aimed at overthrowing the existing structures in the DPRK. Kim also looked less robust than he had done on previous occasions, and the South Korean media carried much speculation about his health. This led Kim to deny that he suffered from diabetes and heart problems. Roh attended the mass performance spectacle 'Arirang', despite some ROK opposition, but he did not allow himself to be overwhelmed as some had feared. The leaders signed a Joint Declaration in which both were referred to by their official titles. In it, they agreed to work towards improved economic and security arrangements and to reduce military tension. There was a nod in the direction of the Six Party Talks and the possibility of replacing the existing armistice agreement with some form of peace agreement. Social and humanitarian co-operation would be expanded. Building on the Kaesŏng experience, the two leaders agreed on the development of further economic zones near the DMZ, turning the West Sea into a 'special peace and co-operation zone'. Work would begin on improving the DPRK's transport infrastructure, including the

[5] For details of the summit and the agreements reached, see 'The 2007 South-North Korean Summit', *Vantage Point* (Seoul), Special Edition October 2007.

Kaesŏng-Sinŭiju rail link and the Kaesŏng-Pyongyang highway, and a direct air service would be introduced between Seoul and Mt Paektu on the Sino-North Korean border. None of this would be cheap; estimates put the bill as high as US$11 billion; expensive, but perhaps worth the money if it continued the process of modifying DPRK behaviour and still less than the expected cost of a North Korean collapse. Further talks and contacts continued after the summit, including a prime ministerial-level meeting in November and the first high-level military talks in seven years in December, while the DPRK New Year joint editorial described the summit as a significant event. But it was increasingly clear, after the presidential elections in December, that the president-elect, the GNP's Lee Myung-bak, would not automatically implement the agreements reached by Roh.

3 Problems and Criticism

South Korean concerns about the DPRK nuclear programme had remained on the agenda, to the annoyance of the North Koreans, who wished to treat this issue as solely between themselves and the US. As usual, the DPRK tried to pre-empt discussions by insisting that its demands be met at the beginning of negotiations, but South Korean officials had stood firm and the North backed down. Hopes that the resumption of governmental contacts after the February agreement might help solve difficult issues such as tensions in the West Sea proved abortive, and despite the agreement on railways, the military on both sides continued to treat each other with great wariness.

The growth of the Kaesŏng zone was also not without its critics. Many in the ROK questioned the basis on which companies established themselves at Kaesŏng, believing that the ROK government was either applying pressure on companies to move there or was directly subsidising at least some of them. The terms and conditions of employment in the zone, which were largely dictated by the DPRK, came in for adverse comment, especially from the US but also increasingly from some groups in the ROK. The fact that salaries were not paid directly to workers was a particular cause of concern, which echoed earlier US criticism of the United Nations Development Programme's projects in the DPRK, but there were also adverse worries about the DPRK efforts to restrict contact to the barest minimum between ROK and DPRK workers.

4 THE ROK PRESIDENTIAL ELECTION AND ITS CONSEQUENCES

But it was the ROK presidential election that had most effect on North-South relations. Although the idea of North-South engagement has an impeccable conservative pedigree, dating back to the days of President Park Chung-hee and the first North-South exchanges of the early 1970s, it had only really taken off after 1997 under the relatively progressive (by South Korean standards) Kim Dae-jung and his successor Roh Moo-hyun. It was thus inescapably linked in ROK political circles with 'radicalism'. The main ROK conservative party, the GNP, could, if it chose, point to its own record of attempting to engage the North. Its former chair, Park Geun-hye, Park Chung-hee's daughter, had visited the DPRK and met Kim Jong Il, who had apparently expressed his admiration for her father's economic and social policies. However, the GNP has generally preferred to take a critical stand on the engagement policy, which it claimed was appeasement of the North, and this scepticism was reflected in the campaign for the party's presidential candidate and, once Lee Myung-bak had been selected, in his own campaign.

Lee tried to move the GNP away from expressing a wholly negative position. He did not reject the idea of engagement with the DPRK; indeed, as the campaign progressed, be developed what he described as a 'pragmatic approach', with a 'Vision 3000 Policy' whereby he would work to raise the DPRK per capita income to US$3,000 per annum.[6] Soon after his election, he said that he would be willing to hold a summit with Kim Jong Il, although since the two previous summits had been held in Pyongyang, the next one should be in Seoul. At the same time, Lee stressed that good relations with the North would depend on progress on the nuclear issue, and that it should not be at the expense of the ROK's relations with the US and other countries and the avoidance of difficult subjects. As he put it soon after his election: 'I will persuade North Korea that the abandonment of its nuclear program will bring greater benefits for maintaining its regime and for the North Korean people. Persuading North Korea won't be easy, but it is necessary.' Lee also argued that human rights issues should not be ignored when dealing with the DPRK, but they

---

[6] Estimates of the current DPRK per capita income vary from around US$500 to around US$1,500, but given the existence of a number of parallel economies and the absence of reliable figures, it is impossible to be certain of the correct figure. It is certainly less than US$3,000, however.

should not be raised in a spirit of hostility: 'Criticism that comes with affection can help make North Korean society healthy ... I will make a change from the previous administration that completely refrained from criticizing North Korea and pandered to it in a one-sided way.'[7] Lee also indicated that the various projects mooted at the October summit would all be subject to review. After his election, Lee proposed abolishing the Unification Ministry and attaching its functions to the Foreign Affairs and Trade Ministry, thus indicating that relations between the two Koreas would be state-to- state relations rather than inter-Korean.

Although the DPRK was critical of Lee before he became the GNP's presidential candidate, it generally remained silent about him during the formal election campaign period from September 2007 onwards.[8] There were no attacks on Lee or the GNP or, apart from the summit, no statements or actions that might have been construed as support for Roo Moo-hyun. But the DPRK media strongly criticised Lee Hoi-chang, the former GNP politician who stood as an independent candidate, and who was extremely hostile to the engagement policy.

This self-denying ordinance continued after Lee's victory as the DPRK waited to see whether election rhetoric would be translated into action. In private exchanges in the margins of meetings, some DPRK officials said that they expected engagement to continue, while others said that if it did not, the South would have to bear the unspecified consequences. Exchanges in fact continued until the last few weeks of the Roh presidency. In December, the DPRK made its first ever repayment to the ROK for humanitarian loans, when 500 tons of zinc, valued at US$1.2 million arrived at the ROK port of Inch'ŏn. In mid-February 2008, the ROK sent steel plates to the DPRK as part of the denuclearisation package, for example, and survey work began on a hospital update programme agreed during the summit meeting. In March, after Lee's inauguration, a group of 159 ROK businessmen visited the DPRK for four days.

But there were signs of DPRK concern over the election outcome. Media comment from the joint New Year editorial onwards stressed the need for North and South to work together in the spirit of the June

---

[7] KOIS (Korean Overseas Information Service) Newsletter, 20 December 2007.

[8] The only exception was a 5 November 2007 article in the party newspaper *Rodong Shinmun*, which drew on South Korean press reports about fraud allegations that had been made against Lee.

2000 and October 2007 summits. There was increasing reportage of alleged protests in South Korea at illiberal policies implemented by the new government. The DPRK cancelled the first working-level meeting planned for 22-23 January 2008, which was due to discuss railway repairs and other matters, pleading that as it was the New Year period, officials were too busy to meet. No new date was set for this meeting, and a number of others that had been planned also failed to materialise. Another clear sign of DPRK concern was that there was no request for ROK fertiliser and food aid, which in recent years had been made in January or February, before the beginning of spring planting. There was speculation but no confirmation that the DPRK was not prepared to risk a rebuff.

By the end of March, it was becoming obvious that it would not be business as before. Although President Lee moved away from one initiative that had worried the DPRK, the proposed abolition of the Unification Ministry, he remained firm in his emphasis that there needed to be a settlement of the nuclear issue before his government would assist the DPRK and that nothing already in place was exempt from re-examination. The tensions came to a head in the second half of March, as the ROK National Assembly elections loomed larger on the political horizon. When Lee's new Unification Minister, Kim Ha-joong, said that further development of the Kaesŏng special zone would be dependent on progress towards denuclearisation, the DPRK responded by demanding that 11 out of the 13 ROK government officials based in Kaesŏng be removed immediately. The ROK Unification Ministry expressed its 'deep regret' over the move, and expressed the hope that the DPRK would agree to normalise economic exchanges as soon as possible.

Instead of an improvement, there was further a deterioration after the chairman of the ROK Joint Chiefs of Staff told the National Assembly at his confirmation hearing that the ROK would take pre-emptive action if it appeared that the DPRK was about to use nuclear weapons against the South. The DPRK responded with a series of test firings of short-range missiles in the West Sea, scene of earlier naval clashes between the two sides, and with accusations of ROK naval intrusions into DPRK waters. Then in its news report for 31 March 2008, the North Korean news agency carried what it said was a note sent to the ROK military authorities dated 29 March, which threatened to ban all movement of ROK military personnel across the Military Demarcation Line at P'anmunjŏm, as well as an item from 30 March headed 'Military Commentator Blasts Outbursts of Chairman of Joint Chiefs of Staff of South Korean Forces'.[9] This mocked the ROK stand, threatened retaliation if the ROK did try pre-emption, and indicated that all North-South contacts would be suspended if the 'present south Korean authorities' continued their 'new policy of the confrontation towards the DPRK.' On 1 April, *Rodong Shinmun*, carried a 'Commentator' article that for the first time since the election attacked Lee Myung-bak and his government by name. Lee was compared to former president Kim Young-sam, who had also meddled in nuclear matters, and dismissed as following the US line.

5 Outlook

The short-term outlook for inter-Korean relations does not look promising. In theory, a spat between the two governments need not affect non-governmental exchanges, but the reality is different. Much of the South Korean involvement in the North since 1997 has been government driven, and if that spur is removed, interest is likely to falter. It now seems unlikely that the development of Kaesŏng or the other planned economic zones will make much progress without ROK government involvement, and planned transport and other infrastructure projects may be put on hold. That said, if agreement is reached between the US and the DPRK on the nuclear issue, it would not be impossible for the two Koreas to restart the process of engagement. President Lee may also find that domestic support for a confrontation policy fades somewhat if there is a marked increase in tension or clashes between the two Koreas, or if popular developments such as family reunions and tourism are affected by the renewed hostility between North and South. At that point, Lee might well want to draw upon the conservative tradition of engagement. But we are some way from that stage yet.

---

[9] 'Notice Sent to Chief Delegate of South Side to Inter-Korean General-level Military Talks', (North) Korean Central News Agency (KCNA), 29 March 2008; 'Military Commentator Blasts Outbursts of Chairman of Joint Chiefs of Staff of South Korean Forces', KCNA, 30 March 2008, both carried by KCNA on 31 March 2008, and available at http://www.kcna.co.jp/index-e.htm, accessed 28 April 2008.

FOREIGN RELATIONS OF THE TWO KOREAS 2007-2008

James E. Hoare

INTRODUCTION

Issues relating to the nuclear programme of the Democratic People's Republic of Korea (DPRK—North Korea) continued to have an effect on the foreign relations of both Koreas. Although the agreement on denuclearisation reached in February 2007 had widespread international implications for the two countries, its implementation was slow and fraught, with deadlines constantly slipping. In addition to the uncertainty over the nuclear issue, the other major development in the period under review was the change of president in the Republic of Korea (ROK—South Korea) in February 2008. President Lee Myung-bak distanced himself from the policies followed by his two predecessors, and reverted to a more avowedly conservative position. He promised a more robust approach to relations with the DPRK, and an improvement in the ROK's relations with the United States (US) and Japan. These changes could conceivably have negative consequences for the ROK's links with the People's Republic of China (PRC) and Russia, although President Lee has pledged to have good relations with all his neighbours. Lee was also somewhat critical of the Ministry of Foreign Affairs and Trade. The kidnapping of a group of ROK Christian missionaries in Afghanistan in July 2007 led to much domestic angst about Koreans' lack of understanding and knowledge of the outside world.

1 REPUBLIC OF KOREA

1.1 *Relations with the United States*

ROK-US relations moved onto a more even keel during 2007, and there seemed to be an abatement of the anti-US feeling that had characterised the earlier years of the Roh Moo-hyun presidency. The less confrontational US policy towards North Korea that developed in the second George W. Bush administration brought the two long-term allies more into line on how to handle the DPRK. The issue of wartime control over ROK forces, which had been so contentious in 2006 and 2007, appeared to be settled by the February 2007 agreement between the US and the ROK,[1] and the debate subsided. The issue was raised again in the ROK presidential election, with calls from the conservative—and ultimately victorious—Grand National Party (GNP) for a renegotiation of the deal, and the incoming president hinted that he might seek to do this. But given that the change has impeccable conservative antecedents and widespread support among the US military, renegotiation seems unlikely. The US also confirmed in February 2008 that it would continue to reduce the number of its forces in the ROK, which should be down to 25,000 by the end of 2008. In the meantime, the relocation of US forces away from forward positions continued, and so did disputes between the two sides over the costs both of the moves and of the clearing of the former US camps.

ROK forces remained in Iraq, although former President Roh said on one occasion that he had made an 'historical error' in agreeing to send them, but that the alliance with the US required the ROK to support its ally. Roh planned to reduce their numbers to 600 from 1,200 and withdraw them entirely by the end of 2008; this looks unlikely under President Lee.

Trade issues between the two countries were somewhat contentious, and scrapping over market access continued. The Lone Star case[2] and the continued difficulties that the Hong Kong and Shanghai Banking Corporation faced over its attempts to acquire the Korea Exchange Bank both raised concerns about the ROK attitude to foreign investment. Indeed, direct foreign investment in the ROK declined in 2007, for the third consecutive year, to US$10.5 billion, down from US$11.2 billion in 2006; some saw this as confirmation of the hostile attitude to foreign business in the ROK. Such concerns were not, of course, confined to US businessmen, but they did feature regularly in the activities of the American Chamber of Commerce and in comments from the expatriate US community. There were high hopes that

[1] See *Korea Yearbook 2007*, pp. 49-50.

[2] For background on this case, see James C. Schopf, 'The Lone Star Scandal: Was it Corruption?', *Korea Yearbook 2007*, pp. 83-111.

the incoming president, with his corporate background, would be more understanding of the needs of business than his two predecessors. His transition team tried to reassure investors that there would be changes after Lee's inauguration in both the attitude to investment and in the provision of facilities for foreigners coming to the ROK. The inclusion of foreign advisors on trade and investment matters in the transition team was also designed to reassure foreigners about the new government's commitment to the encouragement of investment. However, more than one commentator speculated about President Lee's commitment to open markets, given his background and some of his comments about the undesirability of profits leaving the country.

The fraught negotiations on the US-ROK free trade agreement just met the 7 April 2007 deadline that allowed US President Bush to notify Congress of his intention to sign such an agreement. Even as the deadline was met, however, the US side insisted that there were still major areas requiring attention before the agreement would be ratified. By the time the US released the draft text in May 2007, the agreement faced an additional set of hurdles resulting from the Bush administration's adoption of new trade policy guidelines. These meant that there would have to be further negotiations on labour and environmental issues before the agreement was submitted to Congress. The ROK side expressed disappointment and said that renegotiation was not possible, but that it would agree to discussions if there was a formal US proposal. The result was that, despite the high hopes of both sides, the agreement remains unratified. There remains much hostility to it in the US Congress, especially among the majority Democrats, and the forthcoming change of US president may lead to further problems. Domestic ROK opposition did not disappear. The 7 April announcement was greeted by hostile demonstrators demanding the scrapping of the deal, and discontent with it periodically surfaced during the following twelve months.

The importation of US beef brought renewed problems. The ROK had banned all imports of US beef in December 2003 because of fears over 'mad-cow disease'.[3] The ban was partially lifted in 2006, allowing boneless beef from cattle under thirty months to be imported. In July 2007, however, a shipment of beef was found to contain bones, and a partial ban was re-introduced. Later, after a further consignment

---

[3] Strictly, 'bovine spongiform encephalopathy' (BSE), which is linked to a fatal brain-wasting disease in humans, called variant Creutzfeldt-Jakob Disease (vCJD).

was also found to contain bones, the ROK government again banned all US beef imports in October. Soon after coming to office, President Lee decided to lift the ban. However, this led, outside the period of this review, to violent protests and a marked plunge in the new president's poll ratings.

Lee had pledged during his campaign that he would restore ROK-US relations to their former closeness and that he would seek to broaden the alliance. This struck a chord in the US, and while the administration remained formally neutral, there were clearly many in the US who welcomed the departure of the radical Roh Moo-hyun. Members of the transition team made frequent visits to Washington and it was announced soon after Lee's inauguration that his first overseas visit would be to the US. But even conservative ROK presidents have had difficulties with the ROK-US relationship, and Lee is confronted by issues still unresolved. He may not find it easy to manage what remains his country's most important relationship, especially with the prospect of a new incumbent in the White House early in 2009.

1.2 *Relations with the People's Republic of China*

ROK relations with the PRC had steadily developed under President Roh Moo-hyun, symbolised by an agreement on a full-scale co-operation partnership in 2003. There had been problems, notably over DPRK refugees in the PRC and over historical disputes, but these were apparently forgotten in 2007, which marked the 15th anniversary of diplomatic relations between the two countries. The year was designated the ROK-China Exchange Year, and Chinese Premier Wen Jiabao visited in April. Numerous other exchanges also marked the year. The statistics were impressive. From almost nothing, the ROK had risen to become the PRC's third trade partner, after the US and Japan. Trade grew from US$63 million per annum in 1992 to US$145 billion in 2007, of which ROK exports accounted for US$82 billion. The PRC was the largest recipient of ROK firms' overseas investments, which reached US$35 billion in 2006; by June 2007, they had already reached US$28.7 billion. Some 30,000 ROK enterprises were operating in the PRC, and over 70,000 ROK citizens were living in China and some 440,000 Chinese in the ROK. There were approximately 4.8 million ROK visitors to China in 2007, while 1.1 million Chinese visited the ROK. Weekly flights between the two countries totalled 830, compared with 550 between Japan and the PRC. Millions of Chinese watched Korean television dramas.

It was not just a question of statistics. The PRC's role in the Six Party Talks and in restraining the DPRK was seen as important. In deference to Chinese wishes, the ROK was one of the few major countries in the world to refuse a visa to the Dalai Lama, the exiled Tibetan leader, which it did for the third time in November 2007.

Yet doubts were expressed. China's growing economic power was especially worrying. There were fears that cheap Chinese labour would replace Korean workers. That ROK companies were apparently cheerfully engaged in employing such labour either did not occur to commentators or was ignored. At the same time, there was concern at a possible downturn in the PRC economy, which would adversely affect the ROK's huge investment.

Although Chinese Premier Wen Jiabao told a press conference during his April 2007 visit that the PRC distinguished between historical scholarship and current politics, and noted that there were no territorial disputes between the ROK and the PRC, South Koreans were not wholly assured. There were suspicions that the PRC's 'honest broker' role in the Six Party Talks was a mask for wider ambitions vis-à-vis the DPRK, and the ROK media ran scare stories about alleged PRC economic advances in the DPRK.

Incoming President Lee Myung-bak's attitude to the PRC was not clear. In his campaigning, he laid much emphasis on improving relations with the US and Japan but although he talked about upgrading relations with the PRC, he gave little indication of how this might be done. For the Chinese, the combination of a new ROK president with these priorities and direct US-DPRK talks on nuclear issues—see below—raised the unwelcome prospect of a reduction of the PRC's role on the peninsula.

1.3 *Relations with Japan*

There were no major developments in relations with Japan, although old issues such as 'comfort women'[4] and the disputes over the naming

[4] Women from colonial Korea (and several other countries) who were recruited, sometimes forcibly, for Japanese military brothels from the 1930s until 1945. There was particular outrage in May 2007 when Japanese Prime Minister Abe cast doubts on claims that the system was officially sanctioned by the Japanese authorities.

of the East Sea/Sea of Japan and sovereignty over Tokto/Takeshima[5] continued to surface from time to time. Japanese insistence on raising the abductee issue with the North Koreans, rather than concentrating on the nuclear issue, was another irritant. Relations with the ROK had sunk to a low level under former Prime Minister Jun'ichirō Koizumi. His successor as prime minister, Shinzō Abe, had wanted a better relationship and did not visit the Yasukuni Shrine[6] in spring 2007. However, he did send flowers, which were offered on his behalf, and this led to protests from the ROK and the PRC. The ROK's was relatively low-key; the Ministry of Foreign Affairs and Trade said that the ROK government 'greatly regretted' Abe's action, which ran counter 'to the correct interpretation of history that provides the foundation for peace and stability in the region'. Abe's successor, Yasuo Fukuda, has made no pronouncement on the matter, but so far has neither visited Yasukuni nor followed Abe's precedent, a development welcomed in the ROK. The ROK for once found itself on the defensive vis-à-vis Japan in October, when a government enquiry acknowledged that the then opposition leader, Kim Dae-jung, had been kidnapped in Tokyo in 1973 by operatives of the Korean Central Intelligence Agency. The ROK ambassador to Tokyo conveyed a formal apology to Japan for the incident.

Only after Lee Myung-bak's victory in the ROK presidential election did relations begin to improve. Lee talked of 'future-oriented ties' with Japan, and sent a special envoy to Tokyo to invite Fukuda to his inauguration. Fukuda duly attended in February, and his presence was seen as a restoration of the 'shuttle diplomacy' between the two countries, suspended since 2005 because of the Yasukuni issue. For the present, therefore, ROK-Japan relations are on a better footing than they have been for some years, but this new accord could, as in the past, be easily broken if one of the many historical problems that exist once again becomes active.

---

[5] a. Both Koreas and Japan dispute the name of the stretch of water that lies between them. Koreans claim that East Sea or East Sea of Korea has a longer tradition than Sea of Japan, though it depends very much on which map one chooses.

b. Tokto is the Korean name and Takeshima the Japanese name for a group of rocks in the East Sea/Sea of Japan, which Koreans North and South regard as Korean and Japanese as Japanese; they appear as Liancourt Rocks on older Western maps. They are currently occupied by a ROK police unit.

[6] A major Shinto shrine near the Imperial Palace in Tokyo, where the war dead from Japan's domestic and international conflicts since 1867, including a number of those condemned for war crimes at the Tokyo tribunal, are honoured.

1.4 *Other relations*

The ROK's international profile was raised with the election of former Foreign Minister Ban Ki-moon as Secretary-General of the United Nations in late 2006. After a slow start, he began to make more of an impact as 2007 progressed, which pleased South Koreans.

There was the usual round of international visits by the ROK president and other senior members of the government, often with the supply of resources in mind. President Roh visited the US and Guatemala in June-July. He attended the APEC annual summit in Australia in September, and the ASEAN plus 3 meeting in Singapore in November. During the latter visit, the ROK and ASEAN signed a free trade agreement. The presidents of Austria and Indonesia and Italian Prime Minister Romano Prodi were among visitors to the ROK.

Free trade negotiations between the European Union (EU) and the ROK, although far less contentious in ROK domestic terms than those with the US, did not make as much progress as had been hoped at the outset. The ROK side had expected something of a walkover and instead found that the EU negotiators wanted similar terms to those on offer to the US. Rather than the swift accord expected, by January 2008 the talks had gone into a sixth round, which broke up without agreement. The reasons for this failure included the very fact that the negotiations aroused no strong passions. The US negotiations had involved President Roh, but the EU negotiations were left to ministers and particularly to officials who did not bring much fervour to the table. Officials were often more protectionist over issues such as access to financial services and automotive parts. The question of goods produced at Kaesŏng, where the ROK side had not expected problems, did not go smoothly

The most traumatic international incident as far as the ROK was concerned came in Afghanistan in mid-July 2007, when Taliban detained a group of 23 missionaries from Seoul's Saemmul Presbyterian Church; according to the church authorities, the group were engaged in medical and relief work, not in proselytising.[7] Three of the group had been in Afghanistan for some time but most were young and inexperienced and appeared not to have received adequate training or

[7] South Korean missionaries, who number about 16,000, form the second largest group of Christian missionaries after the US. Commentators have often noted a lack of preparation and basic skills among some of the groups who go abroad.

briefing. They had gone against clear government advice about the dangers of living and working in Afghanistan. Once there, they had apparently ignored local warnings about not travelling in large groups and avoiding Kandahar, which was a Taliban stronghold. An immediate consequence was that the ROK government banned ROK citizens from travelling to Afghanistan and asked the Afghan government not to issue visas to Koreans.

The Taliban demanded the release of a number of their followers and when the demands were rejected, two male members of the missionary group were killed in July. When negotiations began between ROK officials and the Taliban, the latter released two women in mid-August as a goodwill gesture. Intensive negotiations continued, with the National Intelligence Service playing a leading role, until the remaining hostages were released at the end of August. Their release was apparently secured by an ROK promise that its troops would withdraw from Afghanistan and that it would ban all Christian missionary activity in the country. The government denied rumours that a large ransom was paid to free the captives but suspicions remained.

The incident caused much soul-searching in the ROK. Many Koreans had hitherto seen the growth of missionary work as a positive example of globalisation, but this attitude gave way for a time to hostile scrutiny, especially in the light of the group's inadequate preparations. Relief at the release quickly turned to recriminations, which soon developed into a criticism of the 'arrogance' of South Korean Christian groups. The media engaged in reflections over lack of knowledge about Afghanistan.

2 Democratic People's Republic of Korea

2.1 *The Six Party Talks and relations with the United States*

The 13 February 2007 agreement[8] and the various subcommittees that it created came under the umbrella of the Six Party Talks (which date from 2003). There was considerable progress towards meeting the talks' declared purpose, namely the ending of the DPRK nuclear weapons-related programme. The group's representatives met regularly during 2007-08, and there was a full-scale session in Beijing in

[8] See *Korea Yearbook 2007*, p. 56.

autumn 2007. Yet in some ways, the six party process largely went into abeyance, as bilateral DPRK-US contacts became both more frequent and more prominent, and, at least until the spring of 2008, the ROK was increasingly hoping for a peace treaty to replace the 1953 armistice agreement. Such developments were perhaps inevitable, since the six party process had been designed to provide an arena where the DPRK and the US could meet without formal bilateral talks, which the US administration preferred to avoid, and where, the US had hoped, the five powers would work together to curtail the DPRK nuclear programme. The reality had proved somewhat different, and it was often the US and Japan that had found themselves in the minority. The developing process did not please all the participants. The PRC and Russia expressed some concern that the DPRK-US and the DPRK-ROK relationships were tending to exclude them, despite the fact that they both had important interests in the way the Korean peninsula moved forward.

As discussed above, DPRK-ROK relations did not always run smoothly during the period under review, especially after the election of Lee Myung-bak as ROK president.[9] DPRK-US relations also had problems. As a consequence of the February 2007 agreement, DPRK funds frozen at Banco Delta Asia in Macau because of alleged counterfeiting and money laundering[10] were to be released in early April. However, having created the issue, the US administration found other problems in solving it, since it proved difficult to persuade any other bank to take the funds that were to be released. Bankers were worried that even if they undertook an action that would help the US government, they might find themselves blacklisted for trading with the DPRK. As a result, it was not until June that the issue was finally resolved, when a Russian private bank agreed to help. Only then did the DPRK begin the process of denuclearisation.

At first progress was good. International Atomic Energy Agency officials were allowed back to the Yŏngbyŏn reactor in July 2007 and reported that work had begun on disabling the plant. Later, US nuclear decommissioning experts arrived to take forward the process. Yet there were soon signs of tension. The DPRK insisted that at some point, it should receive light-water reactors to continue a civilian nu-

[9] See above.

[10] The funds had been frozen in 2005 and included some belonging to foreign businesses operating in the DPRK. There was some international scepticism about the US Treasury claims, which were never publicly backed up with evidence.

clear programme. The US indicated that the DPRK would need to be much more open about its past nuclear programmes before such a move could even be considered. Deliveries of fuel oil to the DPRK under the terms of the 13 February agreement were not as prompt as they should have been, and the DPRK also complained at the failure of the US to take it off the list of states sponsoring terrorism.

The complaints were not all on one side, however. The DPRK was obliged to supply a detailed record of all its nuclear facilities and activities by the end of 2007, but although a list was supplied in November, the US deemed it not satisfactory, and called for a more detailed one. President Bush wrote to the entire six party group, including Kim Jong Il, urging compliance with the deadline. The DPRK's response was that it had done all that was required, and it had offered no further information by the end of December. Indeed, by then a new problem had emerged, arising out of an Israeli air strike against a set of buildings in Syria. The Israeli government refused to comment, but media reports claimed that the faculty was a nuclear reactor being built with DPRK assistance. This was repeatedly denied by both Syria and the DPRK, but the rumours did not go away. Continued US engagement with the DPRK came under regular attack in the US and ROK media and academic circles. Some argued that the Banco Delta Asia affair had shown that pressure could be exerted on the DPRK. Meanwhile, General Bell, commander in chief of US forces in the ROK, frequently and publicly stated that the DPRK was still a major military threat and that the forces under his command were prepared.

Yet the process did not break down. Christopher Hill, the US assistant secretary of state for Asia, travelled to Pyongyang in June 2007, the first such visit since that by his predecessor, James Kelly, in October 2002, which sparked off the current nuclear crisis. Thereafter, Hill went regularly to Pyongyang and to the other six party capitals and, despite the setbacks, regularly announced that he was confident the 2007 agreement would hold. He was backed both by Secretary of State Condoleezza Rice and President Bush; the former publicly rebuked the US special envoy on human rights, Jay Lefkowitz, for comments that appeared critical of engagement. The other six party participants, apart from Japan, also repeatedly expressed confidence that the denuclearisation process was on track.

There were other issues in US-DPRK relations. ROK-US military exercises came in for routine condemnation. In June 2007, earlier US allegations of a diversion of United Nations Development Programme

(UNDP) funds were cautiously backed up by the UN secretary-general, although UNDP denied any wrongdoings. In the same month, the special industrial zone in Kaesŏng became an issue in the debate on the ROK-US Free Trade Agreement. Yet some positive points can also be recorded. In April 2007, the DPRK returned the remains of six US soldiers killed during the Korean War, the first such returns since the US cancelled the Missing in Action programme in 2005.[11] In August 2007, the US offered aid following the devastating summer floods, and in late September 2007, the DPRK was taken off the US list of drug-trafficking countries, on which it had been since 2003. Most spectacular was the February 2008 visit of the New York Philharmonic Orchestra to Pyongyang, which drew world-wide attention, not least because of the large press corps that was allowed in with the orchestra. The visit attracted praise and blame, with some seeing it as a sign of growing DPRK openness and others as pandering to a brutal dictatorship.

2.2 *Relations with the People's Republic of China*

The PRC continued to play an important role in the Six Party Talks, as the main country with influence over the DPRK and increasingly the DPRK's main economic partner. In return, the DPRK expressed public support for the PRC positions on Tibet and Taiwan. As already noted, however, there are some signs of Chinese concern that closer US-DPRK contacts might lead to a reduction of PRC influence.

In economic matters, a lack of competition has allowed the PRC to make considerable economic advances in the DPRK; the tensions in the ROK-DPRK relationship following the ROK presidential elections have already resulted in a further strengthening in the Chinese position. Chinese goods increasingly dominated the markets in the DPRK, and there were reports that Chinese investment in DPRK mineral resources were soaring. Chinese aid also continues to be important and again, the change of president in the ROK will probably make it more so in the short term at least. The Chinese do not publish detailed figures for aid to the DPRK, but observers noted increased grain exports to the DPRK during the year. The Chinese responded to the DPRK

[11] For a fuller discussion of the Missing in Action programme, see the article by Kenneth Quinones in this issue of the *Korea Yearbook*.

appeal for assistance after the summer 2007 floods, and the ROK media claimed in April 2008 that the DPRK was seeking even more Chinese assistance to replace that from the ROK.

At the same time, economic relations between China and the DPRK were not always smooth. In October 2007, the World Food Programme (WFP) office in Pyongyang reported that flood relief aid was held up on the Sino-DPRK border because the Chinese authorities suspended all rail traffic for four days, apparently because of the failure of the DPRK railway authorities to return freight wagons. This is not the first occasion that there have been such problems on the railways, but it was the first time in the ten years of the WFP operation in the DPRK that such a dispute had interfered with aid shipments on a major scale.

The issue of defectors/refugees from the DPRK in China continued to cause international difficulties, as it has since the mid-1990s.[12] Some international non-governmental organisations reported less harsh treatment of those whom the Chinese sent back to the DPRK, but in general the plight of such people remained a major concern for humanitarian agencies and some governments. There had been some expectation among humanitarian organisations that the PRC might be more careful about avoiding bad publicity in the lead-in to the summer 2008 Beijing Olympic Games,[13] but the harsh Chinese reaction to protests in Tibet in spring 2008 did not indicate any Chinese willingness to be more accommodating on human rights' issues. The new ROK government of President Lee Myung-bak has pledged to raise human rights issues, including the case of North Koreans in China, but is unlikely to persuade the Chinese to change their approach.

The growing influence of the PRC in the DPRK was a source of concern to many in the ROK. Although the history disputes of earlier years have faded from view, some ROK commentators have claimed that the long-term Chinese aim is to incorporate the DPRK into China. While this scenario seems unlikely to most outsiders, there can be no doubt that, for the present, Chinese influence is dominant in the DPRK.

---

[12] For background, see Peter Beck, Gail Kim and Donald Macintyre, 'Perilous Journeys: The Plight of North Koreans in China', *Korea Yearbook 2007*, pp. 253-81.

[13] Ibid., p. 276.

2.3 *Relations with Japan*

The February 2007 agreement had provided for a DPRK-Japan subcommittee to discuss the outstanding issues between the two countries as a prelude to normalisation of relations. Two rounds of talks did take place but failed to reach agreement. For Japan, the issue of the abductees remained all important, and the Japanese government refused to lift any sanctions or to contribute to the energy package that had been agreed until it received satisfaction on abductees. The DPRK position was that it had done all that it could, in the context of the two visits by former Prime Minister Koizumi in 2002 and 2004. Exasperation with the tough Japanese line led the DPRK to demand that Japan be dropped from the Six Party Talks as unfit to take part, a demand ignored by the other participants.

The Japanese authorities kept up pressure on Ch'ongnyŏn (Japanese: Chōsen sōren), the pro-DPRK organisation of Koreans in Japan. Even the departure of Prime Minister Abe and his replacement by the generally more dovish Fukuda did not lead to any immediate improvement in relations, and Japan extended its sanctions against the DPRK for a further six months in April 2008. However, Fukuda did promise that he would approach relations with the DPRK in 'a more comprehensive manner' that his predecessors, which may hint at a wish to go beyond the abductees' issue.

2.4 *Other foreign relations*

The DPRK joined the Non-Aligned Movement (NAM) in 1975, and it was at the core of North Korea's foreign policy efforts during the Cold War era. With the collapse of the bipolar world order, the emphasis on the NAM declined. However, in late August 2007, an article in the party newspaper *Rodong Shinmun* re-emphasised the traditional role of the movement. It was described as a means of defending sovereignty and as a tool by which smaller countries could voice their interests in international organisations that are usually dominated by big powers. A further article on 1 September confirmed this position, and also the willingness of North Korea to actively participate in the movement. It called for solidarity among NAM members and close co-operation in the economic and technological fields.

Southeast Asia, traditionally a NAM stronghold, occupied a particularly prominent space in the DPRK's foreign relations. This is relevant for domestic developments as two cases of ongoing socialist transformation are located in that region. From time to time in recent years the North Koreans have expressed particular interest in Vietnamese economic development. Talks were held in Pyongyang in September between the Central Committee of the (North Korean) Democratic Front for the Reunification of the Fatherland and a delegation of the Central Committee of the Fatherland Front of Vietnam. A delegation of the Vietnam General Confederation of Labor visited Pyongyang in late October. Also in October, DPRK Premier Kim Yong Il traveled to Hanoi and met the Vietnamese prime minister. Apart from the prime minister, the delegation included the ministers of foreign trade and agriculture, indicating the priority of economic interests. A 2008-10 Plan for Exchanges in Culture, Arts, Science and Education was signed, as well as a memorandum of understanding on co-operation in the field of agricultural science and technology. The delegation then went on to Laos in early November 2007. In late November 2007, a delegation of the Vietnamese Farmer's Union visited Pyongyang.

Relations with European countries showed no dramatic change. As well as humanitarian assistance, there is some trade and low-key training. Exchanges of delegations included a team from the French foreign ministry, which visited the DPRK in February 2008; France remains the only EU country not to have diplomatic links with the DPRK. Substantive improvements in relations are very much dependent on progress on the nuclear issue but there were some cultural developments. The DPRK film, *A Schoolgirl's Diary,* premiered in Paris in December 2007 and enjoyed some success. David Heather, a British financier, organised the first major commercial exhibition of North Korean art ever to be held in London in a West End gallery in July. The exhibition drew on products from the Pyongyang Mansudae Art Studio, and two of the artists concerned came for the event. The opening night was remarkable in that both the DPRK and the ROK ambassadors attended, as did members of their staff. Heather, together with an opera singer, Suzannah Clarke, who has performed in Pyongyang, is also active in a move to bring the DPRK State Orchestra to Britain in autumn 2008, while the DPRK's London embassy is apparently exploring the possibility that British rock guitarist Eric Clapton would visit the DPRK in 2009.

Russia and the DPRK signed a non-binding agreement in May 2007 on the reconstruction of the rail link between the Russian border and the DPRK port of Rajin. If this were implemented, it might be the first stage in a link to the Trans-Siberian railway.

In 2007-08, the DPRK opened diplomatic relations with the United Arab Emirates, Swaziland, the Dominican Republic, Guatemala and Montenegro, and restored relations with Myanmar and Nicaragua.[14] The official press celebrated these signs of progress on the diplomatic front, explaining that international contacts, especially economic ones, do not contradict *juche*, but rather reflect the new approach of the government in reaction to the changing world environment and to improve the country's standard of living. The DPRK now has diplomatic relations with about 160 countries, although only about 25 have embassies in Pyongyang, and the DPRK has only a relatively small number of embassies abroad. In a move DPRK officials attributed to economic problems, the DPRK announced that it was closing its embassy in Australia.

Following the death of Foreign Minister Paek Nam Sun in January 2007, Pak Ui Chun, a former ambassador to Algeria, Syria, Lebanon and most recently Russia (from 1998 to 2006), was appointed to the post in May 2007. He made his first international appearance at the ASEAN Regional Forum meeting in Manila in July.

---

[14] Myanmar broke off diplomatic relations in 1983, alleging that the DPRK was behind a bomb attack on ROK President Chun Doo-hwan and his entourage during their visit to Myanmar. The attack killed 16 senior ROK ministers and officials. The then Nicaraguan government broke off relations with the DPRK in 1990, following the ousting of Daniel Ortega. When Ortega again became president in 2007, he restored the links.

FISSION, FUSION, REFORM AND FAILURE IN SOUTH KOREAN POLITICS: ROH MOO-HYUN'S ADMINISTRATION

Youngmi Kim

ABSTRACT

This paper discusses the origins, dynamics and decline of the Roh Moo-hyun administration (2003-08). Since the democratisation of politics two decades ago, a distinctive political style has developed in South Korea, marked by weak institutionalisation of political parties with splits and mergers between parties, strong patterns of regional voting, and an electoral system that has often pitted a president against parliament. President Roh Moo-hyun started from a position of apparent strength, having, unusually, achieved a majority in the general election of 2004. His attempts to use this position to initiate reforms in four sensitive areas roused strong resistance, his Uri Party lost its majority through by-elections within a year and finally broke apart through defections. Roh sought to draw in the opposition with a proposal for a grand coalition, but was again rebuffed, as were his attempts to effect further changes to the electoral system. His preoccupations did not please the electorate, who rejected his party and his policies in the 2007 presidential election.

1 INTRODUCTION

For the last two decades, democratic politics in South Korea have been accompanied by two salient political issues: the continuous fission and fusion of political parties, and regionalism. The process of fission and fusion, seemingly unstoppable, was by and large justified by the prevailing administration (which orchestrated them) as a measure necessary to ensure the country's governability by enabling the government to attain a majority status in parliament. Party merger and switching have been the most commonly practiced tools to achieve such a goal. This important 'feature' of politics in the Republic of

Korea (ROK—South Korea) came to dominate and eventually disrupt even the Roh Moo-hyun administration (2003-08).

The political life of the Roh administration was tumultuous. The lowest ebb was reached with the impeachment of the president on 12 March 2004. Outraged by the behaviour of the political class, voters gave the ruling and pro-presidential Uri Party a majority of votes in the general elections of 2004. For the first time in Korea's post-democratisation history, a party was voted into power without the necessity of building coalitions with other political parties. On paper this boded well for Korea's stability and governability. The ruling Uri Party was expected to encounter a less insurmountable opposition in its attempts to pass new laws in the legislature and thus implement the reform agenda it had advocated in the electoral campaign. Instead, Roh and the Uri Party, like all previous governments, had to deal with a strong opposition unwilling to negotiate on controversial issues. The party's majority did not last long enough to secure the approval of any such laws. Disappointment over the party's failure to implement its reform agenda lead to its defeat in the by-elections of April and October 2005. The Uri Party lost its majority in the National Assembly with 144 seats out of a total of 299 seats, down from an earlier 152 seats. An unstoppable process of defection and fragmentation brought the party to its demise before the rounds of December 2007 (presidential) and April 2008 (parliamentary) elections.

In discussing the decline of the Roh administration, this paper pays special attention to the continuous party mergers and splits (in which regional patterns of voting behaviour, although less pronounced than in the past, continued to play a part), to the presidential impeachment and to the virtual implosion of the ruling party. It shows that just like its predecessors, the ruling administration was primarily concerned, in fact obsessed, with achieving a majority status in the legislature. This was perceived, as I have noted elsewhere (Kim Youngmi 2008), as the key to the solution of problems of governability in the country.[1] The

[1] This seems to be in line with the findings of classical coalition research. Minimum winning coalition theories traditionally hold that majority status provides more cabinet stability, especially with a single majority party, in parliamentary systems because majority status can survive confidence votes (Laver and Schofield 1990; Budge and Keman 1990). At the same time, research conducted in very different geographic and cultural settings (Europe) but experiencing analogous political issues (lack of a clear majority in parliament) shows that bare majority or minority status do not necessarily cause political deadlock in the legislature (Strøm 1990; Strøm and Müller 2001; Cheibub 2002; Pech 2004).

Uri Party lost its majority status within a year. Political conflicts within the party and with the opposition brought the country to a standstill. As a way out of the deadlock, President Roh Moo-hyun proposed that the government and opposition should form a 'grand coalition' in order to implement major structural reforms, including amending electoral laws and in the end the constitution as well.[2]

This paper seeks to address two issues: firstly, why the Roh Moo-hyun administration failed in implementing reform laws despite the fact that the ruling Uri Party counted on a majority of seats in the legislature; and secondly, why the president's proposal of a grand coalition met with such fierce opposition from both the ruling and the opposition parties. It shows that the critical factor undermining governability during the Roh Moo-hyun administration was not the lack of a clear majority in parliament, since the 2004 elections actually granted the ruling Uri Party a majority of seats, but rather the low level of institutionalisation of political parties and of the party system, and the administration's failure to connect with ordinary citizens. It was these failings, compounded by an electoral system that often ended up setting the incumbent president against parliament, the paper argues, that prevented Roh's administration from implementing its programme of proposed reforms

The paper is divided into three sections. I start with a brief review of coalition politics in the post-democratisation period in South Korea, which will aim to place the conflict between government and opposition and the Roh Moo-hyun administration's attempt to attain a majority status in the legislature in historical context. Next I look at four major reform initiatives requiring legislation (abolition of the National Security Laws, the Truth and Reconciliation Laws or Laws to Clear Past History, the Media Reform Laws and the Private School Laws) to illustrate the difficulties encountered by the Roh Moo-hyun administration and the ruling Uri Party in the legislature. I then turn my attention to the president's proposal to form a grand coalition to overcome institutional constrains. Final remarks conclude.

---

[2] The constitution of the ROK stipulates that the president is elected for one term only for a total of five years. General elections are often held in the middle of a presidential term, with the consequence that the ruling party finds itself without a majority in parliament, where instead the opposition party/parties dominate (Kim Yongho 2001; Kang 2005; Kim Youngmi 2008). Several scholars have identified in the differing duration of the term for president and the duration of the legislature one of the most critical factors creating problems in new democracies (Mainwaring and Scully 1995; Tsebelis 2002; Figueiredo and Limongi 2000).

2 Korean Politics after Democratisation

While reviewing the process of party merger and split in the period following democratisation, this section also highlights the political prominence of regionalism in Korea. The politics of coalition and party mergers are deeply intertwined with regionalism and the two phenomena have become profoundly entrenched in Korean political life over the past two decades. Both are important for understanding the challenges faced by the Roh Moo-hyun administration.

2.1 *Fission and fusion among political parties*

Many parties have emerged and faded in South Korea since the demise of authoritarian rule. Even party names have frequently changed. Politicians have been engaged in continuous party switching, eventually gaining the nickname of 'migrant bird politicians'. Party mergers and break-ups have become a tool to win elections and achieve majority status in the legislature.

Nevertheless, Korean politics is not the formless entity that the picture above at first suggests. The three main political groupings can be closely identified with the 'three Kims' (Kim Young-sam, Kim Dae-jung and Kim Jong-pil), the leaders who have played a prominent role in the country's politics since the 1960s. This is often referred to as the 'Three Kims' era' (Im 2004). Each leader is associated with a particular region (Kim Young-sam with Kyŏngsang in the southeast, Kim Dae-jung with Chŏlla in the southwest, Kim Jong-pil with the central region of Ch'ungch'ŏng), each region providing loyal support to the leader during the various electoral campaigns. It was not a time, as Lee Gap-yun (1998: 4) notes, when the party system was able to develop, as personalised factions rather than parties grew in importance. During the three Kims' era, party members joined and left political parties following their respective party leaders' decisions.

An example of the process of fission and fusion is provided by the experience of the Millennium Democratic Party (MDP), formed in 1999 by Kim Dae-jung. The MDP underwent serious internal conflicts among a number of factions in the latter years of the Kim Dae-jung administration and the early years of Roh Moo-hyun's presidency. Roh had won a primary election before the presidential election in 2002 with the support of a small faction from among those who went on to make him president.[3] Forty members who supported Roh Moo-hyun defected from the MDP, and, in coalition with five members from the Grand National Party, and two members, (including Kim Won-ung), from the People's Party for Reform, created the Uri Party on 11 November 2003. The following year, Roh Moo-hyun was impeached by the opposition parties which included the MDP, alongside the GNP and the United Liberal Democrats. President Roh was accused of violating electoral laws by supporting a particular party, the Uri Party, during the electoral campaign. The opposition demanded that the president be impeached. The bid was passed with a large majority in the legislature, while Uri Party members physically struggled to stop the impeachment in the National Assembly on 12 March 2004. Clashes between legislators in the National Assembly were broadcast live. President Roh Moo-hyun was then temporarily removed from office. This situation lasted until the impeachment was overturned by the Constitutional Court on 14 May 2004, which deemed it unconstitutional. The impeachment was clearly by far the toughest attack the opposition had ever launched on a ruling administration in post-democratisation Korea. At the general election in April that year the voters granted the Uri Party, backed by Roh, the majority of seats in the legislature. The Uri Party's majority status owed much to voters who resented the presidential impeachment.

2.2 *Regionalism*

Electorally, South Korea appears divided into three main regions: the southeast, the southwest and the centre. Already in the 13th presidential election held in 1987, which was won by Roh Tae-woo, strong patterns of voting along regional lines were clear outside of Kyŏnggi province (where Seoul is located). In 1990, President Roh Tae-woo from the then Democratic Justice Party built a coalition to overcome the large opposition in the legislature by merging parties with Kim Jong-pil's New Democratic Republican Party and Kim Young-sam's

[3] Roh Moo-hyun was able to rely on strong non-party support in society. This was well illustrated by the emergence of 'Rohsamo' (盧思募 Society of people who love Roh Moo-hyun), resembling a kind of fan club, which effectively mobilised support for Roh during the electoral campaign and played a crucial role in his election. The MDP members who later defected and established the Uri Party were also members of Rohsamo.

Unification Democratic Party. The resulting Democratic Liberal Party (later renamed the Grand National Party (GNP)) left Kim Dae-jung, his party, the Peace Democratic Party, and the Chŏlla provinces where the party was primarily based, marginalised. Since 1990 the party system has developed around a split between the Chŏlla provinces, known as the Honam region, and the non-Honam region representing the Ch'ungch'ŏng and Kyŏngsang provinces (the last two known also as Yŏngnam). The three parties forming the coalition later renamed themselves as the Democratic Liberal Party and in February 1990 nominated Kim Young-sam as presidential candidate for the then approaching elections. The politics of coalition-building were successful and led to victory for Kim Young-sam, who in 1992 became the first elected president not belonging to the military establishment since 1961.

The second coalition was built in the run-up to the 1997 presidential elections between Kim Jong-pil from the United Liberal Democrats (ULD) and Kim Dae-jung from the National Congress for New Politics (NCNP). Voters from the Yŏngnam region felt marginalised as a result of this move, and strongly supported the GNP's Lee Hoi-chang.This coalition created a different party configuration in the following general elections: a non-Yŏngnam bloc, made up of Honam and the Ch'ungch'ŏng provinces, versus the Yŏngnam region. (See Table 1 for an indication of regional voting preferences in the 13th to 16th presidential elections.)

In the 15th presidential election (1997), Kim Dae-jung won office with 39.65 percent of the total votes, a margin of only 1.5 percent over the opposition leader Lee Hoi-chang, who gained 38.15 percent. The election results showed evidence of a strong regional cleavage, with Kim Dae-jung receiving 96.3 percent of votes in Kwangju, the capital of South Chŏlla province, and over 90 percent in South and North Chŏlla provinces. Lee Hoi-chang, on the other hand, gained 71.6 percent in Taegu, the capital of North Kyŏngsang province, 60.55 percent in North Kyŏngsang province and 52.6 percent in Pusan (*Munhwa Ilbo,* 19 December 1997; *Seoul Economy*, 20 December 1997; National Election Commission[4]). Two years into the Kim Dae-jung presidency, the results of the 16th general election (2000) showed that these regional differences continued to prevail. Despite the ruling

[4] Percentages are taken from National Election Commission data.

Table 1 Electoral votes in the 13th to 16th presidential elections

Presidential election / Presidential candidates		Province							Total
		Kyŏng-gi	Ch'ung-ch'ŏng	Chŏlla	North Kyŏng-sang	South Kyŏng-sang	Kang-won	Cheju	
13th 1987	Roh Tae-woo	34.4	33.1	9.9	68.1	36.6	59.3	49.8	38.6
	Kim Young-sam	28.7	20.1	1.2	26.6	53.7	26.1	26.8	28.0
	Kim Dae-jung	28.4	8.9	88.4	2.5	6.9	8.8	18.6	27.1
	Kim Jong-pil	8.4	34.6	0.5	2.4	2.6	5.4	4.5	8.1
14th 1992	Kim Young-sam	36.0	36.2	4.2	61.6	72.1	40.8	15.2	42.0
	Kim Dae-jung	34.8	27.3	91.0	8.7	10.8	15.2	32.9	33.8
	Chung Ju-young	19.8	23.8	2.3	17.0	8.8	33.5	15.4	16.3
15th 1997	Lee Hoi-chang	37.8	25.7	3.2	65.7	53	42.4	35.9	38.15
	Kim Dae-jung	41.4	43	93	12.9	13.4	23.3	39.8	39.65
	Lee In-je	18	26.1	1.5	17.4	29.5	30.4	20.7	18.91
16th 2002	Lee Hoi-chang	52	41.3	4.8	75.7	62.4	52.5	40	46.6
	Roh Moo-hyun	50.6	52.6	93.4	20.2	30.76	41.5	56.1	48.9
	Kwon Young-kil	2.6	5.2	1.2	3.8	5.2	5.1	3.3	3.9

Source: Author, from the National Election Commission, available at http://www.nec.go.kr/sinfo/index.html (accessed 17 September 2005).

coalition parties' effort to maximise the number of seats in the legislature through the political reorganisation[5] of the party system, the opposition GNP won 133 out of 273 total seats in the legislature. The MDP gained 115 seats including proportional representation seats and the ULD won a total of 17 seats (*Seoul Shinmun,* 15 April 2000). The GNP gained 39 percent of the total votes, the MDP 35.9 percent and the ULD 9.8 percent. Regional patterns of voting were clear here. The GNP gained 62.5 percent of the votes from the Yŏngnam region, the MDP gained 66.8 percent from the Honam region, and the ULD received 34.8 percent from the Ch'ungch'ŏng region.

After Roh Moo-hyun's victory in the 2002 presidential elections, 40 members defected from the MDP and founded the Uri Party in 2003. Honam voters split their preferences between the MDP and the

[5] To avoid deadlock, the Kim Dae-jung administration (1998-2003) attracted large numbers of defectors from opposition parties. The coalition ruling parties (the NCNP and the ULD) started with 120 seats facing large opposition in February 1998, but after the political reorganisation these parties, by dint of attracting many defectors, in May 1999 had 159 seats out of a total of 293 seats in the legislature

Uri Party and this resulted in a mitigation of the regional cleavage in the 2004 general elections. However, the GNP still received the highest number of votes (50.7 percent) in the Yŏngnam region and the Uri Party 55.2 percent in the Honam region. The decreased influence of strong regional leaders such as Kim Dae-jung and Kim Jong-pil was making itself felt. The ULD only received 14.8 percent in the Ch'ungch'ŏng region, an area traditionally loyal to the ULD under Kim Jong-pil, and the traditionally conservative voters in Ch'ungch'ŏng instead turned to the GNP, giving it the highest rate (25.2 percent) of votes in the region. Thus, outside of the Honam and Yŏngnam regions, the general elections in 2004 show a relative decline in the impact of regional differences. An important development was the emergence of the Democratic Labour Party (DLP) as the country's third largest party. The DLP has benefited from the new electoral voting system (supplementary member system or mixed voting system),[6] introduced on 9 March 2004[7] which has allowed a small party such as this to survive in the legislature. The new voting system allows for seat allocation (56 seats out of 299) based on proportional representation.

2.3 *Effects of the post-democratisation political system*

First, the fission and fusion of political parties became a fundamental strategy to win presidential elections; second, voting behaviour produced no single majority party, but instead spread preferences along regional lines, where the local leader received the largest share of the votes. What made things more complicated was that general elections, coming after presidential ones, produced electoral results at variance with those of presidential elections, typically with the opposition emerging as winner. This institutional set-up provided a clear structural disadvantage to the government in a semi-presidential system where the ruling administration faced a large opposition in the legislature. In order to overcome this situation, the ruling parties sought to

[6] The supplementary member system is a variety of the parallel voting system, which combines plurality voting (also known as single-past-the-post) and proportional representation (party list).

[7] On 19 July 2001 during the Kim Dae-jung administration, the Constitutional Court ruled that the old Single-Seat Districts System was unconstitutional as it restricted voters' rights over choices of party preferences.

gain a majority status in parliament through attracting defectors from other parties.

A salient issue emerging from the evidence of regionalism is how this demonstrates a low level of institutionalisation in the party system as a whole. Randall and Svåsand (2002: 8-9) point out that if a single party is identified with certain groups, this undermines the level of institutionalisation of the party system.[8] The Korean case shows that each party has been strongly identified with a leader and the region where he or she is from. When a party monopolises a region, this undermines fair competition in an election in the region.

What marks the Roh Moo-hyun administration is that during this period, regionalism was less strong than in previous elections. (Roh's political career itself proved that he had challenged regionalism when, in the 2000 general election, he became a candidate for the MDP in Pusan, where his party was expected to have no loyal support base. He failed to be elected.) Furthermore, the pattern of success for one party in presidential elections followed by its defeat in parliamentary ones was broken during his administration. In 2004, the ruling Uri Party received 152 out of 299 total seats in the legislature. Given that ruling parties in Korea have traditionally sought to achieve majority status through all available means, this seemed to be a particularly welcome outcome. On paper, governability seemed to be ensured.

---

[8] Panebianco (1988: 53) defines the institutionalisation of a political organisation as 'the process by which [an organization] incorporates its founders' values and aims'. According to Panebianco, the institutionalisation of political parties can be measured as follows: (1) by the organisation's degree of autonomy toward its environment; (2) and by its degree of 'systemness' (the 'internal structural coherence of the organization', ibid.: 56). Party system institutionalisation is instead understood by reference to four dimensions (Mainwaring 1998: 69): stability in patterns of inter-party competition, party roots in society, legitimacy of parties and elections, and party organisation. Randall and Svåsand (2002) argue that individual party institutionalisation is not always compatible with the institutionalisation of the party system and maintain (p. 6) that the two concepts (party, and party system institutionalisation) are to be kept distinct. This is because of the possible incompatibility arising in two key respects: first, the evenness of party institutionalisation and its identification with an exclusive ethnic or cultural grouping (ibid.: 8-9). By evenness, Randall and Svåsand mean the extent to which the level of political party institutionalisation is relatively uniform across the party system. A second issue concerns the party's identification with certain groups; if a party has absolute support from certain groups (e.g. religious, ethnic) there would be no fair competition between parties but a monopoly of support of one over the entire group. When a party monopolises strong support form a certain group or a region (in the case of South Korea) this may show a high level of institutionalisation of a party but low institutionalisation of the party system.

Reality turned out to be less favorable to the ruling party. Why this was the case and what turned electoral success into political failure in less than a year from the elections is the subject of the next section.

3 Origins of Failure

Roh Moo-hyun's position was vindicated in the April 2004 elections. With impeachment behind him, the president received strong backing from the citizenry, who showed overwhelming support for the pro-presidential Uri Party. The newly elected National Assembly was in fact new in many respects. Two-thirds of the legislators were first-time Assemblymen and women; 13 percent of legislators were female; and finally, the emergence of progressive members from the DLP was expected to bring some form of policy competition between the parties (Lee Tae-ho 2006).

3.1 *Four reform legislative initiatives*

On a wave of enthusiasm, the Uri Party set out to implement 'the four reform laws'.[9] The main legislative initiatives included the abolition of the National Security Laws, the introduction of the Truth and Reconciliation Laws, the Media Reform Laws and the Private School Laws.

The National Security Laws (and their amendment) had already been the subject of heated controversy during the Kim Dae-jung administration of 1998 to 2003. Under earlier authoritarian governments, the National Security Laws had been used to oppress government opponents or political dissidents through jail sentences or execution. Even the former president Kim Dae-jung was once sentenced to death in 1980 on charges of treason under these laws following Chun Doo-hwan's military coup. .

The laws to set up a Commission on Truth and Reconciliation (in other words, laws to clear past history), and to investigate human rights abuses under the Japanese occupation and military dictatorship, were enacted in 2005. However since the so-called Truth and Reconciliation Laws were mainly dealing with cases of human rights abuses under the Japanese colonial period and the period of authoritar-

[9] These reform laws are four different sets of laws.

ian rule, there is still debate about it, as many cases were more than 15 years ago. The Commission was also given duplicated roles (*Donga Ilbo*, 1 March 2007).

The Media Bills were aimed at preventing any media outlet from achieving a dominant or near monopoly status in the media market. This especially concerned the conservative newspapers *Donga Ilbo*, *Chosun Ilbo* and *JoongAng Ilbo*. These three newspapers control 70 percent of the market. The bills set limits on a single newspaper at 30 percent of the print market and on the three newspapers at 60 percent overall. This meant that any newspapers occupying more than 30 percent of the newspaper market were regarded as market-dominating entrepreneurs. The laws were strongly opposed by the conservative opposition. The Media Bills were passed on 1 January 2005 despite the GNP's opposition but in the following year the Supreme Court overruled the bills on the grounds that the laws would have infringed freedom of information.

The Private School Laws were the most controversial bid among the four reform laws; in trying to block approval of the laws, the GNP staged a boycott outside the National Assembly. The Private School Laws were conceived to ensure fairness in school administration by permitting members of the school governing board to be appointed through an open and fair process. These laws were enacted because corruption among family members of the founders of private schools was being raised as a social issue. Some students were being discriminated against in favour of others who had internal connections to board members, mainly family or relatives of the founders of the schools. Grading, teacher's appointments and recruitment were widely seen as lacking in transparency. The Uri Party initiated a proposal that would allow one-fourth of the board members (more than seven persons) of a private school to be appointed by a School Committee and a University Ordinary Committee, with the rest appointed through open procedures. The Private School Laws were passed on 9 December 2005 with support from the Uri Party, the DLP and the MDP, with 140 votes in approval out of the 154 present and attending in the Regular Session (*Hankyoreh*, 9 December 2005). This happened despite the fierce boycott from the Grand National Party. The GNP started a strike which continued for 53 days, during which its members did not attend the National Assembly Session for 31 days (*Segye Ilbo*, 7 March 2007). This conflict showed how deeply embedded political conflict was over state involvement in private school administration.

Chung Min-seung, writing in *Weekly Changbi* (10 July 2007), noted that during the Private School Laws debate in 2005, civil society was entirely left out of the discussion. Chung observes that nine legislators from the Uri Party submitted a proposal to amend the laws governing private schools and this was done under lobbying pressure from civil society groups from 2000 to 2002 with one-man boycotts, public meetings and reports on the corrupt private schools. However, when the laws were under process of amendment in the National Assembly, the Uri Party did not work through the Legislative Counselling Office but raised the issue directly in the Session meetings in the legislature. In other words, the Uri Party could have consulted with civil society organisations to ensure a wide range of public support and at the same time could have discussed the issue thoroughly in the Legislative Counselling Office in the legislature before presenting the bid directly to the National Assembly Sessions. The party could have gathered internal support within a small group in the Legislative Counselling Office and consulted with them on whether passing the reform laws appeared feasible. Such lack of skills in compromise and negotiation stimulated furious boycotts by the opposition. In this case the Uri party's majority status was not helpful but only enabled it to pass the law without any support from the opposition parties, and thus without consensus.

In the same *Weekly Changbi* article, Chung argued that the Uri Party believed that fast-tracking the passing of the law would be accepted, given the significance of the proposed reform. Vigorous boycotting by the GNP undermined the Uri Party's competence over the Private School Laws to the point that even some Uri Party legislators started to have second thoughts on the laws and appeared to be willing to negotiate a re-amendment of the laws. Eventually, to bring the GNP back into the National Assembly Session the Uri Party had to show a willingness to renegotiate the Private School Laws. The new version of the laws allowed family members of school founders who were on the board to be presidents of private schools. The amended Private School Laws in 2005 was intended to prevent corruption by family members of school founders, but the (re-)amended version moved back to the earlier situation, resulting in de facto total backtracking by the ruling party (*Media Today*, 5 July 2007).

Debates over the four reform laws caused relations between the government and the opposition to deteriorate seriously. Prime Minister Lee Hae-chan accused the GNP of being a 'chatteki' party, a slighting reference to allegations that, during one election campaign, a truck was found full of cash destined for the party (*Media Today*, 3 November 2004). As a sign of protest against the prime minister's comments, the GNP refused to attend the National Assembly Session for 15 days. Lee Tae-ho (2006: 2) reports that from the 223rd to the 231st National Assembly Sessions (1 June to 9 December 2004), the legislature had 38 days of deadlock out of a total of 146 days of meetings. These GNP boycotts became more frequent, especially during the sessions to approve the Private School Laws.

3.2 *Uri Party's failure to implement reforms*

The Uri Party's period of majority lasted from April 2004 to April 2005. During this period the party expected to implement its policies without encountering serious opposition in the legislature; however, as shown in the case of the Private School Laws debate, without proper negotiation and compromise between parties, it was impossible to complete the passage of the reform laws. Boycotts and refusal to attend assembly sessions were tools constantly used by the opposition to block government action. While the ruling party leaders were jostled or threatened by the opposition, internal conflicts emerged within the Uri Party between the Chaeya[10] faction and the Progressive faction (*Hankuk Ilbo*, 27 December 2004). These internal factions were also competing over the future leadership among members of the party élite such as Kim Geun-tae, Chung Dong-young and Yu Si-min. Chun Jeong-bae, floor leader of the Uri Party, suggested holding a four-person meeting between the Uri Party chairman and floor leader and the GNP chairman and floor leader as the GNP was boycotting the Assembly over the reform laws. The choice for the Uri Party was between passing the laws without the GNP's attendance in the Assembly and negotiating with the GNP. Meetings went on but failed to produce any substantive result.

[10] 'Chaeya' originally signified social élites who were not involved in practical administration but who were more or less influential in politics. Many members of the Chaeya group became National Assemblymen, especially for the Uri Party. Within the Uri Party the Chaeya faction was less progressive than the other faction.

The Uri Party planned to pass the reform laws, especially the amendment of the National Security Laws, before the end of 2004, but with a complete deadlock in parliament, no reform bids were approved. For the entire year, political life in Korea was to all intents paralysed. This caused voters to become increasingly disaffected with the political class and its excessive in-fighting in the legislature. Voters reacted to the Uri Party's perceived incompetence in government by supporting the opposition in two by-elections in April and October 2005.

3.3 *Proposal for a grand coalition*

Searching for a way out of the impasse, President Roh Moo-hyun proposed in July 2005 that the ruling party and the opposition form a grand coalition. This was after the April 2005 by-election which left the Uri Party with 146 seats, whereas the GNP increased its seats from 120 to 125. The Uri Party had lost its majority status within one year of the general election, at a time when the president was about to enter a period of weakness. Roh Moo-hyun expressed his concern that the Uri Party would lose again at the next by-election in October 2005 and at local elections in 2006. Fearing that the party would be trapped in a series of electoral defeats, Roh Moo-hyun proposed building a coalition with the opposition parties (Grand National Party, Democratic Labour Party and Millennium Democratic Party).

On 5 July, President Roh posted an open letter to the population on the Blue House homepage, entitled 'Korean politics need to return to normal'. In this letter he referred to the situation of the government as it faced an opposition holding a majority of seats in the legislature as a recurrent problem in Korean politics, and complained that the president, despite being expected to govern, was not in a position to do so because of a lack of co-operation from the opposition. The ROK, he argued, needed to change its negative attitude towards building coalitions. In many foreign countries coalition-building was common among parties in order to avoid minority governments; nor were grand coalitions absent from Korean political life. In previous years, party mergers had often been signed secretly, but for this reason coalition-building was perceived by the population as some sort of artificial reorganisation of the party system. Roh Moo-hyun maintained that instead of 'sending a secret messenger to the opposition parties to build a coalition', he was openly suggesting that the coalition should include opposition parties and have an open discussion to overcome the situation of a divided government (*Hankyoreh*, 6 July 2008).

The president's proposal struck South Korea's political landscape like lightning. Made in the realisation that most of the coalitions since democratisation had been built among party élites (mostly party leaders) and that coalition agreements were not open to the public, Roh Moo-hyun's suggestion that a grand coalition be openly discussed was in itself radical. How his suggestion was perceived by opposition parties and within the ruling party was most crucial. Roh Moo-hyun continued to publish open letters to persuade the public of the benefits that a grand coalition would bring to South Korean politics. Some Uri Party members expressed concern about the president's de facto bypassing of the party using what came to be known as 'letter politics'. 'There are roles for the president and roles for the party. If the president goes ahead of the party, the party may be seen as a follower of the president without doing its own job' (*Naeil Shinmun*, 7 July 2005). It seems President Roh did not communicate effectively with his own party on such an important issue. Although his proposal to build a grand coalition to bring about reforms and to mitigate regionalism may have been well intentioned, it is not surprising that the legislators, primarily concerned with their short-term survival in office, were not interested in paving the way for their political demise.

Timing also played a role in destroying the proposal for the grand coalition, which was put forward after the Uri Party had lost a by-election and amid the administration's fears it might lose the following by-election as well as local elections. It seemed more a matter of expediency than of grand strategy. The media and opposition saw the president's suggestion as a make or break move to save his political career (*Breaknews*, 7 July 2007; *Donga Ilbo*, 29 July 2007).

3.4 *A chance to change electoral laws*

A coalition such as President Roh Moo-hyun proposed might have been able to effect a change to the electoral laws, one of the main reasons for a number of structural problems affecting South Korean politics.

Kim Dae-jung had already tried, unsuccessfully, to effect change in this respect. The ruling MDP in 2000 sought to introduce a German-style mixed-member proportional system with a closed party list in order to mitigate strong electoral regionalism. The mixed-member proportional system allows two votes per voter. One vote is for a candidate of a single member district and the other for a party on a closed party list. Early into his presidency in 2003, President Roh Moo-hyun suggested changing the electoral law to allow a multi-seat constituency-based system, which would permit multiple members to be elected in a larger district. He also showed openness in discussing a mixed-member proportional system as well. Both the constituency-based and mixed-member proportional systems have multi-electorates in a larger district that would combine a few existing small districts into one large district. In such electoral systems a single party may not be able to monopolise the majority of votes in a district.

For Roh Moo-hyun, the problem of a divided government facing a large opposition arose from the structural difficulties created by the conventional electoral laws based on the system of a single winner in a small district. The amendment to the electoral laws effected during the Kim Dae-jung administration led to a system of one voter, two votes,[11] which had allowed a small and vulnerable party like the DLP to emerge with ten seats in the 2004 general elections. President Roh suggested introducing a medium-sized constituency to elect multiple members in a larger district. Such a constituency would work against regional votes. With this electoral system the Uri Party would have gained more seats in the Yŏngnam region, where it would be the second most popular party after the GNP. The greater population of the Yŏngnam region means a larger body of electors, and as the second most popular party in Yŏngnam the Uri Party could have hoped to benefit more than the GNP could have from Honam, where the Uri Party was most popular.

While the GNP remained silent, the DLP agreed to the idea of changing the electoral laws. They insisted on moving to a mixed-member proportional system which includes multi-seat constituency allowing multiple-member electorates in larger districts. If a mixed-member proportional system had been implemented at the 17th general election in 2004, the DLP could have gained 39 seats, up from the 10 seats they won with the present electoral system (*Donga Ilbo*, 11 July 2005). However, on the proposal for a grand coalition, even the DLP was in fundamental disagreement.

---

[11] One vote goes to the candidate and the other to the party.

President Roh reached the point of suggesting that he was willing to hand over his presidential powers to coalition partners if they agreed to change the electoral laws (*Breaknews*, 7 July 2005). At the same time, *Donga Ilbo* (29 July 2005) suggested, the proposal for the grand coalition was conceived as an attempt to regain the political initiative and win elections through a change of electoral laws which would ultimately benefit the Uri Party. If the GNP had accepted the proposal, the grand coalition would have created ruling parties with a surplus majority that would have taken 90 percent of the total seats in the legislature.

3.5 *Out of touch with the electorate*

Another element in President Roh Moo-hyun's political decline was his failure to perceive popular needs. A common view among voters was that Roh, with his obsession over the grand coalition, did not pay attention to the people's real needs. The lack of economic growth mattered more than party mergers or coalitions. The gap in housing prices between rich and poor areas grew, and so did the divide between the wealthy and the poor. South Korea's per capita income increased from US$12,826 in 2003 to US$20,081 in 2007, but this 57 percent increase was primarily due to the Korean won's devaluation against the US dollar from 1,200 won to 930 won (*Seoul Shinmun*, 23 February 2008). According to a report from the Korea National Statistical Office, the average monthly income per person was 2,650,000 won in 2003 but increased to 3,220,000 won in 2007, that is, by 570,000 won. However, according to the same *Seoul Shinmun* report, the level of deficit[12] showed that the 20 percent of the population on high incomes had a 2,000,000 won sufficiency of income, but the 20 percent on low incomes had a deficit of 340,000 won a month. When Roh Moo-hyun proposed the grand coalition, public opinion surveys revealed that 84.6 percent saw economic issues as more important than electoral reform issues (*Munhwa Ilbo*, 7 December 2005).

It is widely acknowledged in the literature that political parties play an important role in linking the state with its citizens (Lawson 1988: 15). As shown above, the party plays an important role in linking society with politics. One of the difficulties encountered by the Uri

[12] A deficit is calculated when total consumption is extracted from income.

Party and President Roh was that they came to be regarded as increasingly detached from people's real needs. Lee Myung-bak, a former mayor of Seoul, who campaigned on a platform of economic growth, by contrast received landslide support of 48.7 percent in the December 2007 presidential elections, whereas Chung Dong-young representing the United New Democratic Party (effectively the successor to the Uri Party) received 26.1 percent and Lee Hoi-chang 15.1 percent.

3.6 *Demise of the Uri Party*

As Figure 1 shows, party seat numbers changed after the by-election in October 2005, the second of two by-elections that year, leaving the Uri Party with 144 seats and the GNP with 127 seats. This was the beginning of the end for the Uri Party. After the failure of the proposal for a grand coalition and the two by-election defeats, President Roh Moo-hyun rapidly lost control. In late 2006, fission and fusion among parties began anew in the run-up to the presidential election in 2007. On 6 February 2007, 23 Uri Party legislators switched party allegiance following the defection of a few party leaders including Chun Jeong-bae. The Uri Party became the second party after the GNP and by June 2007 was reduced to 73 seats through further defections. In August 2007, the Uri Party ended its political life after less than four years, merged with the defectors' Democratic New Party and later built a coalition with other small progressive parties (the Centrist Democratic Party, the Millennium Democratic Party, and the Centrist Reform Party) to fight in the presidential election as the United New Democratic Party.

In an interview with the *Ohmynews* newspaper, Roh Moo-hyun, speaking later of his attempt to build a grand coalition, acknowledged: 'I threw a bomb called a "Proposal for a Grand Coalition" to the opposition parties, but it exploded in my own yard, the Uri Party' (*Seoul Shinmun*, 11 October 2007).

Figure 1 Party seat numbers from general election 2004 and two by-elections 2005

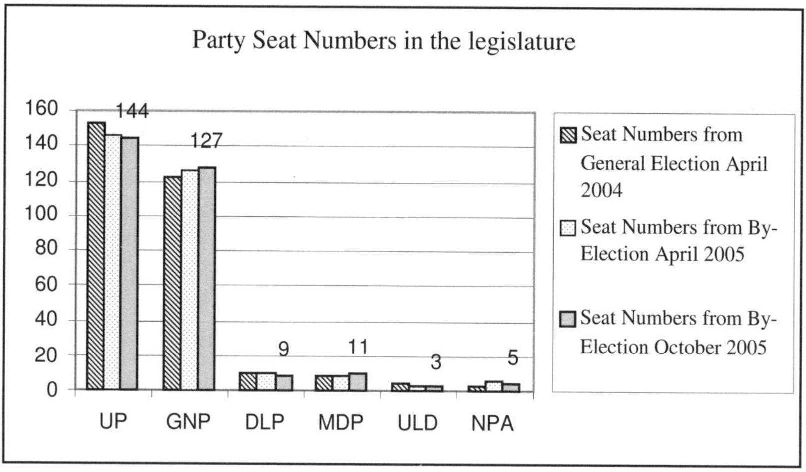

Source: Author, data from National Election Commission.

4 Conclusion

When President Roh Moo-hyun won a majority in the general election that followed his own election to office in 2003, he broke the pattern of a president set against a hostile parliament, but within a year lost that advantage. Thereafter he tried, through proposing coalition government to the opposition parties, to regain a majority. He failed again, his Uri Party fell apart through defections, and the electorate, dissatisfied with what it saw as his incompetence and preoccupation with his own aims, rejected his successor, Chung Dong-young, in 2007. In the end, his administration experienced similar levels of internal disruption and instability to those of preceding administrations.

This article has argued that, although Roh Moo-hyun and his predecessors appeared to see the problem primarily in terms of securing a parliamentary majority for their administration, the basic weakness in the ROK political system is not the difficulty in achieving a government majority but a low level of institutionalisation of political parties. This manifests itself through a constant movement of fission and fusion among parties and is reinforced by strong regional voting behaviour that undermines the institutionalisation process through allowing single party monopolies in certain regions. Scholars (Cheibub 2002; Strøm and Müller 2001; Cheibub, Przeworski and Saiegh 2004; Mainwaring and Scully 1995) have argued that cabinet stability or governability does not necessarily derive from the size of the government but owes much to institutional constraints and party internal mechanisms exerted through party rules that are observed. The ROK may be a case in point, as political instability and sometimes ungovernability owe more to the internal mechanisms of South Korean party politics, I argue, than to the presence or absence of a majority. As suggested by *Kukmin Ilbo* (29 July 2005), the problem for South Korean politics would seem to lie in a political culture that lacks space for compromise and negotiation.

REFERENCES

Budge, Ian, and Hans E. Keman (1990), *Parties and Democracy: Coalition Formation and Government Functioning in 22 Democracies,* Oxford: Oxford University Press

Cheibub, José Antonio (2002), 'Minority Governments, Deadlock Situations, and the Survival of Presidential Democracies', in: *Comparative Political Studies*, 35 (3), pp. 284-312

Cheibub, José Antonio, Adam Przeworski, and Sebastian Saiegh (2004), 'Government Coalitions and Legislative Success under Presidentialism and Paliamentarism', in: *British Journal of Political Science*, 34 (4), pp. 565-87

Chung Min-seung (2007), 'Kaehyŏkchŏk sahakbŏbŭn wae hŏmuhage mu'nŏchyŏnna?' [Why did the laws to reform private schools collapse in vain?], in: *Weekly Changbi*, 10 July 2007

Figueiredo, Argelina Cheibub, and Fernando Limongi (2000), 'Presidential Power, Legislative Organisation, and Party Behavior in Brazil', in: *Comparative Politics*, 32 (2), pp.151-70

Im, Hyugbaek (2004), 'Faltering Democratic Consolidation in South Korea: Democracy at the End of the "Three Kims" Era', in: *Democratization*, 11 (5), pp.179-98

Kang, Wontaek (2005), *Han'gugŭi chŏngch'i kaehyŏkgwa minjujuŭi* [Political reform and democracy in Korea], Seoul: Ingansarang

Kim, Yongho (2001), *Han'guk chŏngdang chŏngch'iŭi ihae* [Understanding party politics in Korea], Seoul: Nanam Publishers

Kim, Youngmi (2008), 'Explaining Minority Coalition Government and Governability in South Korea: A Review Essay', in: *Korea Observer*, 39 (1), pp. 59-84

Laver, Michael, and Norman Schofield (1990), *Multiparty Government: The Politics of Coalition in Europe*, Oxford: Oxford University Press

Lawson, Kay (1988), 'When Linkage Fails', in: K. Lawson and P.H. Merkl (eds), *When Parties Fail: Emerging Alternative Organizations*, Princeton NJ: Princeton University Press, pp. 13-38

Lee, Gap-yun (1998), *Han'gugŭi sŏngŏwa chiyŏkchuŭi* [Regionalism and election in Korea], Seoul: Oreum Publishers

Lee, Tae-ho (2006), 'Kukhoeŭi ŭiwŏn hwaldong p'yŏng'ga' [Assessment of legislators' activity], in: *Parliamentary Politics Review*, Seoul. Online: http://www.assembly.re.kr/research/journal/a18_10.pdf (accessed 5 March 2008)

Mainwaring, Scott (1998), 'Party Systems in the Third Wave', in: *Journal of Democracy*, 9 (3), pp. 67-81

Mainwaring, Scott, and Timothy R. Scully (1995), *Building Democratic Institutions: Party Systems in Latin America*, Stanford CA: Stanford University Press

Panebianco, Angelo (1988), *Political Parties: Organization and Power*, Cambridge and New York: Cambridge University Press

Pech, Gerald (2004), 'Coalition Governments Versus Minority Governments: Bargaining Power, Cohesion and Budgeting Outcomes', in: *Public Choice*, 121 (1), pp. 1-24

Randall, Vicky, and Lars Gerhard Svåsand (2002), 'Party Institutionalization in New Democracies', in: *Party Politics*, 8 (1), pp. 5-29

Strøm, Kaare (1990), *Minority Government and Majority Rule*, Cambridge, UK: Cambridge University Press

Strøm, Kaare, and Wolfgang C. Müller (2001), 'Coalition Agreement and Governance', Annual Meeting of the American Political Science Association, San Francisco CA

Tsebelis, George (2002), *Veto Players: How Political Institutions Work*, Princeton NJ: Princeton University Press

Press sources (in Korean)

Breaknews, 7 July 2007
Donga Ilbo, 11 July 2005; 1 March 2007; 29 July 2007
Hankuk Ilbo, 27 December 2004
Hankyoreh, 9 December 2005; 6 July 2008
Kukmin Ilbo, 29 July 2005
Media Today, 3 November 2004; 5 July 2007
Munhwa Ilbo, 19 December 1997; 7 December 2005
Maeil Shinmun, 7 July 2005
Seoul Economy, 20 December 1997
Seoul Shinmun, 15 April 2000; 11 October 2007; 23 February 2008
Segye Ilbo, 7 March 2007

ASSASSINATION, ABDUCTION AND NORMALISATION: HISTORICAL MYTHOLOGIES AND MISREPRESENTATION IN POST-WAR SOUTH KOREA-JAPAN RELATIONS

John Swenson-Wright

ABSTRACT

Early relations between Japan and the Republic of Korea (ROK) were critically shaped by three decisive events: diplomatic normalisation in 1965, the 1973 abduction of opposition politician Kim Dae-jung from Japan and the attempted assassination of President Park Chung-hee in 1974. These events have remained controversial, not least because much of the detailed information surrounding them has been classified. Prompted by the partial declassification initiatives of the Roh Moon-hyun administration, this article relies on recently released archival material and new scholarship in Japan, South Korea and the United Kingdom to consider the extent to which difficulties in the bilateral relationship were a product of traditional patterns of historical animosity, and to assess the role of the United States in bringing the contending parties together. In the process, the article critically considers the persuasiveness of international relations theory in making sense of changes in the post-war Korea-Japan relationship.

1 INTRODUCTION: AN UNDERDEVELOPED BILATERAL RELATIONSHIP

Relations between Japan and the Republic of Korea (ROK—South Korea) are anomalous. A little like Arthur Conan Doyle's 'curious case of the dog in the night-time' that failed to bark, the puzzle in the Japanese-Korean bilateral relationship has been the relative absence of co-operation and common purpose for much of the post-war period. For many of the past 60 years, since the formation of South Korea's First Republic in 1948, these two states have confronted a common strategic and ideological adversary in the form of the Democratic People's Republic of Korea (DPRK—North Korea), shared a Cold War ally in their more senior security partner, the United States (US), and have increasingly benefited (particularly since the 1970s and the take-off in South Korea's high-speed economic growth trajectory) from a close and interdependent economic relationship. Yet despite the importance of these ties, reinforced in the late 1980s with the shift from authoritarian to democratic government in South Korea, Koreans and Japanese—whether at the level of popular or élite interaction—have rarely appeared comfortable with one another. Despite (or perhaps precisely because of) a common Sino-centric cultural heritage, strong ethnic similarities and shared linguistic patterns, the two countries have more often than not stressed their differences and their divisions rather than their commonalities. The dominant narrative for most of the post-1945 era (indeed for much of the 20th century and into the 21st) has been one of rivalry and bitter disagreement, involving mutual economic boycotts, competing denunciations of either state by the political élites in both countries, frequent disagreements over rival historical interpretations and deep-seated and seemingly intractable territorial disputes. In spite of periodic calls for co-operation and the development, particularly since the ending of the Cold War, of a new regional strategic partnership, either formal or 'virtual' in form (Cossa 1999), Japan and South Korea have frequently remained stubbornly and puzzlingly estranged from one another.

Explanations for this lack of co-operation have varied. The more traditional, orthodox interpretations have focused on animosities and differences born out of the long history of national rivalry, and most importantly the tensions arising from Japan's repressive and often brutal colonial domination of the Korean peninsula from 1910 to 1945 (Kim 2006; Lee Won-deog 2001; Hahm and Kim 2001). Others have elaborated on this theme, suggesting that the past has acted as a perpetual dead-weight, encumbering the relationship with unresolved issues of rival historical interpretation, even to the point where official apologies for the past have exacerbated bilateral tensions by fomenting domestic unrest and internal political 'blow-back' from disaffected nationalist constituencies in the country offering the apology (Lind 2005). Unsurprisingly, it is historians who have often been inclined to identify the past as a particular source of tension, and the relevance of such factors has been highlighted not only by government-to-government disputes, but also by the prominence, especially recently, of depictions in popular culture of past, present, and in some cases future, imagined bilateral rivalry. In 2002, for example, the release in South Korea of *2009 Lost Memories* considered the fanciful notion of what might have happened if Japan had not been defeated in the Pacific War and if Korea had remained under Japanese colonial rule; similarly speculative, the 2006 film *Hanbando* advanced a highly controversial (and arguably very clumsily executed) fictional portrayal of a contemporary Japanese government intent on blocking reconciliation between North and South Korea.[1]

In contrast to these depictions, which focus on the frequently emotional and unpredictable aspects of the bilateral relationship, social scientists have downplayed such elements, preferring instead to stress the role of rational and dispassionate policy-making élites and the more critical role played by contextual factors, Cold War strategic and economic imperatives, and most significantly the key, mediating influence of the US. Foremost amongst the writers working in this tradition is Victor Cha of Georgetown University, whose award-winning monograph, *Alignment Despite Antagonism: The US-Korea-Japan Security Triangle* (1999), presents a picture of Korea-Japan relations in which historical animosities, while not unimportant, are subordinate in significance to the pivotal role played by US government officials. According to Cha, the tendency for decision-making élites in South Korea and in Japan to adopt critical attitudes to one another is directly tied to the level of perceived engagement by the US in regional politics and diplomacy. Cha's thesis is presented as a dynamic model of quasi-alliance behaviour between the Japanese, South Korean and US governments in which alternating fears of abandonment from or entrapment in the alliance partnership with the US have conditioned and shaped the behaviour of individual decision-makers in the ROK and Japan. Simply put, fear of US withdrawal from the region frequently encourages national élites to look beyond historical tensions and rivalries and to work co-operatively; by contrast, when the US commitment to the region has appeared solid and dependable, then the predisposition for Japanese and South Koreans to retreat into old patterns of historical disagreement and animosity becomes more pronounced (Cha 1999: 202-05). Cha is careful to avoid an overly rigid, deterministic model. At points in his analysis of post-war bilateral Korea-Japan relations, he suggests that the relevance of the US role may vary, at times providing a direct and unmistakable set of incentives, at others merely acting in a 'permissive' fashion, encouraging co-opera-

[1] See the article by Mark Morris on *Hanbando* in *Korea Yearbook 2007*, pp. 215-34.

tion, for example, when South Korean and Japanese policy-makers have had reason to worry about the risk of American withdrawal or a dip in US engagement in the Northeast Asian region (Cha 1999: 89).

2 Opening up the Historical Record

Political developments in South Korea in the early 21st century have presented a fresh opportunity to assess the merits of these two competing interpretations of the ROK-Japan relationship. In the autumn of 2004, the government of President Roh Moo-hyun began a process of piecemeal, selective declassification of key government records detailing aspects of the historical relationship between South Korea and Japan. Roh's initiative apparently reflected the administration's and the president's personal commitment to a new style of 'participatory government' in which old patterns of secretive and elitist decision-making would be increasingly replaced by a more transparent and open style of government. Initial disclosure was related to documentation from the negotiations surrounding the normalisation of diplomatic relations between South Korea and Japan in 1965. In particular, the released files provoked controversy in South Korea by suggesting that substantial amounts of Japanese money provided in 1965 to the then governing administration of Park Chung-hee as de facto compensation for Japanese colonial excesses had been intentionally redirected away from the Korean victims of Japan's colonial rule to unrepresentative and frequently corrupt members of the governing élite. Other files released after 2004 exposed other sensitive issues in the post-war bilateral relationship, some relating, for example, to the apparent attempt by the Korea Central Intelligence Agency (KCIA) to kidnap Kim Dae-jung, President Park's principal opposition rival, from Japan in 1973; other material dealt with the attempted assassination of President Park in 1974 by Mun Se-kwang, a second-generation Korean resident in Japan (Underwood 2008).

Each of these incidents was controversial in its own right. However, the declassification generated further controversy given speculation surrounding President Roh's motives in releasing the files. Some observers wondered if the disclosures were an attempt to embarrass the government of Japan at a time when ties between South Korea and Japan were fraying; others suggested that the motives for disclosure were more clearly rooted in domestic politics and efforts by Roh to undermine the position of some of his potential conservative political rivals, most notably Park Geun-hye (daughter of former President Park and a leading member of the opposition Grand National Party) by exposing the weaknesses and shortcoming of past leaders with close ties to contemporary politicians. Indeed, some went so far as to suggest that the disclosures had a much broader remit, allowing the new progressive and self-consciously populist Roh administration to tarnish all those members of the conservative political establishment who could be linked, either directly or indirectly, to past instances of collaboration or collusion with Japan, whether during the colonial or post-colonial period. This suspicion intensified in 2004 when the ROK's National Assembly passed legislation focusing on colonial-era collaboration with Japan and came to a head in August 2005 when President Roh personally called for the confiscation of the property of all those who could be legitimately labelled as colonial collaborators (Swenson-Wright 2008).

Clearly identifying the motives of political actors is always a difficult task, even with the benefit of historical hindsight and access to the archival record. It will almost certainly take the publication of memoirs and/or the disclosure of confidential Blue House papers before we have a better idea of what lay behind President Roh's actions in opening up the historical files as he did from 2004. For now, informed and dispassionate observers of the Korean political scene are inclined to give him the benefit of the doubt and assume that his actions were motivated primarily by the desire to foster a more open and inclusive style of government (Woo 2005; Moon 2005; Yoon 2005). However, the release of new historical material is important for separate, perhaps more fundamental reasons. Much commentary and analysis of relations between Japan and the Korean peninsula, especially among academics in South Korea and Japan, has tended to be concentrated on contemporary and recent developments. Detailed, primary-sourced historical analyses are relatively rare, although younger scholars in both countries are beginning to engage with explicitly historical aspects of the bilateral relationship (Yoshizawa 2007; Shinoda 2006; Lee Jun-won 1996; Koh 2007; Kang 2007). Too often historical issues—especially those of post-1945 vintage and which are relevant in understanding the contemporary interaction of the two Koreas—have been considered too sensitive or politically charged to warrant explicit attention. Even the establishment by the ROK and Japanese governments in 2001 of a joint committee to consider mutual historical issues has yielded disappointing results, with the committee members often failing to resolve key interpretative differences (Kyodo News 2005).

Despite these limitations, the disclosure of new South Korean archival evidence can act as a catalyst for the disclosure of comparable material in other national archives: already the Japanese Foreign Ministry has begun to release new material on post-war relations with South Korea, albeit in a partial fashion. Disclosure is also a salutary reminder of how our understanding of the past can all too often be conditioned and constrained by contemporary perspectives and prejudices and how valuable it is to re-examine the historical record. The following analysis takes this point to heart in looking at the Japan-ROK relationship anew and by focusing on the three core events associated with President Roh's declassification initiative. In particular, it draws upon recently released material from the British and US archives. The relevance of the US material is readily understandable, given Cha's stress on the importance of the US role in managing bilateral relations between Japan and South Korea; the relevance of British sources is perhaps less immediately apparent. Britain's importance is based on three factors: first, the United Kingdom (UK) had a prominent diplomatic presence in both Tokyo and Seoul during the post-war period, and the detailed and high quality of the political reporting provides the historian with a valuable perspective—one that is especially useful given that the UK had less of an immediate, direct stake in events in both countries than the US had and consequently British officials were able to view events locally with perhaps more detachment than their American colleagues; second, both the Japanese and South Korean governments appeared to view Britain as a disinterested, honest broker, prepared to respond dispassionately and potentially favourably to their respective requests for support; third, as a close, if not uniquely sympathetic ally of the US, linked to that country by deep cultural, linguistic and historical ties, the British enjoyed privileged access to the views of senior US officials to a degree that allows us better to assess the views of officials both in Washington and in the region.

3 The Road to Normalisation, 1960-1965

Perhaps the most striking feature in the tortured history of normalisation between Japan and South Korea is the length of time it took for the two countries to reach a mutually acceptable diplomatic accommodation. Following Japan's full return to the status of a formal, independent, sovereign nation-state in 1952, no fewer than 13 years passed before it was possible for decision-makers in Seoul and Tokyo to sit down as nominally equal diplomatic interlocutors in December 1965. For much of the immediate post-war period (particularly the early years), the absence of mutual recognition was a function of deep-seated animosity and resentment, not only between the peoples of both states, but most notably between the leading politicians in either country. Syngman Rhee and Shigeru Yoshida, president and prime minister respectively of the ROK and Japan, harboured a visceral dislike of one another and an abiding suspicion of the peoples on either side of the East Sea, or Sea of Japan, as it is known to the Japanese.

To Yoshida, Koreans—especially the 600,000 who resided in post-war Japan—were a direct threat to the security of Japan, a destabilising fifth column potentially susceptible to the blandishments of communism and at the very least predisposed, given the bitter legacy of the colonial period, to be hostile to the government and people of the former tutelary power. Moreover, any notion of meaningful accommodation or co-operation with Rhee's First Republic was, in Yoshida's judgement, highly questionable given the erratic and self-serving behaviour of a leader who seemed willing to drag South Korea and its political partners into a conflict on the Korean peninsula without a moment's hesitation. For Rhee, Japan remained an implacable opponent, potentially more threatening even than the forces of international communism and one against which Korea needed to mount an unremittingly combative policy of national suspicion and aggressive defence. The clearest expression of this was the Rhee Line of 1952—curiously and misleadingly referred to from time to time as the 'Peace Line'—a maritime defensive exclusion zone extending some 60 miles (97 km) beyond the South Korean shoreline. Despite having no international legal status, the zone was zealously patrolled by South Korean naval forces and any Japanese vessels, commercial or otherwise, foolish enough to venture into these waters risked being seized and impounded, with their crews detained indefinitely at the pleasure of the Korean authorities (Swenson-Wright 2005: 307).

During the 1950s, élite-level tensions acted as a major, albeit not necessarily insurmountable, obstacle to some degree of accommodation between the two countries. However, more often than not such attempts at accommodation exacerbated rather than alleviated hostility. In 1953, Kan'ichirō Kubota, Japan's chief negotiator in talks with South Korea, suggested provocatively, and as a means of bolstering Japan's negotiating position, that aspects of Japan's colonial rule of the peninsula had been beneficial and should be reflected in any future normalisation settlement between the two countries—a proposal that stirred up a storm of protest in South Korea. Even when the Japanese tentatively adopted a more amenable posture, as they did in 1958 when Kazuo Yatsugi, a private envoy of then Prime Minister Kishi, appeared to apologise for the excesses of Hirobumi Itō, the first resident-general of Korea during the Japanese colonial period, political realities quickly extinguished any flickering embers of potential reconciliation. Kishi, when confronted by press reports of his envoy's apparent gesture of historical contrition, swiftly refused to endorse the remarks and rapidly backed away from any public sign of atonement (Wakamiya 1998: 33, 40-41).

Fundamentally, it took a change in the leading political actors to open up a potential avenue, in the first instance, to meaningful reconciliation between the two countries. In mid-April 1960, Rhee was swept from power on the back of a wave of student protests (the 'Sa-il-gu' or '4-19 Revolution') against what many judged to be rigged parliamentary elections in South Korea and the attendant police brutality that killed some 126 student protestors (Lie 1998: 37). Rhee was succeeded by a caretaker administration under Hŏ Chŏng for four months, but it was only with the advent of the Chang Myŏn government in August 1960 that the first signs of a deliberate, serious and sustained effort to improve relations with Japan began to appear (Koh 2007: 269).

3.1 *First easing of tension*

Initial hints of an easing of bilateral tension had appeared with the return of some 200 Japanese fishermen—casualties of the Rhee Line—to Japan in March 1960 and the first post-war visit by Japanese journalists to Seoul in May 1960 (Morland, 13 April 1960). A major breakthrough took place in September, when Zentarō Kōsaka, the Japanese foreign minister, made the first official visit by a serving Japanese government representative to South Korea to engage in exploratory talks regarding normalisation. The talks delivered little of substance, and were more notable for what they failed to achieve—there was no apology from the Japanese, either official or informal, no commitment from the Koreans to allow a Japanese representative mission in Seoul—but they did mark progress in terms of signalling a willingness by both sides to explore the options for an improvement in relations (Koh 2007: 270). Importantly, they set the scene for a flurry of official exchanges in the course of 1961 that demonstrated unmistakably that both sides—at least at the level of élite, government-to-government interaction—were adopting a pragmatic approach to reshaping the bilateral relationship.

The first indication of this new pragmatism was the decision by both governments on 10 March 1961 to approve the release of a 1957 US government document, based on article IV of the 1952 San Francisco Peace Treaty (the collective allied agreement that marked the end of the post-war occupation of Japan), indicating that the Japanese were unlikely in any subsequent normalisation talks to seek compensation for Japanese former colonial assets or property appropriated by South Korea (Chancery, Tokyo, 10 March 1961). Interestingly, at this early stage in the normalisation talks, the Americans played a largely secondary role. Post-war US administrations had, in general, accepted the desirability of improving relations between their two most important East Asian allies, not least because this would help to defray some of America's substantial political and economic costs in meeting the emerging Cold War challenge in Asia (Cha 1999: 28; Brazinsky 2007: 133). Yet the pressure from Washington was indirect and of low intensity, and the real driving forces behind the early push for reconciliation were the local actors, rather than the superpower patron. In the words of one British official, viewing these events from Washington: 'Though the State Department are naturally in full support of this move to improve Japanese/Korean relations, I had the distinct impression that the initiative for it came from Tokyo or Seoul or both' (Denson, 19 January 1961). Even had the Americans wished to regulate or channel this process, there was little to suggest that they were able to exert any decisive influence on either of their junior partners (Foreign Office, 11 August 1961).

Importantly, in terms of any wider historiographical and theoretical discussion about how the process of bilateral rapprochement was effected, it is worth noting the intensity of activity on the part of the South Korean and Japanese governments. In Tokyo, in particular, the governing Liberal Democratic Party (LDP) appeared broadly united in pushing the case for engagement with the South Korean government. In April 1961, some of the most senior members of the party, including former prime ministers Yoshida and Kishi, the incumbent prime minister, Hayato Ikeda, and the promising rising cabinet star and future prime minister, Takeo Fukuda, put their not inconsiderable political weight behind plans for a high-level visit to Seoul by a Japanese parliamentary or Diet delegation, to be headed by the agriculture minister, Uichi Noda (Chancery, Tokyo, 21 April 1961). Typically, the academic literature on Korea-Japan post-war relations has highlighted the divisions within Japanese conservative circles on how best to manage relations with Korea (Wakamiya 1998: 189), but at this critical juncture, not only is there important evidence of unity of purpose, but also a willingness on the part of the country's governing élites to look beyond past historical divisions and cultural tensions.

Japanese pragmatism was matched by the realism of the Chang administration. However, there were limits to how far and how quickly the South Korean government could push the negotiations. Chang himself had worked as a school-teacher during the colonial period and was criticised in some quarters for having 'compromised' himself with the pre-war occupying authorities (Evans, 17 September 1960). In February 1961, the Korean National Assembly voted against establishing closer ties with Japan, and Chang found himself having to move slowly and cautiously to avoid provoking a backlash at home. Ultimately, however, the prime minister's most critical challenge came not from anti-Japanese sentiment, but from the Korean military. Three days after the visit by Noda's Diet delegation to Seoul in May 1960, Chang's government was overthrown in a military coup headed by Major-General Park Chung-hee, and relations with Japan entered a new phase (Brazinsky 2007: 113).

3.2 *Park Chung-hee in charge*

In some respects, Park represented a continuation rather than a departure from the line laid down by Chang. As a graduate of the Japanese

Imperial Military Academy in Tokyo, and having served with the Japanese army in Manchuria in the closing stages of the war, Park had an intimate understanding of Japan and its political establishment. He also recognised that Japan held the key to the ROK's economic regeneration at a time when the South was lagging behind its more economically advanced northern neighbour, the DPRK. Economic modernisation was important not only in its own right, but also as a source of political legitimacy for the new authoritarian government (Koh 2007: 271). Having subverted the democratic political process, Park and his colleagues would need to propel Korea quickly along the economic growth trajectory, and Japan arguably offered the best impetus and model for such a transition.

Park was fortunate too in the reception he received from the Japanese shortly after seizing control of power in the ROK. For leading Japanese politicians such as Nobusuke Kishi (himself no stranger to 'strong' government), Park's arrival on the political scene was a welcome development. It was an opportunity to sweep away some of the corruption that had bedevilled South Korean politics, and offered the prospect of stability and reassurance in a political environment that to Japanese eyes seemed all too vulnerable to change and unpredictability (Koh 2007: 271).

Where the Japanese and Koreans differed at this stage was on the specific formula for promoting rapid and sustainable economic growth. To Japan's economic experts, South Korea in 1961 should have been concentrating on agriculture and light industry, rather than the heavy industry that Park appeared to favour. Notwithstanding these prescriptive differences of opinion, the governments of the two countries were united in agreeing on the need to focus their energies on the task of promoting economic development, and this in turn required a mutually beneficial political and diplomatic accommodation between the two countries (Chancery, Tokyo, 19 August 1961). Critically, this consensus had been achieved without excessive cajoling or prompting by third parties—the initiative for change had emerged locally and only later would it receive added impetus from outside forces, most notably from the US.

With surprising speed, the Japanese and South Korean governments moved quickly to hammer out the beginnings of a settlement. In November 1961, Park, en route to Washington DC for a meeting with the Kennedy administration, stopped over in Tokyo for meetings with his Japanese counterparts. South Korean official documents released in 2005 reveal that the Ikeda administration in Tokyo had taken the lead in proposing these unprecedented talks, the first face-to-face meetings in ten years between the top political leadership in both countries (Koh 2007: 272). By all accounts, the meetings were both frank and cordial and, it seems, that they opened the way to a discussion of the substantive issues separating the two sides (Ogawa n.d.). To the astonishment of outside observers, most notably the British, by early 1962, the two governments were moving towards an understanding on one of the critical issues at the heart of the normalisation discussions, namely, the appropriate size of the financial claims that Japan would agree to meet as a de facto settlement for the colonial period. These would not be presented as formal reparations or compensation, but the eventual financial package would provide the critical monetary stimulus to jump-start the recovery of the Korean economy. Initial discussions between the two governments had the sides separated by a seemingly unbridgeable gap—a ten-fold discrepancy in which the Koreans were demanding US$700 million in compensation and the Japanese were offering a paltry US$70 million. By January 1962, the Japanese had moved far enough to be talking of a possible settlement as large as US$400 million—an indication of the seriousness and urgency with which both sides to the negotiations were approaching the talks (Trench, 18 January 1962).

The talks over compensation/claims reached a decisive turning point in November 1962, when one of Park's closest associates and chairman of the governing Democratic Republican Party, Kim Jong-pil, met with the Japanese foreign minister, Masayoshi Ōhira in Tokyo. The Kim-Ōhira agreement put in place the basis for a financial settlement, a combined package of US$300 million in grants, US$200 million in government loans, and another US$100 million in commercial loans, not far removed from the settlement (US$800 million in total) that was eventually hammered out in the final stages of the normalisation talks in 1965. Most importantly of all, it was clear that both sides were buoyed by a real optimism at the prospect of reaching a full settlement in the near future (Godfrey, 26 November 1962; Cortazzi, 2 November 1962).

It would be a mistake to assume that financial issues were the only important factors in the negotiations. Ultimately, there were a range of issues, of varying degrees of technical complexity, which would need to be resolved. Management and eventual removal of the Rhee Line loomed large for both sides, as did the related question of adjusting fishing rights between the two countries; the status of ethnic Koreans in Japan was a sensitive issue for the Korean side; similarly, South Korean negotiators expressed concern at the willingness of the Japanese authorities to approve the regular repatriation of substantial numbers of Koreans to the DPRK. The programme for allowing Koreans to relocate from Japan to North Korea had been in place since 1959, and by 1961 some 68,000 Koreans had moved to the DPRK from Japan. Japan's foreign ministry claimed that as a Red Cross-administered programme, the repatriation scheme was not something that the Japanese government could or would chose to regulate, but there is little doubt that the Park administration saw it as a serious obstacle to the ROK's interests and prestige globally. In general, South Korean officials worried not only about the relative importance and influence of the North, but also the unforeseen consequences of deepening South Korea's ties with Japan and the risk that economic integration might lead to South Korea becoming subsumed within Japan's wider economic orbit and eventually dominated by the larger economic partner. Japan, for its part, lobbied to be able to open its mission in Seoul and to minimise the size of the compensation package it would need to pay the Koreans. While decision-makers in Seoul worried about the threat of economic domination, the Japanese remained concerned about the risk of political instability in Korea. A leitmotif of the three to four years of normalisation talks, this issue was one that the Japanese negotiators would routinely return to with the Americans and the British, frequently asking if conditions were right to ensure the continuation of stable government in the South. A final, persistent added source of bilateral tension was the vexatious issue of competing territorial claims—most strikingly over a group of rocks known as Takeshima in Japanese and Tokto in Korean—a claim so contentious that it was ultimately omitted from the terms of the eventual agreement as an issue for future resolution.

3.3 *US influence and its limitations*

Despite the promising beginning to bilateral negotiations in 1961-1962, the two sides experienced difficulty in sustaining their momentum. By 1963, the Park government had to contend with considerable local resistance, mainly from opposition parties and from students and university academics who demonstrated regularly and vociferously against normalisation. Kim Jong-pil, in particular, had become a lightening rod and critical focus for anti-government protesters who marched against government corruption and the suspicion that Kim had illegally and covertly enriched himself and his associates via the compensation deal negotiated with Ōhira in November 1962. Such was the intensity of the anti-Kim campaign that by the spring of 1964, Park was forced, at the prompting of US officials, to arrange for his troublesome associate to leave Korea on pretence of taking up a period of sabbatical study at Harvard University—a solution that drew some, but by no means all of the vitriol out of the anti-treaty protests (Brazinsky 2007: 134).

The US role in the bilateral talks increasingly took on a greater significance as international factors weighed more heavily in the decisions of the key political actors. The Park government worried increasingly about the growing regional influence of the People's Republic of China (PRC), reflected in part in its new 1961 mutual defence treaty with the DPRK, and most strikingly in China's acquisition of nuclear weapons in 1964 (Cha 1999: 28-29). For the US administration of Lyndon Johnson such factors loomed large, as did the need to prosecute the war in Southeast Asia. An accommodation between Tokyo and Seoul would be an attractive means of reducing America's financial exposure in South Korea, allowing the Japanese to take over some of the responsibility for promoting the economic health and vitality of the ROK and also possibly allowing the Park administration to deploy South Korean forces to Vietnam—a gesture with powerful practical and symbolic implications, given the importance of demonstrating that the war was not simply a post-colonial conflict between Asians and Caucasians.

Cha argues that the US intervention at this stage played a crucial, if not the decisive role in bridging divisions between the Japanese and the South Koreans and in effecting a successful settlement. There is little doubt that State Department officials (such as the US ambassadors to South Korea and Japan—respectively, Winthrop Brown and Edwin O. Reischauer), and key National Security Council figures such as Robert Komer and William Bundy, had become increasingly involved after 1964 in encouraging an accommodation between America's two key Asian allies. What is less clear, is that such involvement was the decisive factor in prompting an accommodation and meeting of minds between the two protagonists in the normalisation talks. For example, in February 1965, the Japanese and Korean foreign ministers, Etsusaburō Shiina and Lee Tong-won, met in Seoul for a critical set of talks that produced a broad outline treaty draft establishing the framework for a final set of detailed bilateral negotiations that took place in Tokyo in March-April 1965. Shiina's visit to Seoul was, according to Cha, in large measure effected by the US and was especially important because it included a very public expression of 'regret and reflection' from the Japanese foreign minister on his arrival at Kimpo airport in South Korea—a statement that, as British representatives in Seoul noted at the time, '… help[ed] considerably in improving [the] atmosphere for future negotiations' (Godfrey, 22 February 1965). Yet subsequent Korean and Japanese academic analyses as well as accounts from the time, including the memoirs of some of the key participants, suggest that awareness of the importance of acknowledging cultural and psychological sensibilities was keenly appreciated by many of the main negotiators. Shiina himself noted in his memoirs the need to 'understand the emotional and historical viewpoints of the Korean people' and routinely demonstrated his adeptness in defusing bilateral tensions, often by expending the small currency of diplomatic exchange—disarming conversational asides or informal empathetic gestures—in the course of his discussions with his Korean counterparts (Ogawa n.d.).

The importance of gesture politics was keenly appreciated by the Japanese side in general—perhaps not altogether surprisingly given the highly stylised conventions of daily behaviour and linguistic practice in Japan. During the critical final March-April negotiations in Tokyo, the Japanese took every possible means to signal their sincerity to the Koreans, providing full red-carpet treatment to the Korean delegation, laying on for Foreign Minister Lee an honour guard, an unprecedented salute of guns, and a formal audience with the Japanese Emperor. 'The main purposes of these courtesies, according to Japanese officials, was to convince the Koreans of Japan's sincere desire to achieve a settlement' (Rundall, 21 April 1965).

However, empathy alone was not sufficient to bridge bilateral divisions. The final round of negotiations reflected real grievances on both sides, with the Koreans accusing the Japanese of 'slippery conduct' and 'unnecessarily tough, inconsistent and unreliable' negotiating practices. The Japanese retaliated in like kind, complaining privately to the British that the Korean negotiators were 'individually ambitious and collectively unreliable; the most difficult of negotiating teams to deal with' (Rundall, 21 April 1965). There is little doubt that American intervention helped to smooth over some of these differences, not least by providing reassurance to the Koreans that there was no danger that a bilateral settlement with Japan would prompt an American withdrawal from the peninsula or a qualification of its commitment to supporting the political and security interests of the Park administration. This reassurance came in the tangible form of a combined package of technical assistance, agricultural aid and US$150 million in development loans funds presented to the South Korean foreign minister during his visit to Washington mid-way through the course of the extended Tokyo negotiations (Cha 1999: 35).

Significant as this assistance undoubtedly was, it is important to acknowledge that it had very little, if any effect in placating the key critics of the normalisation agreement in South Korea. Yun Po-sŏn, the leader of the country's political opposition, remained implacably unyielding in the face of a two-and-a-half-hour effort by Marshall Green, the State Department's deputy assistant secretary for Far Eastern affairs, to persuade him to drop his resistance to the treaty. Even when it had become clear that normalisation was a near certainty, Yun refused to change course. As the British Ambassador in Seoul noted, '... his hatred of the President, which is almost pathological, blinds him to the inadequacy and incompetence of the Opposition forces' (Godfrey, 5 May 1965).

Importantly, the anti-treaty forces in the ROK were animated by a multifaceted and dogged emotional hostility both to the Park administration and to the agreement with Japan—so much so that they remained apparently impervious to any rational appeal to individual or collective self-interest. The British Japan specialist, Ronald Dore, then a young visiting academic attending a conference in Seoul, was

> ... astonished at the number of younger Koreans, particularly among the more educated, who stated that they would have preferred some form of accommodation with North Korea to what they considered a return of Korea into the Japanese fold (George Buchanan Chalmers, 3 July 1965).

Moreover, the activism of the Johnson administration in seeking to advance the treaty talks may well have heightened rather than dampened local resistance. Seventy-one percent of the Korean population 'actively disliked the Americans' according to one US Army survey, and as British diplomats noted in July 1965, '... [t]here has ... been an increase in anti-Americanism since the Americans are considered to have been one of the major pressure factors forcing normalization with Japan on the Koreans' (George Buchanan Chalmers, 3 July 1965).

If emotional hostility to normalisation was pronounced amongst Koreans, it was just as strikingly muted on the Japanese side. This was remarkable given the political upheaval that had convulsed Japan just five years previously, during the negotiations over another important bilateral accord, the revision and renewal of the US-Japan Security Treaty in 1960. At that time, active opposition from a broad coalition of progressive opinion—trade union groups, radicalised Marxist student organizations, and the principal opposition parties, the Japan Socialist Party (JSP) and the smaller but very active Japan Communist Party (JCP)—had brought chaos to the streets of Tokyo, prompting the cancellation of President Eisenhower's visit to Japan and ultimately contributing to the resignation of Prime Minister Kishi. Yet by 1965, there was little evidence of any such fiery opinion. Zengakuren, the core student group, was fragmented and weakened by internal factional disagreements; the JSP was reluctant to co-operate with the Communists for fear of appearing too radicalised to the electorate; and the mass media had experienced 'a certain amount of maturing' that discouraged it from protesting against the agreement. Perhaps most importantly, the government and the LDP had learnt the lessons of 'Anpo', as the 1960 security treaty crisis was known, and had taken pains to cultivate support for normalisation both in the Diet and in the media. Consequently, despite the continuation of attitudes of condescension and general prejudice against Koreans in Japan, 'the majority of Japanese [were] unconcerned about whether Japan establishes normal diplomatic relations with Korea—North or South, divided or unified …' (Murata 1965; Rundall, 14 July 1965).

Acknowledging these local conditions in Japan and South Korea is important because it prompts legitimate questions about the central thrust of Cha's analysis of the process shaping post-1945 Korea-Japan relations. At the heart of Cha's argument is the stress on the decisive role played by the US in influencing normalisation and also the relevance of the entrapment/abandonment dynamic in understanding the policies of governments in Seoul and Tokyo. Surveying the archival and secondary evidence, it is debatable just how closely this model fits or adequately describes actual conditions in 1965. In particular, there is a risk that in his admirable and justifiable desire to craft a parsimonious and compelling theoretical model, applicable to a series of different negotiating scenarios, Cha may have placed too much weight on analytical leanness at the expense of empirical substance. The messy diversity of historical reality may have been too readily overlooked in favour of the theoretical precision and rigour of the social sciences.

While there were instances in which South Korea's political élites sought reassurance that the US remained committed to maintaining its alignment with the South, it is not clear that this was the main preoccupation of Park and his colleagues. Instead, there appear to have been a multiplicity of factors—not least of which was the desire to foster economic growth at home as a means of enhancing the legitimacy of the ROK government—that shaped the decisions of the Park administration and its predecessor. Domestic politics and political economy then, as much as international relations, determined the process and final substance of the normalisation deal. Nor is it clear, where Japan was concerned, that fear of real or imagined US disengagement or abandonment was a factor in shaping the push for normalisation. Indeed, arguably, the US-Japan relationship in the mid-1960s was conspicuously strong. Reischauer as ambassador had since 1961 assiduously made the case with his superiors back in Washington in favour of treating Japan as an equal partner (the parallel of the UK was often invoked), and as a consequence ties between the Johnson and Satō administrations were secure and the Japanese had no discernible reason to question the US commitment to promoting politic stability and security in the region (FRUS 2006: 46-52). Equally importantly, the vigour with which the Japanese government pursued the normalisation agenda from 1961 onwards reflected a real and unmistakable diminution of historical and cultural antipathy towards the South. That it had not disappeared altogether should come as no surprise—old prejudices are often remarkably resilient, as any cursory glance at the troubled history of post-1945 Europe quickly reveals. Yet there seems little doubt that attitudes had indeed changed on the part of both Japan's élites and popular opinion as a whole and that the Japanese in 1965 was far more ready than they had been ten years previously to begin to bury the political and diplomatic hatchet with Korea.

4 Derailing the Relationship, 1973-1974

Eight years on from normalisation, ROK-Japan relations at the start of 1973 appeared to most objective observers to be remarkably stable and relatively trouble-free. Meeting in London with Anthony Royle, Britain's parliamentary undersecretary at the Foreign Office, Kim Yong-sik, the ROK foreign minister, painted a picture of broadly amicable relations between the two countries. The South Koreans, Kim pointed out, welcomed increased technical and industrial co-operation with Japan and the only significant point of contention dividing the two countries was over how best to promote joint continental shelf developments beyond their littoral waters. Seoul had concerns regarding the likely consequences of a further expansion in semi-official contacts between the LDP government of Kakuei Tanaka and the DPRK, but these were prospective worries rather than a source of immediate tension (Royle, 19 February 1973).

Compared with the political upheaval of 1965, the political waters at home in Korea were noticeably calm. President Park, following the promulgation in the autumn of 1972 of his Yushin constitution and a series of 'revitalising reforms', had buttressed his political position and had largely marginalised any significant political opposition to his increasingly authoritarian administration. Even within the ranks of the government, there were only two nominally viable successors to Park: Kim Jong-pil, his longstanding associate, now installed as prime minister, had a reputation as a 'politically experienced, astute … organizer of skill …' but 'lacked any real political cutting edge' (Petersen, 6 March 1973); Lee Hu-rak, director of the KCIA, was viewed as 'brilliant, sly, and physically brave', but also was judged to be a brutal 'hatchet man' and therefore with a host of enemies and no genuine political backing at home.

Despite these promising indicators, 1973-74 turned out to be a period of immense upheaval and uncertainty in the South Korea-Japan relationship—a sixteen-month interval of high political drama that threatened at points to blow the bilateral relationship dramatically and potentially irretrievably off course. The response of the Japanese and South Korean political establishments during this period demonstrated the continuing salience of volatile emotional and historical tensions in shaping bilateral relations, as well as the relatively limited role for external actors, most notably the US, in mediating between the two competing governments.

4.1 *Abduction of Kim Dae-jung*

The immediate trigger for the rift between Seoul and Tokyo came with the revelation in early August of a dramatic plot to kidnap Kim Dae-jung, a prominent opposition politician who had been defeated by Park in the 1971 presidential election. Kim had been in Japan, liaising with political allies, when on 8 August he was suddenly seized at gunpoint by unidentified Korean assailants, drugged and spirited out of his Tokyo hotel room. Five days later, after his colleagues had raised the alarm over his disappearance, Kim re-emerged bruised and disoriented in Seoul, having been unexpectedly released outside his private residence in the capital and was subsequently placed under house arrest. In the aftermath of the abduction it was not immediately clear what had happened. There was some press speculation that conservative South Korean nationalists might have been responsible for the action, some even suggested that Kim had deliberately staged the abduction to bolster his anti-establishment opposition credentials. For its part, the Park administration denied all knowledge or responsibility for the event (*The Times*, 9 August 1973; Jiji Press, 10 August 1973).

Privately, however, informed observers, both in Japan and amongst Western governments, suspected that the operation had been carried out by the KCIA with Park's direct or tacit approval, in a deliberate effort to rid the president of a troubling political opponent. Philip Habib, the US ambassador in Seoul, on learning of Kim's disappearance on the 8th, intervened immediately with the Korean authorities, making clear in no uncertain terms that bilateral relations between the ROK and the US would be seriously undermined if Kim's safety was compromised—action that Habib argued persuasively in retrospect helped save the opposition politician's life (Petersen, 21 August 1973).

Kim's eleventh-hour rescue merely signalled the start of months of uncertainty surrounding the precise circumstances of the case and in particular a long, protracted set of difficult negotiations between the Korean and Japanese authorities. For the Tanaka administration, the kidnapping represented a major political and diplomatic headache. As a blatant violation of Japanese national sovereignty by a foreign power, it required a swift and comprehensive resolution. The very fact that the abduction had succeeded exposed the security shortcomings of Japan and raised legitimate concerns about the ability of the government to protect its own borders and its citizens. Japan's police authorities, who had formal jurisdiction over the case, were particularly incensed by the event given their past co-operation with the KCIA. Feeling betrayed by the South Koreans, they were therefore determined to get to the bottom of the matter. Failure to push the South Korean government for a full disclosure of the circumstances of the kidnapping would have exposed the Tanaka government to criticism from its progressive political rivals at home that it was colluding with an authoritarian, anti-democratic regime. At the same time, the dramatic nature of the case fed into and exacerbated long-standing anti-Korean prejudices within Japan, fuelling calls for retaliation against Korea and dividing opinion throughout Japan as well as within the Japanese cabinet (Barrington, 12 September 1973).

In response to demands for clarification from Japan, the Park administration denied responsibility, prevaricated and eventually established what amounted to a very desultory and ultimately unrevealing official enquiry. In the immediate aftermath of the crisis, the most divisive point of dispute arose from claims from the Japanese authorities that Kim Dong-woon, first secretary at the ROK embassy in Tokyo, had been directly involved in the incident, along with other senior members of the South Korean mission. Kim himself returned to Seoul in mid-August, where he remained, despite repeated requests from the Tanaka government for him to return to Japan to assist the Tokyo police with their enquiries. Over time, the Japanese police unearthed fresh evidence, including fingerprints, that convinced them of the direct participation of Korean government officials in the kidnapping.

By late September, the Tanaka administration, convinced that they had incontrovertible evidence of the culpability of the Park administration, was lobbying the US for assistance in pressuring Seoul to respond to their demands. However, the Nixon administration chose not to intervene, with representatives of the State Department privately confiding to the British their belief that the Japanese, given their close economic relationship with South Korea, had sufficient independent leverage to force the Koreans to come to terms. Part of this may have reflected economic self-interest rather than a dispassionate assessment of what might prove most effective in negotiating with Seoul. As Jeffrey Petersen, the British ambassador in Seoul noted in a telegram to London, the US position conveniently offered the Americans an opportunity to challenge Japan's growing economic presence in South Korea, since any attenuation of relations between Seoul and Tokyo could be calculated to redound to the benefit of US firms (Petersen, 20 September 1973). Indeed, with the Nixon administration increasingly embroiled in the Watergate controversy, it was no surprise that Korea-related issues had lost the immediate significance they had had in the 1960s. Kissinger, Nixon's secretary of state, remained generally uninterested in Korean matters so long as the country remained stable, and by January 1974 there had been a marked '… decrease in interest in Korea within the Administration' (Pike, 16 January 1974; Petersen, 24 January 1974).

Whatever the motives on the American side, the basic assessment of conditions on the ground proved accurate. South Korea had developed a close and active economic partnership with Japan and was looking to secure valuable Japanese economic development assistance to fund a series of development projects, including the Pohang Steel production facility in the southern part of the ROK. Business pressures helped tip the political balance in favour of an admission of sorts. Following the exchange of secret personal envoys between the two governments in September and October (Westlake, 28 September 1973; Petersen, 30 October 1973), Kim Jong-pil travelled to Tokyo and reached an accommodation with the Tanaka government, under which both sides agreed to treat the abduction as a criminal investigation rather than a political or diplomatic matter, while Japan agreed to resume active ministerial discussions with South Korea on economic collaboration (Blake-Pauley, 8 November 1973). In essence, Kim's admission was diplomatic 'fudge'—a veiled admission of official responsibility in return for the renewal of Japanese economic support. Back in Seoul, the prime minister rebutted opposition claims that he had been engaged in an 'apology mission which [had] damaged national prestige and besmirched the national honour.' Yet in reality, the Koreans had had to offer concessions to buy off critical opinion in Tokyo, accepting that Kim Dae-jung would be eventually released from house arrest (possibly to travel to the US to take up the offer of a visiting professorship at Harvard), while also agreeing to a continuing official investigation into Kim Dong-woon's role in the affair (Blake-Pauley, 8 November 1973). After a decent interval to save face for the government, Lee Hu-rak, the head of the KCIA and therefore the prime architect of the kidnapping attempt, suffered the ignominy of resignation and was forced into temporary exile overseas.

Curiously, and perhaps ironically, the Park administration's attempt to bolster its political position at home by targeting a foreign rival overseas had exposed it to renewed criticism—not from opposition groups critical of the KCIA but from a wave of anti-Japanese sentiment inflamed by Tokyo's apparent efforts to dictate terms to Seoul (Petersen, 4 October and 6 December 1973). Nor did Kim Jong-pil's November trip to Tokyo successfully assuage aggrieved Japanese opinion, even amongst traditionally pro-Korean conservative members of the governing LDP. During ministerial discussions in January 1974 in Tokyo, Yasuhiro Nakasone (who would, as prime minister nearly a decade later, place re-engagement with South Korea at the centre of his foreign policy) had no hesitation in berating his South Korean ministerial counterparts. As one observer noted, Nakasone harangued the Koreans in a '… manner reminiscent more of the playground that bilateral discussions between governments' (Dimond, 4 January 1974).

4.2 *Attempted assassination of Park Chung-hee*

The Kim Dae-jung affair clearly placed the Park administration in a potentially awkward position vis-à-vis Japan. However, on balance there was precious little evidence of any meaningful or sincere contrition on the part of the Koreans. Moreover, by 15 August 1974, just over a year and a week after the abduction crisis, the ROK government was presented unexpectedly with a fresh set of dramatic events that enabled it to turn the tables on the Japanese, dramatically transforming itself in the process from victimiser to victim. The trigger, in this instance, both figuratively and literally, was the attempted assassination at Seoul's National Theatre of President Park by Mun Se-kwang, a 23 year-old ethnic Korean resident of Japan. The attack was witnessed by the foreign diplomatic corps (including the British ambassador), who were in attendance to listen to the president deliver a speech on the occasion of the country's National Independence Day commemorating the end of the war and the country's liberation from Japanese colonial rule. Mun's attack failed to kill the president, but one of the assassin's bullets struck and fatally injured Park's wife, sparking in turn a bitter diplomatic row between the Japanese and South Korean governments and imposing further pressures on a relationship already badly strained by the tensions associated with the Kim Dae-jung incident (Petersen, 20 August 1974).

In the immediate aftermath of the attack on the president, the Japanese government, relieved to discover that the assailant was a Korean rather than a Japanese national, rushed out a public announcement denying any official legal or moral responsibility for the tragic events in Seoul. Technically, Tokyo's position was a sound one, but it demonstrated the tin ear of the Japanese authorities in handling an incident that was bound to be highly sensitive on the Korean side. Public and official opinion in Seoul reacted with predictable outrage, and the Park administration rapidly demanded satisfaction from a Japanese government that it judged was, in practical terms, responsible for the assassination. Mun had entered Korea on a false Japanese passport and had carried out the attack using a gun stolen from a police-box in Osaka in Japan. Under interrogation, Mun confessed to being a member of Chōsen Sōren or Choch'ongryŏn, the pro-DPRK association of Korean residents in Japan, which he claimed had actively supported and plotted the assassination.

Park's government demanded a swift and uncompromising response from Japan, including a thorough and exhaustive investigation of the circumstances leading up to the attack as well as action to proscribe Chōsen Sōren, or at the very least measures to prevent it from engaging in any political activity in Japan. Implicit in these demands also was the Korean insistence that the Japanese government accept official responsibility for the incident and issue some sort of apology.

Park's decision to push for maximum satisfaction from the Japanese government was in part prompted by what appeared to be a genuine outpouring of public sympathy for South Korea's autocratic leader. Huge, sympathetic crowds turned out on 19 August for the funeral for Madame Park which, in the words of a British embassy report, '… appear to have produced a profound effect on the President and to have persuaded him that the overwhelming mass of South Koreans are at heart on his side' (Petersen, 29 August 1974). These scenes were soon followed by mass protests against the Japanese, encouraged by the South Korean authorities but which nonetheless did not require much prompting, such was the intensity of anti-Japanese Korean sentiment. Japan's ambassador in Seoul, Torao Ushiroku, soon found himself virtually besieged. As Petersen, the British ambassador noted in late August,

> … for the past week my poor Japanese colleague has rarely been able to enter or leave his Embassy except through a crowd of Koreans vociferously demonstrating under loose and manifestly benevolent police control; one day schoolboys, another day war veterans and so on. Mr Ushi-

> roku is now driving about in a small Korean car with no marks of identification except a diplomatic number plate (Petersen, 29 August 1974).

The Korean media added further fuel to the diplomatic fire by calling for a formal break in relations with Japan and in one memorably hyperbolic moment by advocating a South Korean guerrilla war against Japan. At its root, the intensity of the South Korean reaction was fanned by an emotional hostility to Japan that in part was shaped by historical legacies that even the most pragmatic of responses could do little to counter—a point that was keenly appreciated by the Japanese ambassador. As his British counterpart noted:

> [Ushiroku] ... considers ... that the anti-Japanese manifestations are based on a solid and deeply rooted foundation of anti-Japanese feeling which even with good will on both sides would only die away over decades rather than years. This seems to be both an honest and an accurate assessment (Petersen, 20 August 1974).

Notwithstanding the emotionally charged nature of the Korean response, Park's hardline position was not surprising nor should it have been unexpected to the Japanese. Park had been the target of assassination attempts in the past, including a 1968 North Korean commando raid on the presidential residence, the Blue House, and in 1970 a failed attempt to detonate a bomb at the National Cemetery. Equally importantly, information had come to light in the summer of 1974 indicating North Korean espionage activities in Japan, but no discernible crackdown had been ordered by the Japanese despite calls for action from the South Korean authorities. Indeed a public statement in the Diet by Kimura, the Japanese foreign minister, suggested that North Korea did not pose a threat to South Korea, indicating a very relaxed, some might argue unduly complacent attitude on the part of the Japanese authorities.

Even allowing for the merits of the South Korean case, there was little that the Japanese government could do to meet the immediate pressures from Seoul. Under Japanese law, the police were only empowered to take action against an organisation if it could be proven that it was engaged in threatening measures intentionally directed against the Japanese authorities. Moreover, Chōsen Sōren vigorously rejected the charge that it had had a hand in the assassination plot and it was legitimate to question the wisdom of basing any action purely on the confession of Mun, the assassin, information presumably obtained in part through South Korea's characteristically vigorous interrogation techniques.

Japan's hesitation in bowing to South Korea's demands was also undoubtedly conditioned by the wider context of the bilateral relationship. Since April 1974, the two governments had been locked in a dispute surrounding the fate of two Japanese students arrested in South Korea and sentenced to lengthy prison terms for conspiring with radical student groups to undermine the ROK government. In addition, on 14 August, the South Korean authorities had finally reported the conclusion of their lengthy investigation into the Kim Dae-jung kidnapping. Their anodyne announcement that there was no evidence to support the claim that ROK government officials had been involved triggered a political storm in Tokyo, with opposition Japanese politicians calling for the immediate end of Japanese economic aid to South Korea. In light of these tensions then, it was perhaps surprising that the Japanese prime minister, Kakuei Tanaka, took the unusual step of attending the funeral of Park's wife and followed this up with a letter expressing his regret for the events of 15 August.

Tanaka's letter, however, became a further source of controversy between the two governments, with Seoul demanding a clearer and more explicit apology and admission of responsibility from the Japanese side. Ultimately, the impasse was resolved through further compromise. This was in part effected through limited pressure from the US, which relied on its chargé d'affaires in Seoul to act as an informal mediator between the Japanese and South Korean officials. The suggestion also that a forthcoming summit visit to Seoul by President Ford might be at risk if the dispute remained unresolved, almost certainly helped to concentrate minds on the South Korean side. Yet, perhaps more important than this, in the final instance, was the value of symbolic, political gestures, deployed once again in a manner that evoked memories of past bilateral disagreements from 1965. Etsusaburō Shiina, the former Japanese foreign minister, was once more deployed to South Korea with some effect. Shiina visited Seoul on 19 September, and photographs published in the local press showing him bowing his head in an unmistakable gesture of contrition appear to have helped to moderate local grievances. Equal importantly, Shiina travelled with a classified letter from the Japanese side. Although not released to the public, the letter made clear that Japan was prepared to go some considerable distance in meeting the concrete demands of the Koreans. As the language of the letter clearly stated:

> Japan will strictly control criminal acts such as terrorist activities aimed at overthrowing the Korean Government and will control criminal acts committed by any other person whether or not they are members of the Chosen soren or any other organization (Dearlove, 9 October 1974).

By mid-December bilateral relations had quietened down considerably, the fall-out from the Mun affair had diminished, and Japan was about to offer another, although unrelated, gesture of contrition, by returning to Korea the ashes of some 300 Koreans killed by Japan during the Pacific War (Dimond, 18 December 1974).

5 Conclusion

Underpinning the crises of 1973 and 1974 was a powerful current of emotional intensity on both sides of the bilateral relationship, especially amongst Korean opinion, at both the élite and mass levels. Some observers, including Cha, have sought to explain the fractured negotiations and pattern of accusation and counter-accusation between Japan and South Korea as shaped primarily by strategic calculations and rational threat assessments, particularly regarding the potential security challenge posed by the DPRK (Cha 1999: 133). This seems to undervalue the importance of the emotional dimension to the bilateral relationship and potentially to assign too much weight, especially in the later stages of the post-war relationship, to the perceived and actual importance of the US to decision-makers in both Tokyo and Seoul. Certainly, there was little, if any evidence, to suggest that Japanese or Korean officials at this point were seriously worried about a diminution of America's presence in East Asia or the risk of any meaningful 'abandonment' of their respective national interests. As with the complicated and drawn-out 1965 normalisation talks, US influence, though not inconsequential, was not the decisive factor. In explaining both the successes and the very real deficiencies in the Japan-ROK relationship, the tensions and the unfulfilled promise of a bilateral partnership that even today has yet to reach its full potential, domestic politics and local interests and actions were key and as important as, if not more important than international conditions or the actions of senior alliance partners.

References

Barrington, N.J. (12 September 1973), 'Barrington to R.B. Hervey', FEK 1/6, FO 371, FCO 21/1178 series, National Archives (NA), Kew, UK

Blake-Pauley, A. (8 November 1973), 'Blake-Pauley to C.J. Denne', FEK 1/6, FCO 21/1179 series, NA

Brazinsky, Gregg (2007), *Nation Building in South Korea: Koreans, Americans, and the Making of Democracy*, Chapel Hill NC: The University of North Carolina Press

Cha, Victor (1999), *Alignment Despite Antagonism: The US-Korea-Japan Security Triangle*, Stanford CA: Stanford University Press

Chalmers, George Buchanan (3 July 1965), 'Buchanan Chalmers to Michael Morgan', FK 103123/37, FO 371 series, NA

Chancery, Tokyo (10 March 1961), 'Chancery, Tokyo to Far Eastern Dept', FK 103123/9, FO 371 series, NA

Chancery, Tokyo (21 April 1961), 'Chancery, Tokyo to Far Eastern Dept', FK 103123/12, FO 371 series, NA

Chancery, Tokyo (19 August 1961), 'Chancery, Tokyo to Far Eastern Dept', FK 103123/20, FO 371 series, NA

Cortazzi, Hugh (2 November 1962), 'Cortazzi to Far Eastern Dept', FK10321/21, FO 371 series, NA

Cossa, Ralph (1999), *U.S.-Korea-Japan Relations: Building Toward a 'Virtual Alliance'*, Washington DC: Center for Strategic and International Studies

Dearlove, J.G. (9 October 1974), 'Japan/Korea Relations', FEK 3/306/1, FO 21/1320 series, NA

Denson, John (19 January 1961), 'Denson to N. Trench', FK 103123/1, FO 371 series, NA

Dimond, Jenny (4 January 1974), 'Dimond to C.J. Denne', FEK 3/306/1, FO 21/1320 series, NA

Dimond, Jenny (18 December 1974), 'Dimond to D. Coates', FEK 3/306/1, FO 21/1320 series, NA

Evans, Hubert (17 September 1960), 'Evans to Far Eastern Department', FK 103123/20, FO 371 series, NA

Foreign Office (11 August 1961), 'Foreign Office to Seoul', FK 103123/18, FO 371 series, NA

FRUS (2006), *Foreign Relations of the United States, 1964-1968*, vol. XXIX, Part 2, *Japan*, Washington DC: United States Government Printing Office

Godfrey, Walter (22 November 1962), 'Godfrey to Far Eastern Department', FK103123)2(c), FO 371 series, NA

Godfrey, Walter (26 November 1962), 'Godfrey to Far Eastern Department', FK 103123/22, FO 371 series, NA

Godfrey, Walter (5 May 1965), 'Godfrey to M. MacLehose', FK 103123/20, FO 371 series, NA

Hahm, Chaibong and Kim Seog-gun (2001), 'Remembering Japan and North Korea', in: Gerrit W. Gong (ed.), *Memory and History in East and South East Asia. Issues of Identity and International Relations*, Washington DC: Center for Strategic and International Studies, pp. 101-112

Jiji Press (10 August 1973), 'Presidential Candidate Kim Kidnapped'

Kang, Sang-jung (2007), *Nitchō kankei no kokufuku* [The triumph of Japan-Korea relations], Tokyo: Shūeisha shinsho

Kim, Samuel (2006), *The Two Koreas and the Great Powers*, Cambridge, UK: Cambridge University Press

Koh, Byung-chul (2007), *Beyond Discord and Cooperation. Japan and the Two Koreas*, Seoul: Yonsei University Press

Kyodo News (27 December 2005), 'Japan-South Korea history group to hold 2nd round of talks in January'. Online: http://findarticles.com/p/articles/mi_m0WDQ/is_2005_Dec_27/ai_n15971576 (accessed 15 April 2008)

Lee, Jun-won (1996), *Higashi ajia reisen to kan-bei-nichi kankei* [US-Japan-South Korean relations and the East Asian Cold War], Tokyo: Tokyo University Press

Lee, Won-deog (2001), 'A Normal State without Remorse: The Textbook Controversy and Korea-Japan Relations', in: *East Asian Review*, 13 (3), pp. 21-40.

Lie, John (1998), *Han Unbound: The Political Economy of South Korea*, Stanford CA: Stanford University Press

Lind, Jennifer (2005), 'Sorry States: Apologies in International Politics': unpublished paper prepared for the American Political Science Association conference, 2005. Online: http://www.dartmouth.edu/~jlind/research/LindAPSA2005.pdf (accessed 25 July 2008)

Moon, Chung-in (2005), Personal interview, Yonsei University, Seoul

Morland, Oliver (13 April 1960), 'Sir Oliver Morland, Tokyo to Far Eastern Department' FK 10323/14, FO 371 series, NA

Murata, Kiyoaki (1965), 'Another 1960? Anti-ROK Pact Agitation Likely to be Less in Scope, Intensity', in: *Japan Times*, 7 October 1965

Ogawa, Akira (no date), 'The Miracle in 1965'. Online: http://www.okazaki-inst.jp/miracle65.html (accessed 20 July 2008)

Petersen, Jeffrey (6 March 1973), 'South Korea: The End of the Ice Age', FEK 1/6, FCO 21/1178 series, NA

Petersen, Jeffrey (21 August 1973), 'Petersen to R. M. Evans', FEK 1/6, FCO 21/1178 series, NA

Petersen, Jeffrey (20 September 1973), 'Petersen to R. M. Evans', FEK 1/6, FCO 21/1178 series, NA

Petersen, Jeffrey (4 October 1973), 'Petersen to R. M. Evans', FEK 1/6, FCO 21/1179 series, NA

Petersen, Jeffrey (30 October 1973), 'Petersen to FCO', FEK 1/6, FCO 21/1179 series, NA

Petersen, Jeffrey (6 December 1973), 'Petersen to E. Youde', FEK 1/6, FCO 21/1179 series, NA

Petersen, Jeffrey (24 January 1974), 'Petersen to E. Youde', FEK 1/6, FCO 21/1308 series, NA

Petersen, Jeffrey (20 August 1974), 'The Attempted Assassination of President Park', FEK 1/3, FCO 21/1309 series, NA

Petersen, Jeffrey (29 August 1974), 'The Attempted Assassination of President Park: the Aftermath', FEK 1/3, FCO 21/1309 series, NA

Pike, M. E. (16 January 1974), 'The Internal Situation in South Korea', FEK 1/3, FCO 21/1308 series, NA

Royle, Anthony (19 February 1973), 'Memorandum of a Conversation', FEK 3/306/1, FCO 21 series, NA

Rundall, Francis (21 April 1965), 'Japan/Korea Relations', FK 103123/14, FO 371 series, NA

Rundall, Francis (14 July 1965), 'Japan/Korea Relations', FK 103123/34, FO 371 series, NA

Shinoda, Tomohito (2006), *Reisengo no nihon gaikō* [Japan's post-Cold War diplomacy], Tokyo: Mineruba shobō

Swenson-Wright, John (2005), *Unequal Allies?: United States Security and Alliance Policy Toward Japan*, 1945-1960, Stanford CA: Stanford University Press

Swenson-Wright, John (2008), 'The Limits to Normality: Japanese-Korean post-Cold War Interactions', in: David Welch (ed.), *Japan as a Normal Nation*, Toronto: University of Toronto Press (forthcoming)

The Times (9 August 1973), 'S Korean exiled politician kidnapped in Tokyo'

Trench, Nigel (18 January 1962), 'Trench to A. de la Mare', FK 103123/14, FO 371, NA

Underwood, William (2008), 'New Era for Japan-Korea History Issues', in: *Oh My News*. Online: http://english.ohmynews.com/articleview/article_view.asp?article_class=2&no=382092&rel_no= (accessed 15 July 2008)

Wakamiya, Yoshibumi (1998), *The Postwar Conservative View of Asia*, Tokyo: LTCB International Library Foundation

Westlake, Peter (28 September 1973), 'Westlake to Foreign Office', FEK 3/306/1, FCO 21/1192 series, NA

Woo, Seung-ji, (2005), Personal interview, Institute for Foreign Affairs and National Security, Seoul

Yoon, Suk-joon (2005), Secretary to the President for Overseas Communication, Ch'ŏngwadae (Blue House), Seoul, personal interview.

Yoshizawa, Fumitoshi (2007), *Sengo nikkan kankei* [Post-war Japan-South Korean relations], Tokyo: Kurein

THE DISPARITY BETWEEN SOUTH KOREA'S ENGAGEMENT AND SECURITY POLICIES TOWARDS NORTH KOREA: THE REALIST-LIBERAL PENDULUM

Alon Levkowitz[1]

ABSTRACT

Since the beginning of the Sunshine Policy, South Korea has pursued a flexible and moderate engagement and economic policy towards North Korea, even at the cost of increased tensions with Washington. But while South Korea's policy on inter-Korean relations has undergone a fundamental change, its security policy continues to be rather conservative, firmly grounded in Cold War parameters. This disparity between South Korea's foreign and security policies forms the theme of this paper. The paper argues that the Kim Dae-jung and Roh Moo-hyun era should be regarded as a hedging period during which South Korea has sought to change the North's behaviour and interests, while at the same time it has continued with its conservative security policy. It concludes that unless North Korean relations with South Korea and with other regional states, including security relations, undergo some fundamental transformation, the disparity between South Korea's engagement and security policies will continue.

[1] I am grateful to Jim Hoare, Rüdiger Frank, Susan Pares, Patrick Köllner and Galia Press-Barnathan for their helpful comments and suggestions on earlier versions of this article.

1 THE DISPARITY BETWEEN SOUTH KOREA'S ENGAGEMENT[2] AND SECURITY POLICIES

The election of Kim Dae-jung as president of the Republic of Korea (ROK—South Korea) in 1997 raised hopes for a change in inter-Korean relations. Expectations (and conservative doubts) were reinforced once Kim presented his new 'Sunshine Policy', which marked a redirection in South Korea's policy towards the Democratic People's Republic of Korea (DPRK—North Korea) from containment to engagement (Son 2006). The philosophy behind this policy was to engage with the DPRK in order to convince it to change incrementally, and to avoid hostility and antagonism between the two states (Kwon and Lim 2006: 134).

Roh Moo-hyun was seen as Kim Dae-jung's political heir, and his election as president in 2002 was expected to lead to a continuation of Kim's Sunshine Policy and once again raised hopes in the liberal camp and doubts in the conservative camp. Roh Moo-hyun added a regional perspective to the Sunshine Policy with his 'Policy of Peace and Prosperity', conceived to create a balance between peace and prosperity in the Korean peninsula and the Northeast Asian region (Kim Choong Nam 2007: 376-80).

The implementation of the Sunshine Policy from 1998 brought many changes to the Korean peninsula but it did not solve the inter-Korean conflict. In fact, from a military and security point of view, the two countries remained in a state of war. Both continued their military build-up and improvements in their strength and technology, although South Korea, with its economic supremacy over the impoverished North, had the clear advantage. South Korea also had the benefit of the continued presence of United States (US) forces, stationed in Korea since the Korean War (1950-53).

The Kim Dae-jung and Roh Moo-hyun North Korean policy raises a puzzle. How was the ROK able to pursue a liberal-oriented engage-

[2] Neither North nor South Korea views relations between them as 'foreign affairs' but as 'inter-Korean relations', hence the use of the term 'engagement' in this paper. This is symbolised by the fact that in both, their mutual relations are not handled by the Foreign Ministry but by other bodies. Hence the North Korean concern early in 2008 when the incoming South Korean president, Lee Myung-bak, announced that he intended to abolish the Ministry of Unification and give its remit to the Ministry of Foreign Affairs and Trade. The decision was later overturned.

ment policy and a conservative-realist security policy towards the DPRK simultaneously?

This paper argues that the Kim and Roh presidencies (1998-2003, 2003-08) pursued a hedging policy in the form of a dual track strategy towards the DPRK. On the one hand, a concrete effort was to be made to change the 'rules of the game' with North Korea and to turn the zero-sum game between the two countries into a win-win situation by fundamentally realigning South Korean policy towards the North and the environment in the Korea peninsula. On the other hand, the South was to be kept safe by adhering to the same security policy that had characterised its behaviour since the Korean War. Under Kim and Roh, the ROK hoped that by providing 'carrots' to the DPRK, it might modify its inter-Korean policy. At the same time, both presidents continued to hold the 'sticks', a conservative security policy, in case the North misinterpreted the South's 'carrots'. The concept of a hedging policy can explain the disparity found in the different and sometimes contradictory policies of the South Korean government over the past few years and may help when we consider possible developments in the near future in inter-Korean relations.

2 TERMS OF ANALYSIS

Two theories of international relations, defensive realism and liberalism, provide us with lenses through which we can understand the hedging behaviour of the ROK.

Defensive realism suggests that states maximise their security and maintain their position in the international system by balancing their rivals' capabilities or deterring them. To avoid inadvertent escalations and to refrain from the quest of primacy, which leads to instability and war, states should maximise security in ways that will be least threatening to others' retaliatory capabilities and vital interests. Otherwise, balancing could lead to destabilising arms races and competing alliances or even to war (see e.g. Miller 2001).

Liberalism suggests that states will use 'soft power' in a bilateral or multilateral manner to affect a rival's intentions. Liberals suggest that this is both desirable for the purpose of peace and security and feasible in different parts of the world. Liberals also argue that illiberal states are more likely to try and accumulate as much power as possible and adopt aggressive strategies (cf. Press-Barnathan 2006: 262-3). While the realist theory assumes a certain pessimistic stance about the international arena, liberalism is more optimistic about the ability to change policies and even the interests and values of states without the need to use force.

The term 'hedging' has been used by different scholars (e.g. more recently Art 2004; Goh 2006; Heginbotham 2002; Medeiros 2005; Roy 2005), who have debated a suitable definition. Here I use Denny Roy's definition of hedging: 'Keeping open more than one strategic option against the possibility of a future security threat' (Roy 2005: 306).

3 South Korea's inter-Korean policy

The adoption of the Sunshine Policy and the later Peace and Prosperity policy (Koh 2006: 7) as South Korea's liberal-oriented policy towards the DPRK brought fundamental changes to the South's inter-Korean policy. The aim of both Kim Dae-jung and Roh Moo-hyun was to try to transform perceptions in the North and within the South Korean public discourse. The intention of the Sunshine Policy, which is based on liberal thought, is to increase the incentives of the two adversaries to pursue peace and not pursue war (Levin and Han 2002: 23-31).

Kim and later Roh reasoned that by changing the rules of the game and adopting a liberal approach based on engagement, they would decrease the possibility of conflict and enhance inter-Korean relations. In order to change North Korea's approach to inter-Korean relations, South Korea decided to pursue a different new strategy in the hope that it would lead to an incremental change in the North's attitudes.

This paper focuses on three different areas of South Korean policy in which major shifts occurred during the past few years: policy towards North Korea based on the principles of the Sunshine Policy; relations with the US; and regional politics. The ROK knew these changes could potentially carry a high price, especially in its relations with the US and Japan, but was willing to pursue the Sunshine Policy even at the cost of disagreements with its allies.

3.1 *Policy towards North Korea*

We can identify several important changes in the Kim Dae-jung and Roh Moo-hyun policy towards the DPRK. Their common ground can be described as a shift from a realist policy to a liberal-oriented aspiration.

3.1.1 *Promoting the goals of economic co-operation and long-term gradual unification*

All South Korean governments have claimed that the quest for unification has been a fundamental policy issue, although the means and strategy to achieve such a goal have changed throughout the years. One of the primary assumptions of the Sunshine Policy, which affected the strategies of the Kim and Roh presidencies, stressed the need to delay the achievement of unification in order to minimise the costs for South Korea (Wolf and Akramov 2005). According to this concept, the cost of North Korea's collapse would have severe implications for the South Korean economy and entail major social and strategic implications for the Korean peninsula. If German unification served as an empirical lesson for South Korean governments, the 1997 financial crisis served to teach the Korean public not only how much a North Korean collapse would cost, but also how it would feel financially, if another economic crisis occurred in South Korea as a result of the collapse of the DPRK (Pollack and Lee 1999; Wolf and Akramov 2005). The 1997 financial crisis also exposed South Korea's vulnerability to the globalised economy and the need to reform and strengthen its economy and make it more competitive (Chung and Eichengreen 2004; Chang 2003). The increased cost of labour in South Korea and the rise of competition from China led South Korean companies to search for alternative solutions in the region, in addition to the transfer of low-tech factories to China or Southeast Asian states.

The Sunshine Policy allowed the ROK to form linkages between different goals. One of the first changes that Kim Dae-jung's government made was to allow South Korean companies to invest in the DPRK. This move indicated a separation of politics from economics, which previous governments had not supported (Koh 2006: 7). The development of the Kaesŏng Special Economic Zone enabled the relocation of industries with high labour costs from the ROK to the

DPRK, allowing them to benefit from the zone's labour force, relatively cheap by comparison with China, and from the subsidies that the South Korean government was offering (Nanto and Manyin 2007: 3-4).[3] Looking to the long term, the Kaesŏng project was seen as a platform for creating additional industrial complexes in the DPRK, which in turn would assist the South Korean economy in becoming more competitive globally. At the same time, the Kaesŏng project also served the goal of developing the DPRK's economy, an essential requirement for assuring North Korean stability and decreasing the cost of a future unification of the peninsula. The gradual development of the North's economy, it was argued, would furthermore reduce incentives for the DPRK to initiate a war, in face of the growing cost of hostilities. Thus, by pursuing a liberal policy that decreased the chances for collapse of the DPRK and sought to convince the states in the surrounding region that the Korean peninsula was progressing towards a less confrontational period, the ROK also served its own economic interests.

It would appear that this economic aspect of the Sunshine Policy has been best integrated into South Korean politics. South Koreans now perceive economic co-operation with the North as inevitable and legitimate. This became clear in 2008 with Lee Myung-bak's presidency, which has already awakened old frictions but has not questioned the legitimacy of the existing inter-Korean economic projects achieved during Kim's and Roh's presidencies.

3.1.2 *Overlooking provocations and 'incidents'*

During earlier presidencies, the ROK reacted severely to any provocation from the North Korean regime, and such provocations were harshly criticised and condemned (Kim Choong Nam 2007). They were seen as part of a zero-sum game, that is, unless the South responded, any incident would be considered as a victory for the North.

Since 1998, this almost automatic reaction has changed. Although one of the principles of the Sunshine Policy was no tolerance for provocation (Levin and Han 2002: 24), and South Korean conservatives expected such a response to any North Korean threat, Kim and

[3] Although there were doubts over the profitability of the South Korean projects in North Korea, for example, the Mt Kŭmgang project. One should remember that the majority of the South Korean companies that are located in the Kaesŏng complex are small- and medium-sized businesses.

Roh pursued a policy that would not increase the tension between the two Koreas. In fact, once the Sunshine Policy had brought about a new relationship with the DPRK, the South Korean government did not pursue a retaliatory line. This less confrontational reaction would appear not only to have been based on fear of escalating tensions in the Korean peninsula but also to have stemmed from a desire to change the rules of the game to which the North was accustomed (Lee Hong Yung 2002; *Korea Herald*, 11 July 2006). By changing the rules of the game, even when North Korean provocations 'crossed the line', the South believed that the liberal flavour of the Sunshine Policy would eventually alter the North's automatic reactions and hinder or modify its challenging behaviour. Conservatives criticised Kim and Roh for pursuing what some even termed an appeasement policy, towards the DPRK, stating that the North still perceived inter-Korean relations in the prism of a zero-sum game.

The South Korean government was aware of the price of the new strategy and the danger of maintaining a softer line towards the DPRK without achieving the desired outcome. Nevertheless, Kim and Roh pursued their policy, even when confronted repeatedly by North Korean brinkmanship, arguing that it would take time for the new approach to penetrate the North's world view and lead to alterations in its policies. Among North Korean provocations was the submarine incident in 1998,[4] when Kim Dae-jung prevented the Joint Chiefs of Staff from making a statement because he wished to handle the issue quietly and cautiously and to return the submarine and its crew to North Korea as a humanitarian gesture (Lee Hong Yung 2002: 328-9). Other incidents included repeated missile firings by North Korea from 1998, though these did not harm relations between the two countries and did not halt the development of the South Korean economic projects in the North. The South Korean government's position was made clear by Park Sung-hoon, deputy minister for unification policy, in 1998, when he was quoted as saying: 'The missile incident is expected to have a negative impact on our government's promotion of inter-Korean reconciliation and cooperation … but the government is not considering retaliating by suspending the tourism project or delaying

[4] In late June 1998, a North Korean submarine intruded into South Korean waters off the east coast of the peninsula. It became caught in fishing nets and was apprehended by South Korean naval vessels. The crew of nine appeared all to have committed suicide. Their bodies were returned to the North.

its pace' (Shin Yong-bae, writing in the *Korea Herald*, 2 September 1998).

The succeeding Roh Moo-hyun administration continued with this policy even when South Korean public opinion polls demanded a harsher stance towards the DPRK,[5] and ignored US and Japanese demands for a firmer reaction against North Korean provocation. In a few cases, the administration did not accept US intelligence evaluation of the DPRK, considering reports in the US and Japanese press that a North Korean missile launch was imminent as unreliable (*Chosun Ilbo*, 19 June 2006).[6] When the DPRK carried out an underground nuclear test on 9 October 2006, questions were raised about South Korean policy and its effectiveness in decreasing tension in the Korean peninsula, but if conservatives hoped that President Roh Moo-hyun would halt South Korean projects in the North and limit relations with the DPRK after the test, they were disappointed. Roh conceded that while it was true that the nuclear test posed an increased security threat to the South, he believed the military balance between the two Koreas had not been upset and that the ROK was 'still capable of defending itself with its own armed forces and with the help of the alliance with the United States' (Kim Ji-hyun 2006a). Speaking in the National Assembly in November 2006, he defended the Mt Kŭmgang and Kaesŏng projects as a 'symbol of peace and stability on the peninsula' and vowed that: 'Under no circumstances can we cut the channel of dialogue with the North. The government may adjust the speed and scope of its policies but will continue to maintain the overall framework and basic principles of the policy of peace and prosperity' (Kim Ji-hyun 2006b).

3.1.3 *Ignoring social and human rights issues*

One might have expected both Kim Dae-jung, who suffered personally from human rights violations during his long years as an opposition member, and Roh Moo-hyun, who was a human rights lawyer, to raise these issues with North Korea. But both presidents, while promoting human rights issues in South Korea itself, preferred to ignore the critical question of human rights in North Korea. Both chose

[5] At the beginning, the Sunshine Policy received 70 percent of public support but later on, public support decreased.

[6] In the event, the DPRK conducted a test launch of seven missiles over the East Sea on 5 July 2006.

to postpone dealing with these issues even when President George W. Bush wanted to raise them, because they viewed them as particularly delicate questions that could potentially halt the progress of inter-Korean relations (Green 2008). Human Rights issues did not feature in the official declarations following the 2000 and 2007 inter-Korean summits. Even on a matter connected to internal South Korean affairs, the ROK agreed to return long-term prisoners to the North without, for a while, raising the issue of South Korean prisoners of war (Lee Hong Yung 2002: 328-9).[7] When the South Korean press brought up human right issues in North Korea, the government declined to participate in the debate and downplayed the reports in order to portray the engagement policy in a positive way (Snyder 2004; Lee Nae-Young 2005).

Behind this reluctance stood the real fear that all of the Sunshine Policy's achievements would be lost if South Korea pressed ahead with such controversial and dialogue-blocking issues. At least at this stage of inter-Korean relations, it appeared unproductive to antagonise Kim Jong Il by insisting on human rights demands and thus jeopardise the continuation of dialogue and confidence-building between the two Koreas. Under Kim Dae-jung and Roh Moo-hyun, the South Korean government preferred to postpone this issue to the later stages of the improvement in inter-Korean relations. Even within the US government, the balance between human rights issues and security issues in North Korea indicated that security issues were judged more important than human rights cases. President Lee Myung-bak, on the contrary, decided to use the issue as one of his first demands on North Korea, not only in order to increase the pressure on the North but to accentuate the difference between himself and his predecessors.

3.2 *Relations with the United States*

The Sunshine Policy led, necessarily, to different perspectives and serious clashes between the US and the ROK, especially with the first George W. Bush administration (2001-05). While Kim Dae-jung and Roh Moo-hyun believed their hedging policy towards the DPRK was decreasing tension in the Korean peninsula and creating an opportu-

---

[7] By early 2006, the two Koreas had agreed to co-operate on the fate of those missing during and after the Korean War, but it remains to be seen whether this will be pursued given the more antagonistic relations between the two Koreas since Lee Myung-bak became South Korean president in February 2008.

nity for change in inter-Korean relations, the Bush administration, with its hawkish and realist worldview, perceived the Korean peninsula as still a remnant of the Cold War and preferred increasing the pressure and sanctions on North Korea. The third corner of this triangle, the DPRK itself, naturally used these tensions as leverage for its own interests. The disagreements with the US created, as one can expect, differences of opinion between the South Korean president and the ROK's foreign ministry over relations with the US (as reported by the BBC on 15 January 2004). Several major areas of policy disagreement between South Korea and the US in recent years can be identified.

3.2.1 *Axis of evil versus the Sunshine Policy*

President George W. Bush included North Korea in his 'axis of evil' when he delivered his State of the Union speech on 29 January 2002 (Bush 2002). At the time, Kim Dae-jung attempted to convince the Bush administration that it should exclude North Korea from the 'axis', claiming that it would only antagonise the DPRK and damage the efforts to bring Kim Jong Il into serious dialogue (VandeHei et al. 2002). Later, Roh Moo-hyun made similar efforts (Niksch 2005: 10-11). From the ROK's point of view, the axis of evil concept promoted an offensive realist foreign policy that could bring the Korean peninsula back to the Cold War era.

Some of the reasons behind these disagreements stem from the different perspectives of the two states. While South Korea analysed its security needs from a regional, mainly bilateral, point of view, the US strategy was based on its global views and interests as it considered how its North Korean policy might influence its policy towards Iran. Regional interests were not always its concern.

3.2.2 *Engagement versus regime change*

A primary goal of the ROK under Kim Dae-jung and Roh Moo-hyun was to prevent the collapse of the DPRK. In contrast to past South Korean governments and to the neo-conservatives in the George W. Bush administration, who hoped for regime change and the collapse of the DPRK (Haass 2005; Lieberthal 2005; Litwak 2007), these two presidents stressed that they would do their best to prevent the implementation of such a policy. In fact, most of their activity towards

North Korea was in complete opposition to US wishes of achieving the downfall of the regime in the North. In the end, the ideas behind the Sunshine Policy prevailed, and helped to bring about a shift in US policy during the second Bush administration on the issue of regime change, at least in public presentations.

3.2.3 *Sanctions*

The concept of using sanctions to apply pressure on a given regime is clearly in complete contradiction to the engagement principles of the Sunshine Policy. As previously mentioned, South Korea preferred not to respond harshly to North Korean provocations, let alone acquiesce in the Bush administration's wish to sanction the North for these provocations. The logic behind the South's liberal policy was that sanctions would only lead to an increase in North Korean brinkmanship, and that the way to change the North Koreans' use of provocation was by bringing them to understand the benefits of international trading. The situation became more problematic for South Korea when the sanctions came from the United Nations Security Council (UNSC). But even when the North Korean missile launch led to UNSC sanctions, the ROK stressed that although the North could be seen as 'crossing the line', there was no need to overreact. As Lee Jong-seok (Yi Chong-sŏk), the South Korean minister of unification noted, South Korea would support only 'limited sanctions' while the important issue was that the inter-Korean Kaesŏng industrial complex in North Korea would not be affected (Lee 2006).

3.3 *Regional policy*

When the second North Korean nuclear crisis erupted in 2002, the Sunshine Policy came to have a profound effect on South Korea's relations with China and Japan. Instead of being marginalised, as was the case in the first crisis, and with the constant fear that a deal would be made at its expense (Snyder 2005: 98-99), South Korea became a pivotal member of the Six Party mechanism, employing a particularly active bilateral and multilateral foreign policy. Its 'open channels' with North Korea allowed it to play an active role both publicly and behind the scenes.

The ROK's generally soft line towards the North significantly influenced its approach in the Six Party Talks. Through the Sunshine Policy, South Korea intended to change the perception of the Korean peninsula confrontation not merely in North Korea and the US but also in the other Six Party states. By promoting its hedging strategy, the South hoped to change the policies of Japan, Russia and China towards the DPRK in a manner that would harmonise with its own policies. On several occasions, the ROK acted in favour of the DPRK, supported its arguments and tried to develop a positive environment towards it. In other instances, the ROK supported the Chinese, who favoured a less hostile attitude towards the DPRK, even against US wishes. The disagreements between South Korea and the US on how to solve the North Korean nuclear issue frequently led the ROK to lean towards China, supporting the latter's efforts to convince the DPRK to return to the Six Party Talks and accept what was agreed upon between the parties. It is obvious that the Sunshine Policy drove South Korea much closer to China, especially over their shared perspective on sanctions, which both saw as a useless, if not counterproductive, tool. While South Korea and China stood on the side opposing sanctions, the US and Japan represented the other side. In fact, the Sunshine Policy significantly complicated the already complex and sensitive relations between South Korea and Japan. The growing fear in Japan of the North Korean threat (Niksch 2005: 8; Kliman 2006: ch. 5), together with Japan's demands for a more active policy against the DPRK's provocations only caused South Korea to blame Japan for increasing the tensions, and widened the gap between the two countries.

4 South Korean Security Policy

South Korea hoped that the modification of its policies would lead to a change in the North's behaviour and later, even to a change in its interests and values. Meanwhile, however, it could not jeopardise its security merely on the premise that the DPRK would assimilate change and bring inter-Korean relations from a zero-sum to a win-win situation in a short span of time.

This situation forced South Korea to pursue a parallel track that was the centre of its hedging policy: a policy towards the North that was dominated by the liberal-based Sunshine Policy, and a more conservative security policy influenced by defensive realism. From the ROK's point of view, it was imperative to formulate a defensive policy that would deter the DPRK but would not be too offensive, in order not to trigger any misunderstanding or miscalculation by the North or inflict damages on its own policy of engagement.

The changed atmosphere between the two Koreas did affect the tense situation that had characterised the relationship prior to the Sunshine Policy, and included the important step South Korea took in no longer formally defining North Korea as an enemy state. But a closer examination indicates that South Korea was not yet ready to alter its strategic and military posture. In fact, in contradistinction to Roh's anti-American polemics and his promotion of the concept of security 'self-reliance' (Roh 2003) and to his administration's problematic foreign policy relations with the US, South Korea worked hard to preserve its security dependence on the US. This dependency, clear even in Roh's leftist presidency, was based on South Korea's fear of being abandoned by the US and the fundamental fear of North Korea's adventurous military nature. The fear of unintended or intended war through miscalculation by the DRPK was one of the main pillars of the ROK's security policy, even with the advance of the Sunshine Policy. The ROK also continued with its programmes to prepare the South Korean army for a possible military clash with the North by increasing its military budget, particularly stressing the 'force improvement' factor. This conservative South Korean security policy is the focus of the next four sections: reclassifying North Korea as the enemy; the withdrawal of US forces from Korea; the wartime command; and the defence budget and force improvement in South Korea.

4.1 *Changing North Korea's classification as an enemy*

From the establishment of the ROK in 1948, and especially after the Korean War, the ROK's foreign and security policies were based on the existence of the North Korean military threat. The definition of North Korea as its main enemy shaped the South's military strategy, including its extended military dependence on the US, and dictated the location of South Korean and US military forces in Korea. As part of the Sunshine Policy and of the South Korean government's efforts to promote economic co-operation with North Korea, as well as changing the North's menacing and irrational image in the eyes of the South

Korean public, the ROK decided in 2005 to remove the definition of North Korea as the enemy from the Defence White Paper and to treat the DPRK as a 'partner' and not as the 'enemy' of the ROK (BBC, 4 February 2005). This change of definition, especially while the DPRK continued its provocations, was not easy to promote and justify, not only because of conservative internal opposition and US global policy, but also from the government's point of view. This new classification of North Korea should have been an important step in helping to promote the new liberal-oriented policy towards the North. However, it raised questions about whom the South Korean army should deter. If the DPRK was not the enemy, then what were the implications for the security alliance with the US and the status of the US forces in Korea? Although the ROK officially declared that the DPRK was no longer the enemy, it was not ready yet to change its security policy.

In fact, South Korea security policy in the Kim Dae-jung and Roh Moo-hyun era faced the same dilemma as had previous South Korean regimes over the balance between its security dependence on the US and its aspiration for security autonomy. Since Kim Dae-jung's period in office, this issue had become more prominent and in some cases led to noted high tensions between South Korea and the US. This was especially so under Roh Moo-hyun. Roh's administration not only pursued a very independent policy towards North Korea, but also, especially at the beginning, did not hide its ambitions to promote an independent security policy with an anti-American twist. Yet, when the US voluntarily offered more freedom and independence, the ROK chose to continue with the conservative and dependent option. Two important examples that demonstrate this dissonance in South Korea's policies are the planned partial withdrawal of US forces from Korea and the negotiations on the transfer of wartime command.

4.2 *Withdrawal of US forces from Korea*

During his presidential election campaign and even after his election, President Roh Moo-hyun expressed his support for a possibly earlier than expected withdrawal of US forces from Korea. For the first time, a South Korean president publicly discussed an issue that had been taboo for many years except among radical students and left- wing groups. He even instructed the army to begin preparing the Korean defence forces for the day the US troops would leave (Niksch 2003: 14).

Concurrently, as part of its global posture plan of reorganising US forces around the world in order to cope with the needs of the wars in Iraq and Afghanistan and a limited defence budget (Garamone 2004; Jung 2006a), the US was planning a reduction of forces stationed in bases around the world. The plan envisaged the reduction of 12,500 soldiers from Korea by 2005 (Roehrig 2007: 3).

The US expected that the South Korean administration, which was pursuing a liberal policy towards the DPRK and objected to its hard-line stance towards the North, would fully support its initiative. The withdrawal of US forces from Korea might have assisted South Korea's policy of easing tension in the Korean peninsula, but the South's response showed that it was not ready to make the leap forward when its security was concerned. Instead, South Korea was initially shocked by the plan, refused to support it, and responded by requesting that the US postpone it. The main reason for the official objection was that the ROK would not be able to prepare itself for the withdrawal in such a short time-frame (Kim Mikyoung 2005: 22-23), while it worried that the North could misinterpret the US plan and would use it as a pretext to increase tension on the peninsula.

The reaction of the Roh Moo-hyun administration to the US withdrawal proposal in June 2004 was identical to the South Korean reaction to all of the five withdrawal plans that had preceded it since the establishment of the ROK (Levkowitz 2008: 139-40). The possible withdrawal of some of the US forces from Korea has been an ongoing subject of debate between the US and South Korea. Since the Korean War, which followed about a year after the withdrawal of US forces from Korea in 1949 had left the ROK almost defenceless against North Korea's attack (Hong 2000), the South has carried the scars of this traumatic first withdrawal, fearing it would be abandoned by the US once again. All South Korean administrations have reacted nervously to every US withdrawal plan, claiming they were not yet ready to stand alone and fearing the implications of a pull-out of troops on their relations with the US and their deterrence capabilities towards North Korea (Cavendish 2004; Hwang 2006; Wood 1996; Gleysteen 1999).

After lengthy discussions, South Korea accepted the 2004 US plan to withdraw a portion of their forces and to relocate some of the remaining forces but in a lengthier and more gradual process in order to allow the ROK to prepare itself (Fifield 2004). At South Korea's request, the withdrawal would be accomplished by 2008 and not by 2005, as the US had originally wanted.

4.3 *The issue of wartime command*

The issue of transferring wartime command[8] to South Korean hands has been under discussion since the beginning of the 1990s. In 2002, South Korea and the US began the latest round of talks concerning the issue, as part of the discussion on the new framework of the ROK-US alliance. The pattern of relations between the two sides repeated itself along the lines of the withdrawal negotiations. The US was willing to pass the responsibility for wartime command to South Korean hands as early as 2009, but the ROK asked to postpone it to 2012. (A date of 17 April 2012 has now been fixed.) South Korea asked for the delay in order to allow it to prepare the military for the new command change. The South Korean opposition and retired high-ranking army officers criticised President Roh Moo-hyun for hastening the command change without readying the army (Jung 2006b). Again, the South was worried that a hastened transfer of command without proper preparations would leave the country without an appropriate deterrence and could lead the DPRK to misinterpret it as a sign of US abandonment of the ROK.

Although President Roh repeatedly stressed in public how South Korea should overcome the psychological barrier of being left alone without the US command and US forces in the future (Park 2007: 10-11; Roh 2007), in reality his administration made great efforts during the 2002-06 negotiations to persuade the US to postpone its plans (Jin Dae-woong 2006a; 2006b; 2006c).

[8] The root of the issue lies in the Korean War, when South Korea voluntarily placed operational control of its military under the American-led UN Command (UNC) (Jung 2007). After the war, operational control was handed over to the US Forces in Korea (USFK) as part of the ROK-US Mutual Security Agreement. Later, with the creation of the Combined Forces Command (CFC) in 1978 (Rich 1982: 18), wartime command was placed under the authority of the CFC commander. Peacetime control of Korean forces was transferred to Korean hands in 1994, but wartime control remained under the control of the CFC, led by a four-star US general (Bechtol and Bush 2006).

4.4 *Defence budget and force improvement*

North Korea's declassification as an enemy did not affect the defence budget or force improvement projects of Roh Moo-hyun's administration. The increase in the defence budget and the South Korean defence reform 2020 (Han 2006: 117) shows how the ROK continued to perceive the DPRK (even if not officially in the Defence White Paper) as a potential threat. Although it was part of Roh Moo-hyun's efforts to gain a more self-reliant and independent security policy (Roh 2003), it is obvious that these force improvements are based on scenarios in which North Korea is still the main enemy.

During the Roh administration, there was a steady 9.5 percent annual growth in the ROK's defence budget (Cordesman and Kleiber 2006: 9-10; SIPRI 2007). This growth was the result of the budget implementation plans for the financial years 2004-08 put down by Roh's administration, which included a specific emphasis on increasing the budget for force improvement by an annual 15 percent (Park 2005: 5). It is clear then that the Sunshine Policy did not turn the ROK into a pacifist country neglecting its security; on the contrary, it seems that this kind of defensive realist security policy enabled the South Korean government to go forward with its liberal engagement policy.

5 Conclusions and a View of the Near Future

An analysis of the disparity between South Korean inter-Korean and security policies under Presidents Kim Dae-jung and Roh Moo-hyun suggests this disparity can be explained by the mixture of different world views and strategic assessments pursued by the same two governments during the same period.

The ROK's hedging policy towards the DPRK included a dual track strategy. The first track—the Sunshine Policy—was aimed at influencing North Korea's behaviour by pursuing a liberal theory logic, which argued that trade would increase the chances for peace and decrease the possibility for conflict (McDonald 2004; Owen 1994; Press-Barnathan 2006). South Korea hoped that pursuing the liberal-oriented Sunshine Policy would change the perceptions of North Korea, the US and Japan, as well as the political arena and public discourse in the ROK, and subsequently the outcome of the confrontation on the Korean peninsula. Concurrently, the South pursued a second parallel track in which it continued with its long-time security policy based on deterrence and prevention of a new war, and its security dependence on the US; this approach could be described as conservative defensive realism.

As this paper has sought to show, South Korea's hedging policy allowed it to keep more than one strategic option open against the possibility of a future security threat by the DPRK. In this context, the Kim Dae-jung/Roh Moo-hyun era can be seen as a transition period in inter-Korean relations, from a Cold War balancing mentality towards a more positive interaction within the Korean peninsula through changing North Korean behaviour. Kim's and Roh's hedging policy enabled them to try to affect inter-Korean relations, on the basis that their ongoing security policy and capabilities would not fail them if North Korea should not fulfill the Sunshine Policy's goals and hopes. The selection of a hedging policy for this kind of transition period, which was bound to be a risk-taking period, seemed rational and careful. During the first five South Korean republics, there was a correlation between foreign policy and the security policy towards the DPRK. As long as the Cold War played such an influential role in the Korean peninsula, no gap could exist, but the introduction of the Sunshine Policy created an interim situation. The goal of this policy was to alter perceptions and the rules of the game, but this is an incremental process that will require not only a short-term change, but a mid- and long-term realignment of values and interests. However, this attempt to achieve incremental change does not mean that Seoul has become an 'idealist liberal' that is willing to compromise its security. That is why the liberal policy towards the North had to be accompanied by a dual track of a conservative and defensive realist security policy.

The election of the new president, Lee Myung-bak, in December 2007 will put all these developments to the test, particularly in light of his prospective 'anything but Roh' approach (Kang 2008). In his presidential campaign, Lee stated that he would pursue a more conservative approach to the North than his predecessors, which will be based on a greater demand for reciprocity from the DPRK. Lee's presidency has begun with attempts to redefine the rules of the game with the DPRK and will probably be characterised by increased tension between the South and the North as the DPRK attempts to test the limits and boundaries of Lee Myung-bak's policy by pursuing its well-known brinkmanship.

Some changes are likely in the Sunshine Policy, which some in the conservative political wing have for quite some time perceived as an appeasement policy. However, it is important to stress that the change of attitude towards the North, especially its economic aspect, has become so embedded in South Korean society that it seems mostly irreversible. Thus, although a more conservative, suspicious and critical policy towards the DPRK is anticipated, it is unlikely it will return to the level of hostility and animosity of the past.

Another issue that will probably witness some changes is US-ROK relations. During the Kim and Roh presidencies, relations between the two states were rather tense, especially after the election of George W. Bush, who did not fully agree with the two Korean presidents over policy on North Korea. Lee Myung-bak has made it clear that during his term, relations between the two countries would improve.[9] This improvement mainly depends on a similarity of attitudes towards the DPRK, the security relations between the ROK and the US (Kim Ji-hyun 2008), and the policies of the next US president.

The process of changing values and interests in the DPRK is a long one, with quite a few anticipated 'bumps in the road' while North and South agree on the new rules. As long as the North does not fully adopt these changes, one can expect the continuation of some degree of disparity between South Korea's engagement and security policies. Only if the North's relations with the ROK and other regional states undergo some fundamental transformation, one can expect a future change in the South's hedging policy and a greater correlation between its engagement and security policy towards the North.

[9] However, despite President Lee's wish to see better relations with the US, his administration has had to cope with a strong outbreak of anti-US feeling over the issue of US beef and mad cow disease.

References

Art, J. Robert (2004), 'Europe hedges its security bets', in: T.V. Paul and James Wirtz (eds), *Balance of Power Revisited: Theory and Practice in the 21st Century*, Palo Alto CA: Stanford University Press, pp. 179-213

BBC News (15 January 2004), 'S. Korea foreign minister resigns'. Online: http://news.bbc.co.uk/2/hi/asia-pacific/3398203.stm (accessed 1 February 2007)

BBC News (4 February 2005), 'Seoul drops "enemy" tag for North'. Online: http://news.bbc.co.uk/go/pr/fr/-/2/hi/asia-pacific/4235701.stm (accessed 1 February 2007)

Bechtol, Bruce E., and Richard C. Bush (2006), 'Change of U.S.-ROK Wartime Operational Command', Washington DC: Brookings Institution. Online: http://www.brookings.edu/views/op-ed/bush/20060914.htm (accessed 31 December 2006)

Bush, George W. (2002), 'State of the Union Address', 29 January 2002. Online: http://www.whitehouse.gov/news/releases/2002/01/20020129-11.html (accessed 1 February 2008)

Cavendish, Richard (2004), 'Troops Withdrawals from Korea', in: *History Today*, 54 (8), pp. 54-55

Chang, Sea-jin (2003), *Financial Crisis and Transformation of Korean Business Groups*, Cambridge, UK: Cambridge University Press

Chosun Ilbo, 19 June 2006, 'Seoul Skeptical About N. Korean "Ballistic" Missile Test'. Online: http://english.chosun.com/w21data/html/news/200606/200606190022.html (accessed 6 April 2007)

Chung, Duck-Koo, and Barry Eichengreen (eds) (2004), *The Korean Economy Beyond the Crisis*, Cheltenham, UK: Edward Elgar

Cordesman, Anthony H., and Martin Kleiber (2006), *The Asian Conventional Military Balance in 2006*, Washington DC: Center for Strategic and International Studies

Fifield, Anna (2004), 'US Set to Delay South Korea Troop Withdrawal', in: *Financial Times*, 6 October 2004, p. 3

Garamone, Jim (2004), 'Global Posture Part and Parcel of Transformation', in: *American Forces Press Service*. Online: http://www.defenselink.mil/news/newsarticle.aspx?id=25053 (accessed 14 September 2007)

Gleysteen, William H. (1999), *Massive Entanglement, Marginal Influence: Carter and Korea in Crisis,* Washington DC: Brookings Institution Press

Goh, Evelyn (2006), 'Understanding "Hedging" in Asia-Pacific Security', in: PacNet 43, Washington DC: Center for Strategic and International Studies. Online: http://www.csis.org/media/csis/pubs/pac0643.pdf (accessed 10 April 2008)

Green, Michael (2008), lecture presented to Panel on the Human Rights Crisis in North Korea, 8 April 2008, Edmund A. Walsh School of Foreign Service, Georgetown University, Washington DC

Haass, Richard N. (2005), 'Regime Change and Its Limits', in: *Foreign Affairs*, 84 (4), pp. 66-78

Han, Yong-sup (2006), 'Analyzing South Korea's Defense Reform 2020', in: *Korean Journal of Defense Analysis*, 18 (1), pp. 111-34

Heginbotham, Eric, and Richard J. Samuels (2002), 'Japan's Dual Hedge', in: *Foreign Affairs*, 81 (5), pp. 110-21

Hong, Yong-Pyo (2000), *State and Security and Regime Security: President Syngman Rhee and the Insecurity Dilemma in South Korea*, 1953-1960, London: St Martin's Press

Hwang, Y. Balbina (2006), 'The U.S.-Korea Alliance on the Rocks: Shaken, Not Stirred', Heritage Lecture 970. Online: http://www.heritage.org/Research/AsiaandthePacific/hl970.cfm (accessed 10 October 2007)

Jin, Dae-woong (2006a), 'GNP Rejects Wartime Control Plan: Defense Ministry Outlines Roadmap for an Independent Command', in: *Korea Herald*, 18 August 2006

Jin, Dae-woong (2006b), 'Timing of Wartime Control Transfer Flexible: Seoul', in: *Korea Herald*, 18 September 2006

Jin, Dae-woong (2006c), 'Uri Members Revolt over Troop Control', in: *Korea Herald*, 20 September 2006

Jin, Hyun-joo (2006), 'Parties Divided over Roh Speech', in: *Korea Herald*, 7 November 2006

Jung, Sung-ki (2006a), 'Ministry Reaffirms US Base Relocation Plan', in: *Korea Times*, 10 April 2006

Jung, Sung-ki (2006b), 'Ex-Defense Chiefs Oppose President', in: *Korea Times*, 10 August 2006

Jung, Sung-ki (2007), 'Korea-US Alliance Will Grow Stronger', in: *Korea Times*, 14 November 2007

Kang, Hyun-kyung (2008), ' "Anything But Roh" Policy?', in: *Korea Times*, 22 January 2008

Kim, Choong Nam (2007), *The Korean Presidents: Leadership for Nation Building*, Norwalk CT: EastBridge

Kim, Ji-hyun (2006a), 'Roh Champions Defense Abilities', in: *Korea Herald*, 3 November 2006

Kim, Ji-hyun (2006b), 'Roh Pledges Support for N. Korea Project', in: *Korea Herald*, 7 November 2006

Kim, Ji-hyun (2008), 'Lee, Bush Agree to Boost Alliance', in: *Korea Herald*, 24 January 2008

Kim, Mikyoung (2005), 'The U.S. Military Transformation and its Implications for the ROK-U.S. Alliance', in: *IFANS Review* 13 (1), pp. 15-39

Kliman, M. Daniel (2006), *Japan's Security Strategy in the Post-9/11 World*, London: Praeger

Koh, Yu-hwan (2006), 'Roh Moo-hyun Administration's North Korea Policy and Nuclear Crisis Management', in: *Korea and World Affairs*, 30 (1), pp. 5-30

Korea Herald, 11 July 2006, 'Low-key reaction' (editorial)

Kwon, Eundak, and Jae-Cheon Lim (2006), 'Crossing the River that Divides the Korean Peninsula: An Evaluation of the Sunshine Policy', in: *International Relations of the Asia Pacific*, 6 (2), pp. 129-56

Lee, Brian (2006), 'Seoul Links a Missile Test to a Halt in Aid', in: *Joongang Ilbo*, 22 June 2006. Online: http://joongangdaily.joins.com/200606/21/200606212201245679900090309031.html (accessed 1 February 2008)

Lee, Hong Yung (2002), 'The Domestic Determinants of South Korea's Policy towards North Korea', in: *Korea and World Affairs*, 26 (3), pp. 313-34

Lee, Nae-Young (2005), 'Changing South Korean Public Opinion on the US and the ROK-US Alliance', paper presented at the conference 'America in Question: Korean Democracy and the Challenge of Non-Proliferation on the Peninsula', 10-11 May 2005, Seoul

Levin, D. Norman, and Han Yong-Sup, (2002), *Sunshine in Korea: The South Korean Debate over Policies toward North Korea*, Santa Monica CA: Rand

Levkowitz, Alon (2008), 'The 7th Withdrawal—Has the U.S. Forces' Journey Back Home from Korea Begun?', in: *International Relations of the Asia-Pacific*, 8 (2), pp. 131-48

Lieberthal, Kenneth (2005), 'The Folly of Forcing Regime Change', in: *Financial Times*, 11 March 2005. Online: http://us.ft.com/ftgateway/superpage.ft?news_id =fto031020050097002215 (accessed 1 February 2008)

Litwak, Robert S. (2007), *Regime Change: U.S. Strategy through the Prism of 9/11*, Washington DC: Woodrow Wilson Center Press and Johns Hopkins University Press

McDonald, Patrick J. (2004), 'Peace through Trade or Free Trade?', in: *Journal of Conflict Resolution*, 48 (4), pp. 547-72

Medeiros, Evan S. (2005), 'Strategic Hedging and the Future of Asia-Pacific Stability', in: *The Washington Quarterly*, 29 (1), pp. 145-67

Miller, Benjamin (2001), 'The Global Sources of Regional Transitions from War to Peace', in: *Journal of Peace Research*, 38 (2), pp. 199-225

Nanto, Dick K., and Mark E. Manyin (2007), *The Kaesong North-South Korean Industrial Complex,* Washington DC: CRS Report for Congress

Niksch, Larry A. (2003), *Korea: U.S.-Korean Relations—Issues for Congress*, Washington DC: CRS Report for Congress

Niksch, Larry A. (2005), *Korea: U.S.-Korean Relations—Issues for Congress*, Washington DC: CRS Report for Congress

Owen, John M. (1994), 'How Liberalism Produces Democratic Peace', in: *International Security*, 19 (2), pp. 87-125

Park, Juhyun (2005), *Medium-term Expenditure Framework and Year 2005 Defense Budget*, Seoul: Korea Institute for Defense Analyses

Park, Yong-ok (2007), 'Post-CFC Korean Security: Key Issues and Suggestions', in: *Korean Journal of Defense Analysis*, 19 (2), pp. 5-20

Pollack, Jonathan D., and Chung Min Lee (1999), *Preparing for Korean Unification: Scenarios and Implications*, Santa Monica CA: Rand

Press-Barnathan, Galia (2006), 'The Neglected Dimension of Commercial Liberalism: Economic Cooperation and Transition to Peace', in: *Journal of Peace Research*, 43 (3), pp. 261-78

Rich, Robert G. (1982), *U.S. Ground Force Withdrawal from Korea: A Case Study in National Security Decision Making*, Washington DC: United States Department of State

Roehrig, Terence (2006), *From Deterrence to Engagement: The U.S. Defense Commitment to South Korea*, Lanham MD: Lexington Books

Roh, Moo-hyun (2003), 'Presidential Address on the 58th Anniversary of National Liberation', 15 August 2003. Online: http://english.president.go.kr/cwd/en/archive/archive_view.php?meta_id=en_speeches&page=12&m_def=2&ss_def=1&category=&sel_type=1&keyword=&id=e40ebd562d49a29648670f87 (accessed 10 September 2007)

Roh, Moo-hyun (2007), 'Presidential Address on the 62nd Anniversary of the National Liberation of Korea', 15 August 2007. Online: http://english.president.go.kr/cwd/en/archive/archive_view.php?id=a578c6383a9b6beac4c5ebe1&m_def=3&ss_def=1&meta_id=en_speeches (accessed 9 October 2007)

Roy, Denny (2005), 'Southeast Asia and China: Balancing or Bandwagoning?', in: *Contemporary Southeast Asia*, 27 (2), pp. 305-22

Shin, Yong-bae (1998), 'Seoul's Inter-Korea Policy to Stay on Course', in: *Korea Herald*, 2 September 1998

SIPRI (Stockholm International Peace Research Institute) (2007), *SIPRI Yearbook*, Oxford: Oxford University Press

Snyder, Scott (2004), 'Managing Diminished Expectations for U.S.-ROK Relations', in: *Comparative Connections*, 26 August 2004. Online: http://www.csis.org/media/csis/pubs/pac0436.pdf (accessed 10 January 2008)

Snyder, Scott (2005), 'South Korea's Squeeze Play', in: *The Washington Quarterly*, 28 (4), pp. 93-106

Son, Key-young (2006), *South Korean Engagement Policies and North Korea*, London: Routledge

VandeHei, Jim, Susan Lawrence, and John Larkin (2002), 'Bush to Maintain Tough Line on Weapons during Discussions with Leaders in Asia', in: *Wall Street Journal*, 15 February 2002, p. 18A

Wolf, Charles, and Kamil Akramov (2005), *Circumstances, Costs, and Consequences of Korean Unification*, Santa Monica CA: Rand

Zelikow, Philip, with Joe Wood (1996), *Persuading a President: Jimmy Carter and American Troops in Korea,* Case CRI-96-1319.0, Kennedy School of Government, Harvard University

HIGHER EDUCATION REFORM IN SOUTH KOREA: SUCCESS TEMPERED BY CHALLENGES

Peter Mayer

ABSTRACT

This article first describes the rapid and fundamental transformation of South Korea's system of tertiary education since 1945. It then identifies five challenges for higher education in South Korea: an appropriate response to demographic change, the introduction of a new governance model, the implementation of a coherent quality assurance system, the development of competitive graduate education at home and finally the process of internationalisation in higher education. These five challenges will force Korea to continue with reforms. However, a simple continuation of changes that were instituted in the past will not be sufficient. A change in direction is required in all five dimensions.

1 INTRODUCTION

'Korea's Educational Competitiveness Surges High: Strong Improvements Achieved in Higher Education': this was the headline of a press release when the Organisation for Economic Co-operation and Development (OECD) presented its newest 'Education at a Glance' publication to the public. The Republic of Korea (hereafter South Korea or Korea) repeatedly scored well in the OECD programme testing the skills of school children in OECD countries, with its students being among the best in mathematics, reading and problem-solving skills (OECD 2008). Recent studies showed that no other country increased as much as South Korea did the number of published articles in science and engineering, highlighting the extraordinary growth in research output of Korean scholars (Marginson and van der Wende 2007: 317). And the 'Global Competitiveness Index 2007-2008' of the World Economic Forum saw the quality of South Korea's educational system ranked 19th among 131 countries, up from earlier weak positions, seemingly reflecting improvements in recent years (World Economic Forum 2008).

International attention, however, was also high when the prominent Korean stem cell researcher Hwang Woo-suk was found to have forged laboratory tests, a discovery that cast a dark shadow over the South Korean attempt to be among the leading nations in research and development. And when a considerable number of cases were uncovered where scientists had forged their curriculum vitaes there was widespread frustration in Korea. Publicly voiced disappointment with higher education is a standard theme in newspapers and other media (*Korea Times* 2007; Song 2007). It seems sometimes as if true competitiveness in international competition is still elusive.

Which direction is South Korea's higher education taking? This paper gives an overview on South Korean's tertiary sector, its transformation in the past and some of the most fundamental reforms ahead. It will argue that key policy-makers face a formidable task in instituting a substantial change in direction in five policy dimensions:

- Demographic changes, which will lead to an almost inevitable decline in the number of students and number of higher education institutions.
- The governance system in higher education, which in the past rested on strong direct control of public universities and strong government guidance of private universities. Change is to be directed towards a system of indirect control and more autonomy for higher education institutions.
- An end to concentration on quantitative expansion brings a need for a clear focus on quality in higher education. This requires the development of a sound system of quality assurance.
- The development of graduate education, which has not received much attention in the past. Only a small number of students finish their graduate education in South Korea. A considerable number of students move abroad to obtain their master's degree and especially their PhD. This is seen as an outdated division of labour between Korea and other industrialised countries, and government policy now focuses on increasing the output of highly qualified graduate students who receive their graduate education at home.
- The internationalisation of Korean higher education institutions was not a prominent goal of higher education policy in the past. Attention is now shifting towards internationalisation at home.

This article describes important changes both instituted and planned in South Korea's higher education. It focuses on a description and analysis of the policy of the South Korean government, the main player in higher education, and tries to put the government's response into perspective by briefly comparing it with respective changes in other OECD countries.

2 Successful Transformation of Higher Education in the Past: Key Facts about South Korea's Higher Education

When Korea gained independence in 1945 from Japan, literacy levels were low; a higher education system barely existed. Less than 8,000 students were enrolled in higher education in 1945. The number of Koreans with higher education degrees was extremely small. Immediately after independence, interrupted only by the Korean War, South Korea concentrated efforts on developing the educational system (Park 2006: 867-71; Woo 2002: 7-8; KEDI 2007: 9-13). The number of students steadily increased. In 1960, around 100,000 students were enrolled in higher education institutions; by 2005, the number had risen to 3,555,115. The student population increased on average by 8 percent per year over a period of 45 years! The number of instructors in universities, colleges and specialised higher education institutions increased as well, as did the number of institutions offering programmes in tertiary education.

Table 1 Students enrolled in tertiary education

Year	Students	Institutions	Teachers and assistants
1945	7,819	19	1,490
1960	101,041	85	3,808
1970	201,436	232	10,435
1980	601,494	357	20,900
1990	1,490,809	556	41,920
2000	3,363,549	1,184	79,136
2004	3,580,549	1,473	68,448

Source: MOE & HRD 2007: 20.

The dynamic development that has taken place in South Korea can be grasped by looking at the percentage of age groups who have attended a tertiary institution. Korea is now among the leading nations when comparing the percentage of people between 25 and 34 who have earned a tertiary degree. Almost 50 percent of this age group have finished their studies with a degree at a tertiary institution, only surpassed by Canada and Japan. The respective figure for the age group of 45-54 years is below 20 percent, much below the average of OECD countries. And only 9 percent of the age group 55-64 finished education with a tertiary degree. The comparison shows the extraordinary change in participation in higher education in a relatively short period of time (McGaw 2005: 6-9; OECD 2008).

There are in essence four kinds of institutions offering programmes in tertiary education. Universities offer four-year programmes leading to a bachelor's degree and programmes leading to master's degrees. Industrial universities or polytechnics offer programmes which are more applied in nature. They run four-year programmes leading to a bachelor's degree. There are a considerable number of junior colleges offering two- or three-year programmes ending with so-called associate degrees. And there are the group of 'other universities' such as broadcasting universities or more recently cyber universities, offering distance-learning programmes supported by the extensive use of new technologies. The importance of colleges has increased over the years. Now around 40 percent of students are enrolled in colleges (KEDI 2007: 27-9). A specific feature of Korean higher education is the dominance of private establishments offering educational programmes. More than 70 percent of all students in higher education study at private institutions. Only Japan has a higher percentage studying at such institutions. The financing of most private institutions rests almost exclusively on tuition fees (Woo 2002: 27).

A relatively large percentage of students are enrolled in science- and technology- related fields, which is in line with Korea's economic priority sectors. In 2002, 27 percent studied engineering or manufacturing-oriented programmes, with respective figures for the United States (US) and Germany standing at 6.3 percent and 17.6 percent. In social sciences, business and law-related programmes the figure for Korea was 22.3 percent, with the figures for the US and Germany being 41.4 percent and 27.4 percent respectively.

Spending on education measured as percentage of gross domestic product (GDP) is among the highest around the world. In 2004, South

Korea devoted 7.2 percent of GDP to educational purposes, compared with an OECD average of 6.2 percent. Only Iceland and the US have higher rates. While government spent 4.4 percent of GDP, which is below the OECD average of 4.7 percent, the opposite is true as far as private spending is concerned: 2.8 percent of GDP was spent by the private sector, by far the highest rate among OECD nations, with an average of 1.4 percent in OECD member states (OECD 2008). However, when the large number of students is considered, the per capita spending in Korea is not extraordinarily high and is even below the OECD average. While the high level of private expenditure might be interpreted as a sign of Koreans' willingness to pay and their appreciation of education, there is the other side of the coin, which is the comparatively high burden for the private sector. Tuition costs per student per year at a low tuition-cost institution represent 19 percent of the average total yearly salary in South Korea. And when a high-cost institution is chosen, this ratio is 38 percent (Grubb et al. 2006: 12; Webb 2007: 23; Woo 2002: 22-23).

3 The Need for Further Higher Education Reforms: Five Challenging Tasks

I argue here that higher education in South Korea is in a process of fundamental transformation and faces five challenges:

- Fewer students imply a shrinking tertiary sector in terms of number of students. This changes the overall conditions for competition and co-operation in higher education.
- The old governance system in higher education does not deliver required results. A new framework for the system emphasises autonomy instead of direct control.
- Instead of increasing quantity, the emphasis in tertiary education is now on increasing quality.
- Given the need for highly skilled personnel in the South Korean economy, the government intends to transform the tertiary educational system so as to offer more postgraduate programmes producing the human resources required by industry.
- The one-sided pattern of internationalisation, whereby students and professors go abroad but only a few foreign students and instructors come to Korea, is to be changed.

3.1 *Demographic development and its impact on higher education*

Demographic trends in South Korea are as important as in other industrialised countries for explaining new policy priorities. The ratio of population aged 65 and above has doubled in the last 20 years. It is now around 10 percent and is expected to grow further to 15 percent by 2020. Birth rates have continued to decline as in most industrialised countries. The number of children born to women aged 15 to 49 is as low as 1.16. This is the lowest among all OECD countries, if compared with the OECD average of 1.6, and is substantially below the replacement rate of 2.1 (OECD 2008).

Schools felt the impact years ago, and universities have started to be affected since the beginning of the new century. The demand for higher education fell below the supply for the first time in 2002. More than 50 percent of local junior colleges have had to manage with enrolment rates of less than 80 percent of capacity, creating serious financial difficulties for institutions (Lee Man-Hee 2005: 85). Mostly institutions outside Seoul are affected. The gap between demand and supply is expected to increase. According to some estimates there will be a drop in the college-bound population from 3.2 million in 2000 to less than 2.5 million in 2020. While there might be some room for further increases in the number of school children finishing secondary education and moving on to tertiary education, the potential is estimated to be small. Currently around 90 percent of all children in school already complete secondary education, of which the vast majority continue with tertiary education (MOE & HRD 2007: 5).

It therefore seems almost inevitable that the number of students and the number of institutions providing tertiary education will decline. The government has started to support the necessary structural adjustment by facilitating mergers of institutions. Ten public tertiary institutions were merged into five in 2004-05, and eight were merged into four in the following period 2006-07. In the same period twelve private institutions were merged into six (MOE & HRD 2007: 169). While the government is able to take decisions concerning closure or mergers of public institutions, they cannot do so as easily in the case of private universities. However, public policy needs to address the problem posed by private universities that fail to respond to a lack of revenues. The economic crisis, which began in 1997, showed the fragility of many private universities and the implication of the composition of their funding. And when universities have easy access to credit and have accumulated high debt, there might exist a moral hazard if the founder or chairman of the board sought to avoid closure because of personal benefits derived from the operation of the university, like salary or free housing (Kim and Lee 2006: 580), thereby delaying the necessary adjustment.

A decline in the number of students, number of programmes and number of tertiary institutions presents an opportunity to adjust the structure of higher education. It might be of benefit to South Korea if the relative share of different kinds of tertiary institutions changes, and a system emerges that is characterised by more specialisation and differentiation. The Ministry of Education, Science and Technology favours the emergence of a system where universities focus on their strengths, not one where each university is offering the same kinds of courses. The needed structural adjustment might, furthermore, be used to respond to over-education in some fields: unemployment rates and the time needed to find a job are high for graduates in quite a number of disciplines, and the private benefit of educational expenses varies a lot. Here a careful evaluation might be necessary to reduce the high cost to society. In addition, the government wants to use the adjustment process to address the regional distribution of higher education institutions by controlling the enrolment of students in Seoul (KEDI 2007). It has repeatedly announced it will use structural adjustment to improve the ratio of students per professor, as pressure on tertiary institutions to offer more attractive conditions for students has increased. The intention is that the number of students per full-time instructor at national universities should be reduced to 21 by 2009 (MOE & HRD 2007: 168; KEDI 2007: 39). Demographic development creates an opportunity to revise the trend of the last decades. There is support for universities that open up for adult learners who aspire to get degrees and are in a position to enhance their job-related skills. Innovative methods such as a 'credit bank' where adult learners can accumulate credit points in tertiary institutions have been developed; and institutions have started to develop a new focus on professional programmes and to offer interesting courses for new target groups.

There seems to be no real alternative to the structural adjustment course adopted. Demography sends clear signals to all the institutions in tertiary education. While the extent of downward adjustment cannot be specified exactly, the direction seems to be clear. Most OECD countries face similar challenges. Declining birth rates have a direct impact on higher education. This effect is strongest when no compensatory effect is forthcoming through an increase in the ratio of school graduates entering higher education. Structural adjustment due to low birth rates is delayed in countries such as Germany, where a relatively small percentage of school graduates enters higher education. Where adjustment in Korea differs from the experience in other countries is in the significant variation in Korea in terms of the high percentage of private institutions offering programmes. While in other OECD countries public policy must respond directly by redirecting public funds, the challenge in Korea is rather the facilitation of such an adjustment in the private sector.

3.2 *A new concept for governance in higher education*

The South Korean development model was based on a strong role for government in guiding the private sector. This general approach characterised all spheres of public policy even though the number of public servants was relatively limited as compared to other OECD countries. Tools and instruments were developed in such a way that government effectively determined the course of affairs. This state-led philosophy—which started to change in the 1990s—was dominant in higher education as well. Public universities were managed almost as if they were units of the relevant ministry; and the private tertiary institutions, which offered the majority of programmes and absorbed the majority of students when the system expanded, were guided by the state. The state opted for a set of detailed regulations. There was a clear understanding in society that the state determined the direction in education, justified by the importance of education for Korea's development and by the 'public good' character of education, and based on the philosophy of state-led development. This top-down system of guiding higher education institutions, whether they were public or private, dominated South Korea's higher education for half a century (KEDI 2007).

With the growing number of institutions and students and with more diverse challenges in tertiary education, it became increasingly clear that this approach would not serve the country's future interests best. There was growing awareness among those concerned with education that such a top-down management style did not allow for enough flexibility and inhibited opportunities for dynamic responses to new challenges. The government started to accept that potentials for innovation would not be exploited unless more autonomy were introduced (MOE & HRD 2007: 170; Grubb et al. 2006: 42). This change in attitude towards a new concept of the state was part of the broader discussion about South Korea's state-led development model, which reached its peak in the 1990s. It was no coincidence that this debate took place at the same time that Korea reached income levels typical for industrialised countries and became a member of OECD.

The move towards a new governance model in higher education gained momentum in the mid-1990s when Kim Young-sam received recommendations from the Presidential Commission for Educational Reforms, an advisory body for the president (Woo 2002: 13-15; KEDI 2007: 12-13). 'By many accounts, the 1995 reform is regarded to mark the shift in the paradigm of Korea's higher education policy' (Woo 2002: 15). The proposals to government emphasised the need to adopt a new governance model, one which economists describe as 'new public management'. The model calls for a more market-based approach in managing public institutions in higher education; it emphasises incentives to guide institutions instead of directives to control them. The governance model calls for the granting of more autonomy to the leadership of higher education institutions, and prefers the introduction of mechanisms where external stakeholders can influence strategic decisions of higher education institutions.

Now, more than a decade after the recommendation by the Presidential Commission in 1995, there is less strict and less detailed government guidance, there is more autonomy and strengthened leadership by tertiary institutions themselves, there is more involvement of external stakeholders in the management of universities and there is more competitive pressure when applying for scarce resources. Regulations have been simplified and clarified and obsolete regulations eliminated. Co-ordination across ministries has improved. Boards of trustees have gained importance in selecting the presidents of private universities. And despite the failure in 2007 to get parliament to vote on a new law that would formalise the role of a board of trustees in managing a public university, introduce new instruments to guide public universities and give more power to their leadership, other measures have been implemented and realised (KEDI 2007; Grubb et al. 2006; Woo 2002; Han 2003). The new government of President Lee Myung-bak is expected to start a fresh attempt to change the law in this respect. The issue of autonomy featured prominently in the inaugural address of President Lee: 'Autonomy for universities and colleges is key not only to national competitiveness but to the advancement of Korean society' (Lee 2008).

The government has improved rules concerning accountability and transparency, an important corollary to autonomy and delegating authority to a lower level. This is because improved information flow and opportunities for members of a board of trustees or the public to scrutinise the way higher education institutions act are important in ensuring that influence and power are not misused by the leadership of universities.

Many experts in the field of educational policy call for further reforms, requesting government to abolish many more of the existing regulations. Some argue that Korea's higher education regulations still compare unfavourably with those of other OECD countries: 'Korean higher education system is far more regulated by the state when compared to western countries, and remains highly centralized and inflexible to market needs' (Woo 2002: 21). Others argue that the organisational culture in the Ministry of Education, Science and Technology and operational procedures must change, for example in the field of budgetary and financial provisions (Han 2003). Critics argue that government is still too much the institution that picks winners and losers, and not just the institution that makes the rules and ensures enforcement of them (Kim and Lee 2006: 574-6).

Other such experts fundamentally challenge the wisdom of a new public management and of introducing market-style co-ordination into higher education. They claim that education with its strong public good character requires different solutions. They are in favour of reforming the governance model, but reject the government's proposals. Some fear that the proposed model will imply that only such programmes are offered which bring immediate economic benefit to the institution, and that long-term objectives will be neglected. They see basic sciences or arts and sciences threatened, and some fear the reduction of jobs (Chung 2007; Jeon 2004; MOE & HRD 2007: 170; Woo 2002: 21).

The reform of the governance model intended by the government does move South Korea closer to the governance model favoured in most other OECD countries. In countries where more autonomy was introduced some time ago, as in Germany, it was and partly still is equally difficult to move from an old model to a new model, given the various dimensions of university governance. Criticism voiced in

Korea is quite similar to criticism in other countries. There is considerable scepticism concerning the alleged positive results of the reform. The challenge in Korea differs from most other OECD countries because of the strong role of private universities. When looking at official statements concerning university governance it seems as if this problem of university governance and private higher education institutions does not receive the required attention.

3.3 *The quest for quality: reforming the different elements of quality assurance in higher education*

Whether the tertiary education system fulfils its role in economic, social and political development depends not only on the quantity of human resources provided. With Korea's economic development progressing, it is of strategic importance that the quality of teaching and research accompanies the quantitative expansion. There is a consensus in public and increasingly in academic circles that the existence of a sound quality assurance system is important in this respect. Well-established quality assurance systems are characterised by a definition of the responsibilities of bodies and institutions involved, the establishment of a system of evaluation of programmes and/or institutions, agreement on the instruments of internal assessment, external reviews, and possibly a system of accreditation.

It is widely accepted that the Korean system of quality assurance is complicated, lacks coherence, and in many respects lacks power (MOE & HRD University Support Bureau 2007; KEDI 2007; Grubb et al. 2006: 30-37). On the national level there is the instrument of accreditation and evaluation involving the Korean Council for University Education, the Korean Council for College Education, the Korean Education Development Institute (KEDI) and accreditation boards for specific disciplines. Institutions use different procedures. In some cases accreditation is voluntary, in other cases it is mandatory. Quality management systems used in higher education institutions differ in character as well. Some universities can boast of fine and well-established systems, others have no systematic approach. Sometimes there is no visible consequence when evaluation results show weaknesses (Grubb et al. 2006). There seems to be a consensus that the fragmented system of quality assurance in South Korea does not satisfy the demands of modern times, produces unnecessary costs for higher education institutions and needs to be overhauled. The Korean government has proposed overhauling the national system of quality assurance by establishing a coherent system and introducing a single and independent quality assurance agency (MOE & HRD University Support Bureau 2007). The government has started to increase transparency in higher education by publishing input and output data which allow observers watching institutions from the outside to judge various aspects of academic life which have direct or indirect bearing on quality. The University Information Disclosure System was presented to the public at the end of 2007 and a full-fledged implementation is planned for 2008. The system is meant to allow easy access to data such as the number of full-time faculty, research output, enrolment rates, scholarship provision, etc. It will make it easier for those choosing between alternatives to make sound judgements.

A sound debate on quality assurance requires a common understanding of the issues at stake. The authors of a thematic review on South Korea's higher education published by the OECD's Directorate for Education argue that 'there is apparently no agreement on the meaning of quality, or how to measure quality' (Grubb et al. 2006: 30). Once such an agreement is reached, it remains to be decided which kind of quality assurance Korea wants to implement, which system is most appropriate and functional, how much responsibility is delegated to tertiary institutions, and how many resources should be invested in quality assurance activities. There is good reason to reflect on these matters. International comparative studies of quality assurance in higher education show that substantial differences exist, that performance of systems depends on many factors such as ownership structure, traditions in the educational sector and government attitudes, to name just a few (Kis 2005).

South Korea has signalled its interest to OECD in participating in an international test of skills of students at universities, similar to the well-known PISA[1] study. This could be an important factor in quality assurance because it would give some objective information about the output of Korea's educational system. From the Korean government's perspective it seems that Korea can only gain from such a test: if tests show weak results, then the government can use such information for

[1] *Ed.* PISA: OECD Programme for International Student Assessment, which conducts regular surveys of students nearing the end of compulsory education in the principal industrialised countries.

further reforms; if results are better than generally expected, it will help in responding to harsh public criticism and claims that tertiary education does not meet international demands.

While the official quality assurance system lacks transparency, an unofficial quality control takes place through rankings. The newspaper *JoongAng Daily* publishes annually a ranking of universities and colleges, claiming to identify the quality of tertiary institutions. This ranking, which had Pohang University of Science and Technology, Korea Advanced Institute of Science and Technology (KAIST), Seoul National University, Korea University and Yonsei University leading in 2007, is most influential in the public discourse. Parents, students and employers watch the results with keen interest; tertiary institutions direct their investments so as to improve their rank. International rankings receive considerable attention as well. It is widely observed that 'only' Seoul National University was ranked among the best 100 in the Times Higher Education Supplement—QS World University Rankings in 2007, where it was ranked 51st; KAIST was placed 132nd (Paked.net 2008). Other rankings, which show Korea's 'success or failure', are equally watched with anxiety and are subsequently debated in the academic arena and by the public. Despite the arbitrariness in calculating ranks when putting together different quantitative figures into one or few indicators, there is little criticism of the validity and reliability of rankings as is the case in other countries.

South Korea is less involved in international networks which would drive the process and give this process the necessary momentum and possibly direction. Internal demands and internal drivers of change dominate and fuel the discussion. This existence of truly national drivers of change is an asset. This might not be true for all European countries, in some of which the quality assurance debate is mainly externally driven. However, Korea could benefit from being more deeply involved in international debates on quality in higher education. It is difficult to predict what kind of quality standards will dominate global debate on quality in higher education in a few years, whether for example the European approach[2] now emerging will go beyond the

[2] Quality assurance is one of the cornerstones of the Bologna process in currently 45 states. The standards and guidelines for quality assurance in the European higher education area provide for a common framework for internal and external quality assurance in higher education (European Association for Quality Assurance in Higher Education 2007). Based on this platform, which has been agreed upon for all signatory states, higher education policy makers and academics in virtually all these

current 45 members and will become a worldwide standard, or whether other approaches like those used in the US will dominate. But whatever the result will be, it is difficult to imagine Korea developing its own standard.

The focus on rankings is very strong in Korea. They are keenly observed, and not just in the field of higher education. International rankings are taken very seriously. This indicates a competitive attitude and reflects the basic approach to have international standards as a benchmark. However, it seems as if the arbitrariness of some of the rankings is rarely reflected upon, and some distance towards the results of rankings would be advisable.

3.4 *Increasing the output of high-level graduates: adjusting the system towards the needs of an industrialised Korea*

The large majority of South Korean students finish their tertiary education with a first degree and then enter the labour market. It is still quite rare, when compared to traditions in many developed countries, for students to come back to university after a few years of work and continue with a master's degree, full time or part time, or attend short-term programmes at universities. In 2004, more than 92 percent of all students were enrolled in programmes leading to a bachelor's degree. Only 6.5 percent studied in master's programmes, and 1.1 percent of all students were doctoral students. However, interest in postgraduate education is much higher than revealed by such figures. There has been a long-standing tradition of highly qualified students seeking postgraduate degrees abroad, especially in the US. For outstanding students the preference for getting a doctoral degree from a prestigious university abroad is very strong (Park 2006: 877).

This feature of distribution of labour with the US and other industrialised countries is increasingly seen as inadequate and outdated. Given the level of development of the South Korean economy, there is little doubt in Korea that the country needs more high-level research and more excellent graduate schools. Although total spending on research and development has been consistently above the OECD aver-

---

countries discuss which specific configuration of quality assurance serves the purpose best, which institutions are needed and what kind of procedures should be established (Kis 2005). (*Ed.* The Bologna process is a series of reforms aimed at introducing greater compatibility and comparability into higher education in Europe.)

age since 1995 and accounted for 2.85 percent of GDP in 2004, experts still see the need to develop a considerable number of centres of excellence in higher education. This is because around 75 percent of research and development funds are currently spent by corporations and only a meagre 10 percent in universities. The large number of highly qualified graduates moving abroad creates, moreover, the problem of a brain drain. Some of the best graduates do not come back to Korea. And Korea increasingly worries about the balance of payment effect inherent in neglecting high-level education and research in the country. Koreans pay much more for education abroad than foreigners pay for education in South Korea. Worries about net payments for patents, showing South Korea's reliance on research and development in foreign countries add to this perspective (MOE & HRD University Support Bureau 2007).

With the ambitious Brain Korea 21 programme, a project to 'nurture highly qualified human resources', the Korean government has aimed at increasing research capabilities in South Korea (Song 2008; KEDI 2007: 19-20). Substantial funds were allocated in the first period of 1999-2005 and now for 2006-13 in order to initiate high-powered research and development. Brain Korea 21 concentrates funding on the development of graduate schools where it is expected that scientists would focus on high-level research and would offer opportunities for bright students to do their master's degree or PhD in Korea. The stated goal of the first tranche was to nurture more than 1,000 doctorates in each year in natural sciences and engineering. Funding was on a competitive basis, using 'performance contracts' to guide institutions into output orientation. The principle of selection and concentration of funding and the creation of a competitive research climate were even more pronounced in the second period starting in 2006. Brain Korea 21 is meant to help Korea set up a number of world-class graduate schools and with that to help to propel Korean higher education institutions into the world league: ten world-class universities by 2012 has been the publicly announced goal. Brain Korea 21 has enabled a number of institutions to be innovative and to produce research results as intended. The number of doctorates has increased substantially. However, there is criticism because of the omission of arts and science. The claim is made that the project unduly favours highly reputed institutions and does not leave not enough room for promising but younger and less-established institutions or give them a chance to excel.

If the premise of a lack of graduate schools is accepted, then such a forceful approach to attract public attention, to highlight the need to act and to get people to think about ways to do better might be considered necessary. Industrialised countries such as Germany opted for similar forceful rhetoric and allocation of funds when 'universities of excellence' were identified and large amounts of money were distributed for the development of graduate schools. However, at the same time it might be argued that excellence cannot be developed in a matter of a few years and that the rush for public subsidies might create an income for some people in the system, but not really the results which were intended. The allocation of funds and decision-making procedures create government bureaucracy, which Korea wants to reduce.

The OECD thematic review of 2006 argued that a further expansion of Korea's educational output was not required: 'the expansion of tertiary education seems to have outpaced the demand for jobs requiring high levels of schooling' (Grubb et al. 2006: 23). On postgraduate education, it argued further that 'it is not clear that there is a shortage of post-graduate degrees, at least not in the economist's sense' (Grubb et al. 2006: 23).

From a strictly economic perspective it is efficient to develop higher education in line with economic priorities in the economy. The congruence of supply and demand of skills is an issue in other countries as well. This is so because of scarcity of resources for higher education and because of the need to have the required human resources for the economy. With South Korea's economic transformation continuing at a high speed, there is a need to constantly review the appropriateness of the supply of skilled personnel. It is, however, an important question whether government is still able to anticipate the strategic requirements of the economy and can do so better than the higher education institutions themselves. It can rightly be asked whether the active involvement of government is in line with the new philosophy of decentralisation. Other OECD countries where autonomy has been practised for a while would be reluctant to guide higher education institutions into offering more master's programmes in a certain field and would leave decisions to higher education institutions. It would be up to universities to react to anticipated or realised demands by industry. It remains to be seen which approach is better.

The idea of developing graduate education in close alliance with industry is an approach increasingly favoured in other countries as well. High-level research, especially in the field of science and technology where South Korea wants to excel, requires access to laboratories and to networks which go much beyond the academic sphere. Korea's strategy in this respect is in line with strategies pursued elsewhere.

3.5 *Internationalisation*

South Korea's higher education system shows a very ambivalent picture when indicators of international orientation are considered. In 2003, around 90,000 Korean students were studying abroad, mainly in the US (52,000), followed by Japan with 19,000 and Germany with 5,000. Only China and India have a higher number of students studying abroad (OECD 2008), and the mobility of Korean students is clearly high. The percentage of professors who received their postgraduate education abroad is equally high. In the case of the renowned Pohang University of Science and Technology, more than 90 percent of the academic staff had received their PhD in the US (Kim 2005). Curricula quite often resemble curricula in US universities.

However, when looking at foreign students in South Korea, the country is much behind other countries. Only a tiny 0.2 percent of all students in Korea come from abroad, while the respective figure for OECD countries was 6.4 percent in 2003 (OECD 2008). Despite some recent improvements, the number of foreign scholars teaching and doing research in Korea is still small, the total figure being 2,100 in 2005. The government emphasises the need to change course and increase the attractiveness of Korean universities for foreign students and foreign lecturers. Institutions are asked to offer programmes in English and are encouraged to increase the number of instructors coming from abroad. The government backs the development of dual degree programmes with international partners and supports institutions that endeavour to develop international joint research activities. Financial support for universities is offered for improving infrastructure such as dormitories, and additional grants and scholarships are available. The government-supported Korea Research Foundation has expanded its programmes considerably. The policy objective is clear: to present Korea as an interesting place to study, to work in and to work with in the academic field. The Korean government signals its interest in having foreign universities invest in South Korea if they offer programmes in free trade zones (MOE & HRD 2007; KEDI 2007; Woo 2004).

Internationalisation has become one of the standard goals of higher education policy. It is one of the key objectives of the Bologna process. European policy-makers encourage internationalisation for economic, political, social and cultural objectives. Mobility of students and of teaching staff is intended to strengthen regional cohesion in the long run. Korea stresses the need for internationalisation, and equally is starting to focus on the regional perspective: 'Korea had traditionally made educational exchanges mainly with the United States, England and other advanced Western countries, but it began to shift the focus to Asia-Pacific countries from the late 1990s to diversify partners for exchanges and cooperation in education' (MOE & HRD 2007: 109). Bilateral agreements with countries such as China, Mongolia and Russia have been signed. The intensity of co-operation, however, is small as compared to the degree of co-operation currently realised in Europe.

The large exodus of students from South Korea is quite atypical and cannot be found in any other OECD country. With further development of the Korean higher education system in terms of quality and of international outlook, this exodus might well decline. Instead of students doing all their tertiary education abroad, they might instead go for shorter stays. The government has announced its intention to have more foreign professors teaching and researching in South Korea. However, it will take some time to move successfully in this direction, given the various barriers for foreign staff to becoming members of a Korean university, be they in terms of language, culture, remuneration or otherwise (Kim 2005). The case of Professor Robert Laughlin, the Nobel prize-winning physicist who served as president of the Korea Advanced Institute of Science and Technology and whose reappointment was rejected by professors of that institute is a reminder of the difficulties for foreign professors in finding acceptance in Korean higher education.

4 Conclusion

This article has highlighted some of the important changes taking place in higher education. It is interesting to see how far South Korea has arrived in mainstream OECD thinking on higher education when revisiting the topic. Demographic change and its implication for higher education is an important issue in many OECD countries, with many countries facing similar challenges. The governance model favoured by government has become the standard model in many other OECD countries: Germany, France and many other countries have overhauled their regulatory system with the same objectives and ideas in mind. The quality debate has been a key feature of public discourse in higher education in OECD countries and beyond, and there is little doubt that quality considerations will gain importance in future. The need to match the output of the higher education system with the requirements of the economy has become a topic in many countries as well. The debate about preparing societies for international challenges by integrating international dimensions into tertiary education is a debate in other OECD countries as well. The Bologna process is motivated by the thrust that higher education systems should openly embrace the challenges of internationalisation and globalisation.

While the discourse on transforming higher education in Europe has been deeply influenced by the Bologna process and its numerous benchmarking processes, there is no equivalent in South Korea. There is little reference in public or academic discourse to Asian educational reform efforts. The United Nations Educational, Scientific and Cultural Organisation is playing a role in looking at a common higher education area, but its influence as compared to European experiences is rather limited. There are many similarities, however, for South Korea with higher education reforms in Japan. Given the strong orientation towards the US since 1945, there are many trends, moreover, which reflect lessons learnt from US debates on higher education.

Higher education reform is driven by Korean organisations. This is helpful in terms of having an authentic desire for change, which might not be true for some countries in Europe. At the same time it is a disadvantage because benchmarking and the elaboration of reforms after a careful look at other countries' experiences is not as automatic as, for example, in Europe.

Public discourse in Korea about education will continue. This is because of the ongoing transformation, which will not be just a combination of marginal shifts. The changes ahead for Korea will alter the landscape of tertiary institutions. Public attention is guaranteed because, with 3.5 million people enrolled as students, changes affect so many people directly. Parents whose children are or will be in tertiary education are watching reforms. The corporate sector is also paying attention because of the need to secure the human resources required to accomplish its mission to be highly competitive in advanced technologies. The new government inaugurated in 2008 has announced fresh efforts to improve tertiary education performance. 'Autonomy for universities and colleges is key not only to national competitiveness but to the advancement of Korean society. Universities and colleges must be able to enhance their education and research capabilities so that they can compete with other institutions of higher learning abroad. Indeed, they must rise to lead the forming of a knowledge-based society' (Lee 2008). This was President Lee's statement on education as part of his inaugural speech. Transformation will continue to be the overall theme for tertiary education in South Korea.

REFERENCES

Chung, Yungsup (2007), 'Die Hochschulpolitik Südkoreas zwischen Staat und Markt', Arbeitspapiere des Zentrums für Bildungs- und Hochschulforschung, Mainz. Online: http://zope.verwaltung.uni-mainz.de/zbh/ver_mat/veroeff/bericht_skorea.pdf (accessed 30 March 2008)

European Association for Quality Assurance in Higher Education (2007), *Standards and Guidelines for Quality Assurance in the European Higher Education Area*, Helsinki: European Association for Quality Assurance in Higher Education. Online: http://www.enqa.eu/files/ESG_v03.pdf (accessed 14 April 2008)

Grubb, W. Norton, et al. (2006), *Thematic Review of Tertiary Education: Korea Country Note,* Organisation for Economic Co-operation and Development, Directorate for Education, Paris: OECD. Online: http://www.oecd.org/dataoecd/37/21/38092630.pdf (accessed 30 March 2008)

Han, You-Kyung (2003), 'Higher Education in Korea: Context, Issues, and Prospect'. Online: http://www.sri.or.jp/forumandsympo/asia/8th/pdf/Han(R).pdf (accessed 10 April 2008)

Jeon, Jae Ah (2004): 'Corporatization in Higher Education Policies of Australia and Korea in the Era of Global Market', Stanford CA: Stanford University. Online: http://suse-ice.stanford.edu/monographs/jeon-04.pdf (accessed 31 March 2008)

KEDI (Korea Educational Development Institute) (2007), *Understanding Korean Education*, vol. 4, *Higher Education and Lifelong Learning in Korea*, Seoul. Online: http://eng.kedi.re.kr/09_edu/koreduse.php (accessed 14 April 2008)

Kim, Sunwoong and Ju-Ho Lee (2006), 'Changing Facets of Korean Higher Education: Market Competition and the Role of the State', in: *Higher Education*, 52 (3), pp. 557-87

Kim, Terri (2005), 'Internationalisation of Higher Education in South Korea: Reality, Rhetoric, and Disparity in Academic Culture and Identities', in: *Australian Journal of Education,* 49 (1), pp. 89-103. Online: http://www.thefreelibrary.com/Internationalisation+of+higher+education+in+South+Korea:+reality,...-a0131499548 (accessed 14 April 2008)

Kis, Viktoria (2005), *Quality Assurance in Tertiary Education: Current Practices in OECD Countries and a Literature Review of Potential Effects*, Paris: Organisation for Economic Co-operation and Development. Online: http://www.oecd.org/dataoecd/55/30/38006910.pdf (accessed 14 April 2008)

Korea Times (2007), 'Poor Rankings – Universities Must Improve International Competitiveness', 12 November 2007

Lee, Man-Hee (2005), 'Social Concerns in the Liberalization of Korea's Higher Education: Between Regulation and Deregulation', in: *KEDI Journal of Educational Policy*, 2 (2), pp. 79-101

Lee, Myung-bak (2008), 'Together We Shall Open a Road to Advancement', address by President Lee Myung-bak at the 17th Inaugural Ceremony. Online: http://www.korea.net/news/issues/issueDetailView.asp?board_no=18994 (accessed 14 April 2008)

Marginson, Simon and Marijk van der Wende (2007), 'To Rank or To Be Ranked: The Impact of Global Rankings in Higher Education', in: *Journal of Studies in International Education*, 11 (3/4), Fall/Winter, pp. 306-28

McGaw, Barry (2005), 'International Perspectives on Korean Educational Achievements', in: *KEDI Journal of* Educational Policy, 2 (2), pp. 5-21

Ministry of Education & Human Resources Development University Support Bureau (2007), *Higher Education in Korea 2007*. Online: http://english.mest.go.kr/main.jsp?idx=030201 (accessed 5 April 2008)

MOE & HRD (Ministry of Education & Human Resources Development) (2007), *Education in Korea 2006-7*, Seoul: Ministry of Education and Human Resources Development

OECD (Organisation for Economic Co-operation and Development) (2008), OECD Stat Extracts, Korea. Online: http://stats.oecd.org/wbos/viewhtml.aspx?queryname=322&querytype=view&lang=en (accessed 30 March 2008)

Paked.net (2008), 'World University/College Rankings'. Online: http://www.paked.net/higher_education/rankings/times_rankings.htm (accessed 14 April 2008)

Park, Namgi (2006), 'Korea', in: James J.F. Forest and Philip G. Altbach (eds), *International Handbook of Higher Education*, Dordrecht, NL: Springer Publishers, pp. 867-79

Song, Ho-keun (2007), 'The Shining Seoul National University', in: *Korea Focus*, November 2007. Online: http://www.koreafocus.or.kr/design1/Society/view.asp?volume_id=66&content_id=101768&category=D (accessed 11 June 2008)

Song, Somi et al (2008), *Brain Korea 21 Phase II – A New Evaluation Model*, Santa Monica CA: Rand Corporation. Online: http://rand.org/pubs/monographs/2008/RAND_MG711.pdf (accessed 30 March 2008)

Webb, Molly (2007), 'South Korea: Mass Innovation Comes of Age – The Atlas of Ideas: Mapping the New Geography of Science', London: Demos. Online: http://www.applygroup.com/Korea_Final.pdf (accessed 30 March 2008)

Woo, Cheonsik (2002), *Upgrading Higher Education in Korea: Context and Policy Responses*, Seoul: Korea Development Institute. Online: http://www.kdi.re.kr/kdi_eng/database/report_read05.jsp?1=1&pub_no=10066 (accessed 14 April 2008)

World Economic Forum (2008), *The Global Competitiveness Report 2007-2008*, Geneva: World Economic Forum. Online: http://www.gcr.weforum.org/ (accessed 14 April 2008)

THE NEW KOREAN CINEMA LOOKS BACK TO KWANGJU: *THE OLD GARDEN* AND *MAY 18*

Mark Morris

ABSTRACT

In 2007, two South Korean films appeared which place the May 1980 Kwangju uprising at the heart of their stories: *The Old Garden* (*Oraedoen chŏngwŏn*), an adaptation of the novel of that name by Hwang Sŏk-yŏng; and *May 18* (*Hwaryŏhan hyuga*), the first big-budget narrative film to propose tackling the May uprising head-on. Mixing elements of romance and comedy, the latter film tries to recreate in the form of a docu-drama the extraordinary period of 18-27 May 1980. This essay will look in some detail at the two films to consider the artistic and commercial choices made by these two very different productions. It will set the films alongside earlier cinematic treatment of the Kwangju uprising and will briefly take into account two other film visions of insurrection: Luo Ye's *Summer Palace* and Paul Greengrass's *Bloody Sunday*. Finally, the article will attempt to assess what significance the films may have beyond the context of the South Korean film industry.

1 THE KWANGJU UPRISING

The assassination of Park Chung-hee (Pak Chŏng-hŭi) in October 1979 was followed by a coup d'état engineered by another military figure, Chun Doo-hwan (Chŏn Tu-hwan), in December of the same year. Yet the forces for change and democratisation which had been building through the long years of Park's regime, one characterised by its mix of forced economic development and suppression of political and human rights, carried on organising and protesting. By the time university campuses reopened in March 1980, the situation was still volatile, despite waves of arrests of students and their teachers. After mass demonstrations in the capital on 15 May brought out some 150,000 people, leaders of the Seoul protests decided to pull back temporarily and see how the new regime would respond to such a massive show of solidarity on the part of ordinary citizens. The new regime chose Kwangju to show its intentions.

Protests had continued after 15 May in Kwangju. As news of the hardening of current martial law restrictions became known by the morning of 18 May, students protesting outside the gates of Chŏnnam University challenged the soldiers occupying the university. Troops like these had been sent to occupy university campuses elsewhere, but the students and citizens of Kwangju found themselves facing shock troops especially trained for combat against North Korea, not civilian crowd control. The soldiers waded into the students with long-handled clubs, boots and bayonets. When protestors reassembled closer to the city centre, the troops went after them there. The unprovoked violence continued over the next two days, leading to a confrontation before Province Hall on 21 May. Although it has never been made clear who gave the order, on this occasion the soldiers opened fire on the crowd massed in front of them, then hunted down survivors. Some people, students but also significant numbers of young working-class men, seized arms where they could and began to fight back. Troops were pulled out of the city centre to its outer perimeter, from where they continued to snipe at individuals while sealing Kwangju off from the outside world.

From 22 to 25 May the battered citizens of Kwangju engaged in an exhilarating if frantic experiment in grass-roots political and defensive organising, while senior members of the community tried to negotiate a settlement with the military. It was clear after a few days the new regime had no intention of making deals with people labelled hooligans and reds by the media it controlled. A small group of young men from the hastily organised citizens' militia defiantly remained in Province Hall when the troops returned in the early hours of 27 May to retake the city. Gi-Wook Shin has called the ten days between 18 and 27 May 'the single most important event that shaped the political landscape of South Korea in the 1980s and 1990s' (Shin and Hwang 2003: xi).

In 2007, two South Korean films were released which place the May 1980 Kwangju uprising at the heart of their stories. *The Old Garden* (*Oraedoen chŏngwŏn*) appeared in January. It is a rather free adaptation of one of the most significant works of fiction to appear in the last decade, the novel of that name by Hwang Sŏk-yŏng. The second film, *May 18* (*Hwaryŏhan hyuga*),[1] which opened in July, was the first big-budget narrative film to propose tackling the May events directly. Mixing elements of romance and comedy, the film tries to recreate in the form of a docu-drama the extraordinary period between 18 and 27 May almost three decades ago.

Before considering some of the artistic and commercial choices made by these two very different productions, it should be worth taking a brief look at the immediate context in which they were made: the South Korean film industry.

2 South Korean Film in 2007

The South Korean film industry seemed to continue on its upward curve during 2007, at least in terms of output. A record number of films were released, 112, and almost 159 million admissions recorded at the box offices. The average cost of production, around 5 billion won (US$4.7 million+), made up of 3.7 billion won for production costs plus 1.2 billion for promotion and advertising, had not changed significantly from previous years. However, there was a widely held consensus that 'the film industry is currently facing a "knife wind" due to the drastic negative profitability levels last year', and production companies began to have serious worries about how to slim down costs while maintaining quality (Han 2007:10). To add to industry woes, a predicted downturn in the Korean Wave of cultural exports seemed to be taking hold: whereas in 2005 the South Korean film industry had exported films worth some US$76 million abroad, a full 79 percent to Japan, the figures for 2007 were down to a total below US$13 million and Japan's share of 27 percent seemed to reflect a chill in the Hallyu air.[2]

Within a less than confident financial mood came more bad news from the part of ordinary film-goers and the critics, who reported 'fewer strong films than in previous years, local audiences beginning to cool on Korean film, exports showing a continued decline, and the film industry suffering through a recession of sorts. The first half of

[1] The Korean title *Hwaryŏhan hyuga* means 'elegant/stylish vacation'. This was the cruel euphemism given by the military planners to the operation directed against Kwangju.

[2] Unless otherwise noted, all statistics are gleaned from the koreanfilm.org website. For a somewhat different, concentrated breakdown, see *KC* 2007: 492-8.

the year was particularly tough, with hardly any Korean films stirring up any excitement among viewers' (Paquet 2007). If in 2005 almost 59 percent of tickets sold were for Korean rather than imported films, the domestic market share eventually slipped to just over 50 percent in 2007. *The Old Garden* appeared on 4 January, making it the first major release in what would prove to be a disappointing year

May 18 opened in late July. It was one of two blockbuster-scale films, which were to be the major commercial successes of the year. Box office success and critical success along with artistic achievement do, of course, often seem to inhabit different planets. *The Old Garden* was made for a modest budget (3.7 billion won—US$3.5 million, according to *KC* 2007: 126). It was directed and scripted by Im Sang-su, a well-respected director known for mixing artistic style with a coolly ironic view of Korean society, and shot by Kim U-hyŏng, one of the most talented young cinematographers in the business. The two had collaborated before on the 2003 film *A Good Lawyer's Wife* (*Paramnan kajŏk*) and in 2005 on Im's political black comedy *The President's Last Bang* (*Kŭ ttae kŭ saramdŭl*). *The Old Garden* opened on 212 screens, yet struggled to sell 300,000 tickets. On the other hand—and on that other planet—*May 18*, produced by the media *chaebŏl* CJ Entertainment with a budget of some 10 billion won and backed by an extensive advertising campaign, opened on 551 screens and went on to sell over 7.3 million tickets. Even this success needs to be balanced against the overall picture for CJ Entertainment, out of whose 36 films for 2007 only five surpassed break-even point (*KC* 2007: 5).

3 *The Old Garden*

Adapting a well-known work of literature can be both a blessing and a curse. Almost all Koreans will know of Hwang Sŏk-yŏng. He is widely considered the country's most likely candidate for the Nobel Prize and, in the eyes of readers and critics in many countries (reading translations in English and French), Hwang's short stories and epic-scale novels seem overdue for their place in the sun. *The Old Garden* was seen as a return to form upon its publication in 2000, even if many readers would come to prefer the next work in his 20th-century trilogy, *The Guest* (*Sonnim* 2001). (A French translation of the third, *Shim Ch'ŏng* (2004), will appear soon.)

A film carrying the title *The Old Garden* can thus hope to attract audiences via the novel's success and the esteem many hold for its writer. The connection implies a seriousness and an artistic register that might seem rather unusual in a cinematic marketplace dominated by commercial imperatives and the rom-coms and various permutations of the gangster film which that marketplace has favoured in recent years. That Im Sang-su is very much positioned as an 'art' director is clear through the support system his films have depended upon in order to exist in a business that can provide more than three times the budget of *The Old Garden* for a film such as *May 18*. The film was backed up by the Korean Film Council (KOFIC), a government-funded organisation which, while promoting mainstream commercial films, is a crucial support, among other things, for independent small and middle-scale film-making (*KC* 2007: 8-11). KOFIC provided funding for subtitling and print production, which in turn allowed the film to supplement its limited domestic box office through participation in film festivals from South America to Europe, and four cities in the US (*KC* 2007 : 126).

Literary adaptation and art-film status do, however, carry certain expectations. For one thing, Hwang Sŏk-yŏng's reputation rests on much more than his writing. He is intimately linked in fact and in the popular imaginary with the best aspects of the Korean left, in particular the deeply ethical moment of the democratic citizen's struggle that followed the Kwangju uprising[3] and massacre. When in 1985 Yi Chae-ŭi (Lee Jai-eui) and his friends sought to publish the results of the first systematic investigation into what had happened in Kwangju, Hwang took a considerable risk in allowing his name to be used as that of the work's author; he even made a draft of the manuscript in his own writing to provide extra cover for the young Kwangju researcher-authors behind the project. When police raided the publisher in mid-May of that year, they seized 20,000 copies of a book eventu-

[3] Yi Chae-ŭi (Lee Jai-eui)'s *Kwangju Diary* (Lee 1999) is still the most important account of the days from 18 till 27 May 1980, now memorialised as 5.18, the day the troops started their rampage. (The book includes invaluable essays by Bruce Cumings and Tim Shorrock on US involvement.) A concise overview of the democratic movement is found in Cumings 1997: 337-93. A brief account with chronology and valuable links can be found in the English *Wikipedia*; the Japanese version is short but provides some statistics about the compensation scheme and other links; the version on the fledgling Korean *Wikipedia* is short but with useful links. The May 18 Memorial Foundation now has an English website: http://eng.518.org/eng/. A very helpful overview is provided by Gi-Wook Shin's 'Introduction' to Shin and Hwang 2003: xi-xxxi; a moving account of both the uprising and its painful aftermath is Lewis 2002.

ally known internationally as *Kwangju Diary*, and arrested Hwang for good measure (Lee 1999: 14). (Some people still identity Hwang as the author of the book, including, it seems, the young director of *May 18*, Kim Chi-hun; *KFO* 23: 44). After self-imposed exile in Berlin, Hwang served several years in prison for an unauthorised visit to North Korea; he was finally released in 1998 thanks to the arrival in the Blue House of Kim Dae-jung.

The narrative of Hwang's *The Old Garden* is complex, a performance in two voices. It follows a former activist, O Hyŏn-u, who after 16½ years of prison emerges blinking into the rather superficially self-confident society of mid-1990s South Korea; he goes on the traces of a woman, Han Yun-hŭi, who had sheltered him in her countryside studio during the crackdown that continued most brutally during the first years of the Chun Doo-hwan dictatorship. Hyŏn-u had been one of many 'submarines' hiding from the police after May 1980. He and Yun-hŭi shared life together till the following autumn, until Hyŏn-u felt compelled to rejoin the struggle, this time in Seoul, where he was soon arrested.

Yun-hŭi has been dead for several years before the novel begins. Her voice emerges mainly from the notebooks she left behind in the simple cottage she used as painter's studio and retreat from the pressures of family back in Seoul. The older Hyŏn-u has fled there in turn, attempting to gain some sort of purchase on a world bewildering in its forgetfulness of the violent recent past. There he discovers the notebooks, reads them, and pauses to reflect on his long hard years of incarceration. Some of the most compelling pages in Hwang's novel detail in all its grubby chaos the life of the activist 'submarine': the dull cold ache of fear, the difficulty of getting fed or staying clean, the frantic, almost comic efforts to stick up posters or hurl pamphlets in the face of tanks, guns and torture chambers. Other sections lay out the routine of life inside. Korea's modern history has been generous in providing many writers with fieldwork opportunities in the prison underworld developed first by the Japanese, later by home-grown military strongmen such as Park and Chun. Hwang has skilfully drawn upon his own years in prison to fill in the minute oscillations between hope and despair of a man on a life sentence. Chapters shift back and forth between the voices, and jumps in chronology keep the reader wary as one chapter hands over to the next. It is big book, with ambitions to tell the story of 'a generation which had followed the dream of a better life'.[4]

3.1 *From novel into film*

Im Sang-su, in recasting this long text into a filmable scenario, had to make some major excisions and simplifications. Before considering them, it might be worthwhile to examine the skill with which the director has transformed Hwang's prose into visual and sound imagery in the powerful opening sequences of the film. The opening shots are close-ups of a sleeping man, apparently bundled up in rags and a scruffy woollen cap, being woken by the drip of water from the scaly concrete ceiling above him. It is Hyŏn-u's day to leave prison. From the dark interiors he is accompanied outside the prison by a large, avuncular guard who, recalling his sixteen years and eight months spent locked up, wishes him well; this guard is quite a different figure from any of the anonymous police or prison guards inhabiting the world of Hwang's work. Hyŏn-u exits the prison into a dark snowy night. Snow will return later as a kind of aesthetic echo in key scenes of the film. Night and snow, black and white, will be invested with much beauty, as is the visual design of the film overall: harmony of staging and set design with Kim U-hyŏng's camera-work throughout the film mean that whatever its shortcomings, *The Old Garden* always looks good.

After less than five minutes of the opening prison sequence, Im cuts to a completely different scene. It is night, but now rain is falling. Hyŏn-u—whose greying hair is now noticeably black—and a young woman wait under an umbrella as a small bus comes bumping along a country road toward them. They say silent farewells, he boards the bus, then moves to the back to look from the window out at the young

[4] 'In 1993, as soon as I returned to my country, I had been arrested; while taking a walk where you could circle about in the narrow, confined space between the walls, I thought of the legend of Wulingyuan and that of Shangri-La, and the title "The Old Garden" came to me. Recalling days spent in the company of my comrades, I felt a need to recount what we had lived, not abstract ideas about the future and prophesies, but the concrete process which had brought changes to reality. I wanted to show the world through the prism of days lived by ordinary, fragile individuals caught in a whirlwind, not through the epoch or history … "The Old Garden" would be the portrait of a generation which had followed the dream of a better life': Postface, Hwang 2005: 565.

woman standing in the rain. Cut: close-up on Hyŏn-u, now in a regular bed, though with the same scruffy woollen cap over his grey hair. He has returned home from prison. He remains silent while those around him, and most eagerly his mother, try to bring him back into their world: scenes follow of a doctor's consultation and a visit to a trendy clothing shop. While he was inside, Hyŏn-u's mother had grown rich through property speculation. She is that new Seoul/Kangnam cliché, the 'mega-rich middle-aged woman living the good life' (Yi Yŏng-jin 2007), who shops in places offering champagne to the patrons. Her son's prison rags are replaced by designer clothes topped by a 13-million-won overcoat. This later scene is carried off in a few minutes, with a light, gently humorous touch.

The family is next seen sharing a meal. Mother casually asks about Han Yun-hŭi. She has to repeat the name when he seems to remain blank; she goes on to ask if he had heard from her family about her death. Cut: back to the previous young couple waiting in the rain. Then another jump, one that moves into the future: Hyŏn-u is somewhere outside Seoul, in a dilapidated house, taking down a book from a shelf. It's a diary which he begins to read. Cut: the family is still at the table. Hyŏn-u seems more concerned about a painful molar; tears roll down his cheeks, as he gets up to go to check the state of the tooth in a bathroom mirror. The face in the mirror seems devastated by the double shock of physical agony and this sudden intrusion of memory in the shape of the name Han Yun-hŭi.

Some 11 minutes into the film, we are abruptly relocated to contemporary Kwangju. The older Hyŏn-u arrives at Kwangju Airport, to be met by an old comrade. The old friend is balding and has a nervous twitch; life and years of political struggle have done him few favours. His simple working-class demeanor contrasts with the elegant-looking middle-aged passenger from Seoul. Then comes the most dramatic cut so far. We suddenly realise that the camera is following the younger Hyŏn-u and his friend through a blood-spattered plastic curtain into what looks like a school gymnasium full of coffins, bodies wrapped in plastic sheeting and mourning family members. This scene will last less than two minutes, but it is the historical and emotional gravitational centre of the film. We are in the Sangmu Hall, the gym-cum-judo school on the other side of the central fountain and public plaza from the Province Hall, where the final stand of the uprising would be crushed a few days later.

The iconography of Kwangju as uprising is most directly derived from photos and scraps of film footage made of the street demonstrations and/or citizen army trucks, jeeps and armoured personnel carriers on Kŭmnamno, the broad avenue running east-west which leads towards the fountain and Province Hall; other clusters of powerful images remain of rallies and speeches made from a stage improvised over the fountain or of rallies at the Province Hall itself. Kwangju as massacre, eventually given symbolic shape in the newer memorial cemetery, is in its less symbolic and more visceral form forever associated with the bodies collected in the impromptu morgue-funeral hall of the Sangmu Hall.

In Hwang's novel, what happened in Kwangju is left to the imagination; Hyŏn-u got out of town before the worst of the violence. One of the desperate tasks of those like him working underground was to try to find out what actually did happen and somehow to relay that fragmentary story to a public kept well in the dark by media censorship. Regarding his use of this sequence, Im has said simply that 'I tried to recreate the photographs of record that were taken at the time. Those are the representative images that we all remember, right?' (Huh and Jung 2008: 145). Im has not only chosen to use cinematic form to give visual form to what for the literary Hyŏn-u remains a nightmare occurring off-stage. He has given the scenes a few 'unrealistic' touches as well; they tie into the particular poetics and ethos of the film.

For example, one of the best remembered photos from the hall is that of a little boy kneeling at the head of his young father's flag-draped coffin, a funerary photo of the man in his arms. (*May 18*, in its simpler realism, includes in one extensive sequence at Sangmu Hall a scene of the photographer in the act of taking the photo; a later scene shows the photo as it appeared on the front page of the *New York Times*.) Im places what appears to be an older sister, standing beside the boy, touching his shoulder. The pietà-like couple of nurturing female and suffering male is echoed through the film in flashbacks to the brief, intense relationship of Hyŏn-u and Yun-hŭi: a similar portrait made by Yun-hŭi of herself with Hyŏn-u becomes one of the final images on screen as the credits roll. Here, roughly a dozen minutes into a 112-minute film, Im and his team allow this poetic recasting of Kwangju iconography to remain in the background, only partly in focus and occupying only a matter of seconds on screen. This kind of restraint and attention to detail is characteristic of much of the director's best work.

So in place of Hwang's mixed voices and jumps from one to the other through 27 chapters treating various eras between 1980, and even earlier, until the late 1990s of the novel's present, Im uses this technique of staccato flashbacks and, when needed, flashes-forward. Im is good at teaching the viewer to negotiate shifting planes of time and event, but it is important to learn the grammar through these opening minutes of *The Old Garden* as he begins giving visual clues as to the sources of Hyŏn-u's anguish and the lost object of his longing. It has long been observed that 'art cinema is less concerned with action than reaction: it is a cinema of psychological effects in search of their causes' (Bordwell 2008: 153). In asking the viewer to do the work of connecting past to present, Im can assume we are familiar enough with the basic rules of 'plot manipulations of story order (especially flashbacks)' to know that they will 'remain anchored to character subjectivity' (ibid.: 154).

3.2 *Characters and characterisation*

The actors chosen to embody Hyŏn-u and Yun-hŭi, Chi Chin-hŭi and Yŏm Chŏng-a, are at least as well known from roles on television as for any of their work in film. You should probably never judge a South Korean movie by its poster: it is much more likely to represent the visions of the P&A office than anything the director may have wanted to emphasise or that you will see finally on the screen. In this poster the central couple strike a love-struck pose before a lurking knot of police in riot gear. The male lead Chi Chin-hŭi is mainly associated with comic roles in film or romantic ones in TV drama, as is Yŏm Chŏng-a, though she is probably best known outside Korea for her part as the evil, albeit implausibly elegant, stepmother in the horror film *A Tale of Two Sisters* (*Changhwa, Hongnyŏn* 2003).

In casting these two as his lead actors, Im certainly did not chose to emphasise gritty realism. Chi does a reasonable job with what is a fairly limited role. When a flashback mid-way into the story takes us back to his years in prison, he can look haggard and worn. In one violent scene Hyŏn-u is bound and gagged, then carried off to solitary. The gag is finally removed, but not the cords binding his arms and legs. Once the door is slammed shut, Im allows the screen to remain pitch black. All we are aware of is a man sobbing. Chi's invisible performance is more moving than any overworked close-up. On the other hand, when Hyŏn-u slips into his mother's choice of male wardrobe, for all his embarrassment, he looks quite at home. The wear and tear of almost 17 years in prison seem to have produced few physical effects other than tingeing his hair a bit greyer a bit more quickly. Yŏm's Yun-hŭi has more to do, a wider range of experiences, and people to negotiate—from her down-to-earth mother or her own little daughter to the student activists she finds herself spending time with, first as partner of an incarcerated comrade, later as friend. For the most part, she maintains a cool elegance, even when chemotherapy takes away her long hair.

One point of comparison between film and novel that should be worth considering has to do with the politics of gender. The film is, as Im and others have pointed out, more Yun-hŭi's than Hyŏn-u's in several ways. Sometimes the female role has obviously been expanded in the direction of the melodramatic. There are two dream sequences in the film: in one, Hyŏn-u dreams that he has returned home to the old house to find his lover and their toddler daughter waiting for him; in one other, Yun-hŭi dreams that Hyŏn-u comes to visit her in her Seoul studio and to play with the little girl. Neither is like anything in Hwang's book. At the end of the film, when the father finally meets his teenage daughter for the first time, Yun-hŭi's spectre walks through the snowy night-time scene of her two loved ones meeting, invisible but her presence sensed for a moment by Hyŏn-u.

There is also the question of Han Yun-hŭi's life outside either political widow-hood or romance. She is an art teacher and painter by profession. Im mentions in an interview reproduced on the DVD extras that he gave her more prominence, in a sense, than Hwang was able to. It is an overstatement, however, to claim that 'he transformed the boundlessly modest and devoted leading female character of the novel into a polished and challenging woman' (*KC* 2007: 5). Many of Hwang Sŏk-yŏng's works do represent a very male universe. One other big, sprawling novel written during the 1980s, *The Shadow of Arms*, reproduces the shabby world of black marketeering and political corruption surrounding the Korean involvement in the Vietnam War.[5] Female characters seem stereotyped, either innocent victims or scheming survivors. In the author's *The Old Garden*, however, the character of Yun-hŭi does take on a life of her own, quite apart from her imprisoned lover and apart even from South Korea. Hwang drew upon his own experience of exile in Berlin to allow her to live there as well. She works on her art, loves another man, witnesses the coming down of the Wall. She reflects on the art which moves her most: the epic, intensely socialist work of Käthe Kollwitz is prominent in her thinking, though we learn how Yun-hŭi's own style evolved in a more abstract direction. None of this makes it into the film.

3.3 *Resistance to political nostalgia*

Im saw the role of Han Yun-hŭi as crucial to his way of transforming Hwang's *The Old Garden* to something more relevant to the present:

> Many of the people who have seen this film view it with the opinion that it is Han Yoon-hee's film. There were also various opinions in the production company, but I think so too … since the stage of preparing the film, I made up my mind to minimize the sequences in the prison (Huh and Jung 2008: 118).

Rather than display loyalty to Hwang's own loyalty to the sacrifices of the movement for democracy of the 1980s, Im wanted to question the negative effects of political nostalgia. To one critic's comment that it seemed cynical of Yun-hŭi, at one point late in the film, to say of her absent partner's imprisonment: 'What a tremendous waste. Of a life and talent,' Im replied: 'Could she say about his life, "He lived passionately, giving all of my [*sic* his] heart and soul"? I think there's nothing else to say but that it was a waste of life and talent' (Huh and Jung 2008: 119).

---

[5] For an important introduction to the work, see Hughes 2007.

It can be difficult to judge whether Im Sang-su wanted to de-politicise or re-politicise the kind of left-wing democratic ethical commitment that Hwang Sŏk-yŏng's work continues to reflect.

> When I complained that the characters in the novel were too lofty, one friend of mine told me, 'There are some really noble people that you just don't know.' Frankly, I don't believe that. I said that to Hwang Sok-yong, the book's author, and all he did was laugh (Huh and Jung 2008: 120).

There are scenes of violent confrontation in the film other than the flashback to Kwangju. Midway comes a university occupation brutally ended by riot police. The long (4-minute) dialogue-free sequence (derived from the violent suppression of the student movement at Kŏn'guk University in the wake of Kwangju; Huh and Jung 2008: 122, 146) is not tied to either of the focal characters or given a particular connection to the rest of the narrative, nor does it appear in Hwang's novel. An incident which does feature there, a strike of young female workers and the subsequent immolation of a student activist, is part of Yun-hŭi's story. In a scene where student radicals are meeting in Yun-hŭi's Seoul studio, Kim U-hyŏng's camera shoots first of all the moving lips of the debating students in extreme close-up; then the camera pulls back to show the group. Later scenes, in which Yun-hŭi's growing disenchantment with the doctrinaire atmosphere of politicking is made clear, prepare for her later conclusion that the sacrifice made by O Hyŏn-u was a waste of life and talent. The immolation of her young female friend leaves her with no different conclusion.

It would be possible, but mistaken I think, to conclude that Im used the framework of the novel merely to make a more mainstream melodrama than critics might have been prepared for from a director with his artistic credentials, and that the novel's politics were only acknowledged superficially. The three sequences of undeniably political confrontation are more than 1980s local colour. What he seems to distrust is the way that the struggle from Kwangju till the election of Kim Dae-jung has become a fetish, a clichéd reservoir of political nostalgia that says nothing about contemporary South Korea.

> There are common characteristics to the characters in my memory who participated in the 1980s student movement. They devoted themselves enthusiastically to the movement at one time, but at some point they dropped the movement and entered the mainstream of Korean society.

Yet inside, they think they are living meaningful lives in some sense (Huh and Jung 2008: 118).

You can, however, accept Im's scepticism about political nostalgia without wanting to go so far as to dismiss the long struggle for democracy as irrelevant for present or future generations.

Im's personal history may perhaps go some way to explaining the distance he maintains from any positive political identity in interviews. Huh Moon-yung has noted that Im, himself a university student at Yŏnsei during the turbulent early 1980s, did not fit in at all with an increasingly sectarian, dogmatic climate of political debate. Huh speculates as well about a more distant family connection with politically motivated violence that could explain a deeply ingrained suspicion of activist ideology. It seems his grandfather and father were survivors of the atrocities committed by all sides during the Korean War in their hometown of Sunch'ŏn (Huh and Jung 2008: 153-7). (Hwang Sŏk-yŏng's *The Guest* is a powerful shamanistic summoning of the ghosts of this massacre which preceded Kwangju by three decades.)

The relative lack of success of *The Old Garden*, Im's fifth film, is not surprising given the general downturn in confidence and profitability experienced by the film industry in 2007. Im's third film, *A Good Lawyer's Wife* (2003) and his fourth, the political thriller-comedy *The President's Last Bang* (2005),[6] were seen by far greater numbers of viewers; the box office for the latter film was increased to some extent by the controversy stirred up by the film's sharp irony aimed at Pak Chŏng-hŭi and cronies. It may be that in trying to connect with the seriousness and political ethics of Hwang Sŏk-yŏng's novel, while simultaneously casting in the lead roles actors better suited to romance or rom-com, trimming the original story to fit better with melodramatic conventions and shooting most scenes in an aesthetic palate of soft muted tones, Im Sang-su and team created a film that fell between audiences. Too serious to win over the kids, not sufficiently politically informed or innovative enough in cinematic terms to generate much debate among the critics, even though reviews were generally positive. Outside Korea, both of Im's previous films have had greater success as well. In yet one more interview about *The Old Garden*, Im wryly observed, 'Well, in Korea the film wasn't debated much … But, on the other hand, it looks like outside the country

6 For an interpretation, see Morris 2008.

people accepted the film just the way I wanted, not taking it so seriously' (Im 2005).

3.4 *Tiananmen*

There is one Chinese film, released only some six months before *The Old Garden*, that resembles it in the general shape of its narrative and that seems to show that, even in our era of political disenchantment, it is still possible to set a love story in the context of a suppressed insurrection and produce a very powerful film. Luo Ye's *Summer Palace* (2006) takes one couple, and several of their lovers, through the days leading up to and beyond the 1989 Tiananmen massacre and the brutal crushing of student protests on Beijing's campuses. The 'film' was shot on hi-def video, which can impart aesthetic softening to the images, but the love is raw and sexual and the characters have nothing of the rather chaste, safely contained passion which seems to accompany the visual aesthetics settled upon in *The Old Garden*. Luo Ye's people drift—through rooms and corridors and through alienating urban landscapes—to no greater purpose than Hyŏn-u or Yun-hŭi. They do so with a gritty realism that shows one road not chosen by, or perhaps no longer realistically available to, contemporary South Korean film-makers aiming for access to the commercial marketplace.

4 *May 18*

4.1 *Elsewhere*

Imagine a middle-sized insular country facing a political crisis sometime in the second half of the 20th century. The conservative government of the time is faced with growing unrest in a region which, left behind by much of the economic development of recent years, often has justifiably felt discriminated against. In one particular city this bitterness and a growing desire for a more democratic society has brought about serious conflict with the local forces of order but has also spurred the formation of a vocal yet peaceful civil rights campaign. The more democratic elements are able to keep the lid on more violent youthful protestors. Rather than chose to negotiate, the government decides to crack down on the perceived rebellion. They have already incarcerated representatives of the region's people. Now they send in the troops.

And in so doing, the government and military commanders make a terrible mistake. The men have all been told they are facing what are at best 'hooligans'. From among the different forces deployed to the area, senior officers decide to set loose the toughest soldiers in a famously tough army: the special forces men, the ones proud of their snappy berets, the ones trained for the most brutal combat.

The predictable happens. The soldiers attack and hunt down their fellow citizens, killing them with seeming indiscretion. Student protesters, working-class youth and older inhabitants are beaten and shot down. And when initial investigations are first held, the military are exonerated, while many of the dead are labelled 'terrorists'. It will take many more years for anything like the truth to be widely known. None of the soldiers will ever face charges, nor will their commanders all the way up the line. The latter will instead receive medals.

I may have oversimplified things in attempting to draw parallels between what happened on Bloody Sunday, 30 January 1972, in the Northern Irish city of Derry (Londonderry) and the Kwangju uprising of May 1980. Such parallels are, however, easy to make, sometimes eerily close (Korean black berets/UK maroon berets) and are a stark reminder, certainly for those of us in the United Kingdom, that not only can it happen here but it did.

The death toll in Londonderry was fourteen, which in numerical terms is a mere fraction of the some 200-plus killed outright in Kwangju. The peak of violence, the rampage of the 'paras', lasted perhaps 16 minutes—not whole days as in Kwangju in May 1980. In Kwangju the protracted brutality left a swathe of damage through the community which can perhaps only be compared with that generated in Northern Ireland by the long years of the Troubles. It is very much to the credit of director Paul Greengrass and his collaborator-producer Mark Redhead that in their film *Bloody Sunday*, they are able to give a concrete demonstration of how this violent incident sparked a decades-long guerrilla war. Screened originally on ITV television in 2002 for the 30th anniversary of Northern Ireland's own small Kwangju, *Bloody Sunday* has left a docu-drama record of what happened on 30 January 1972, why and how it happened, and what the results turned out to be. It is perhaps the greatest political film ever made in Britain.

It must be to the credit of CJ Entertainment not to have waited quite 30 years to commission the first full-scale feature film concerning the events between 18 and 27 May 1980 in Kwangju. It is more significantly to the credit of South Korea's hard-won democracy that *May 18* could be seen by millions of viewers. Compare the case of Luo Ye's film, discussed above. Luo and his producers took *Summer Palace* to the Cannes Film Festival in 2006, where it was deemed impressive enough to be included in the official competition. The film-makers had not, however, secured government approval for screening the film abroad or anywhere else. Rather than being celebrated, Luo Ye and colleagues were given a five-year ban from all film-making activity, a ban still in force. *Summer Palace* has been screened all around the world, but not (legally) in China.

Within South Korea, several previous films have treated the Kwangju uprising and aftermath in a much more tangential manner akin to *The Old Garden*. Chang Sŏn-u's *Petal* (*Kkonnip* 1996), like Im's film, is based on a polished literary text. Chang adapted the novella by Ch'oe Yun: 'There a Petal Silently Falls' ('Chŏgi sŏri ŏpsi hanjŏm kkonnip'i chigo' 1988).[7] Ch'oe writes in a modernistic, fragmented style. In choosing to tell the aftermath of Kwangju, she created a narrative of memory jumps and flashbacks which assault the shattered mind and feelings of a young female survivor of the massacre. Kwangju is not depicted but rather continually recreated in the violent memories which leave the young woman no peace, no escape.

Chang adopted a similarly fragmented narrative, adding sequences of animation to literal flashbacks to produce a small masterpiece. Cinema of course makes things visually concrete. Scenes from the

[7] For an English translation, plus valuable biographical note about Ch'oe, see Ch'oe 1997/8. Ch'oe, herself a scholar of French literature, has co-operated with Patrick Maurus on French versions of her work: see Ch'oe 2000. An excellent overview of both film and literature dealing with the Kwangju uprising is Baker 2003.

Kwangju uprising were physically reproduced with the co-operation of local government and citizens. Chang chose, however, to keep faith with Ch'oe Yun's non-heroic, psychological realism of scenes as refracted through a young woman's damaged mind. Flashbacks are shot in black and white—a standard enough practice. But Chang and his team have managed to give the images a washed-out, over-exposed texture that allows shapes and movement to emerge almost like abstract strokes from an ink brush. Added to this is slow motion and slow sound; in early flashbacks, crowd noises register not like cheers and shouts but the groaning of souls in torment.[8]

4.2 *The film and its production*

The plot of *May 18* moves in straightforward chronological fashion. From about 23 minutes in, titles appear several times locating the viewer in the progression of events, from the first violence at the entrance of Chŏnnam University on 18 May to the final attack by government forces on Province Hall on 27 May. Woven through the main chronology are the stories of three couples of characters who represent the ordinary people of Kwangju. There is a duo of earthy working-class characters, a cab driver and the small-time hood he met through a fistfight: they will join the struggle and die heroically at Province Hall. More significant is the couple formed by a widower, retired army officer Pak Hŭng-su, and his young daughter Shin-ae: he will act as commander to the citizens' army, hers will be the last voice of the uprising, calling out from a jeep-mounted loudspeaker for people to remember the men like her father about to be sacrificed. The last and most important couple is made up of two parentless brothers: the older, Kang Min-u, drives a cab in order to send his younger brother Chin-u through school, with a dream of sending him on to study law at Seoul National University. The three couples will, over the course of the two hours of the film, have their stories woven to-

---

[8] When *Petal* appeared in 1996, the marketplace for Korean film looked very different from today's supermarket of glossy products. Korean films occupied barely 23 percent of it, there were only some 511 screens (by contrast with the 2000+ of today) in the country, and the average budget for a feature film was around 0.9 billion won, less than US$900,000. Chang's film was number four among Korean releases that year: its Seoul box office of 214,000 still looks strong compared to that of *The Old Garden*, 64,000.

gether: Shin-ae, a friend of Chin-u, will be courted amidst the chaos by Min-u who works for her father: her father will lead the last stand at Province Hall where all the male characters will perish, except Chin-u, who is gunned down on 21 May.

The team assembled by CJ Entertainment for the making of *May 18* was generally young and commercially orientated. Rather than look for any narrative model to realistic prose or the stylistic tour-de-force of a Ch'oe Yun, director Kim Chi-hun claims to have depended most on Yi Chae-ŭi's *Kwangju Diary* and the sort of documentation which went into its writing. In his initial approach to the subject, Kim seems to have made a decision which would have repercussions for the overall shape of the film: 'The most important extracts [of testimony] were from grassroots people during the ten days … rather than those who set out to change the course of history' (*KFO* 23: 44).

In more practical terms, the Kwangju uprising was first reshaped for director Kim into a basic narrative by Pak Sang-yŏn, the writer who provided the story for Pak Chan-uk's hit *Joint Security Area* (*Kongdong kyŏngbi kuyŏk JSA*, 2000). Kim Chi-hun himself had directed only one film before, a genre comedy-gangster film. Care seems to have been taken to surround him with industry veterans: special effects expert Kim Pyŏng-gi has since 1998 worked with many of the best and most successful directors; martial arts choreographer Shin Chae-myŏng has been acting and designing on-screen mayhem since 1991. Producer Yu In-taek had worked with avant-garde directors such as Chang Sŏn-u and Pak Kwang-su in the past, before producing Kim Chi-hun's first film.

A big-budget film such as *May 18* pays special attention to casting since however controversial or serious the topic itself, the film has to appeal to the widest demographic. Kim Sang-kyŏng in the part of older brother Min-u has to play a character far removed from the roles he is known for in the work of art-film director Hong Sang-su; as Shin-ae, Yi Yo-wŏn retains the sort of fragile innocence shown in her first major role in Chŏng Chae-ŭn's *Take Care of My Cat* (*Koyangi-rŭ put'ak hae* 2001). Her father is played by Korean cinema's most ubiquitous actor, veteran An Sŏng-ki. Perhaps the most tactically astute casting concerns the youngest of the main characters, Chin-u. He is played by Yi Chun-ki [Lee Joon-ki], popular across the East Asian cultural market. The Japanese and Korean Wikipedia pages devoted to him link on to a world of cyber-enthusiasm that seems extraordinary for a slight, gender-bending twenty-something from Pusan. With An

Sŏng-ki for the older audience and Kim Sang-kyŏng or Yi Yo-wŏn for somewhat younger film buffs, Yi Chun-ki's presence could practically ensure the film would do well with the all-important youth audience. It may seem almost a by-product of casting that, as it turns out, Yi happens to be fairly good actor.

4.3 *Conventions and actuality*

One could attempt to test how historically accurate *May 18* managed to be despite the pressures of genre convention threaded all through it, although less than eight minutes in, these conventions have been laid out with little subtlety: peaceful sunny countryside surrounding small city of poor but honest citizens versus the preparations for war begun in the dark; the down-to-earth good humour of working-class people (usually speaking exaggerated dialect); innocent romance; loving, simple relations between parents and children and/or between siblings. *May 18* indeed starts out to be, as an advertising slogan for the film put it, 'A film to make us aware of the importance of family love' (cited in Kim 2007). We might insist, for instance, that there was no retired officer leading the young men who fought at Province Hall; but middle-aged former soldiers had been part of the hasty training of the citizens' army, so An Sŏng-ki's character could be considered a kind of proximate synthesis. The final scenes of Shin-ae riding through the night-time streets of the city calling out for help at the Province Hall, or for at least the memory of the martyrs to be recalled, is not pure fiction. Many accounts of the final hours remember such a voice. One of the three disks on the special edition DVD of *May 18* is an independent documentary of testimony from people caught up in the events; it includes an interview with one of two women who broadcast through the last moments during the pre-dawn of 27 May. The scene of coffins and grieving relatives at the Sangmu Hall is placed midway through the narrative. The realism is effective, particularly because the scene has been preceded by harrowing recreations of the violence which produced all this suffering. Yet even here genre convention and sentimentality are brought forward as though to blunt the edges of the moment. The iconic little boy grieving beside his father's coffin is there, and so is Min-u grieving for brother Chin-u lying in his box nearby. The soundtrack plays in voice-over Chin-u's farewell letter to big brother.

It is in the key scenes of the attacks on students—in the climate of the time, spurred on by the anti-Communist fervour of their senior officers, the élite units generally saw students as combatants-in-waiting—and civilians that the film goes beyond safe conventions. The first sequence at Chŏnnam University lasts only a minute. It is followed some five minutes later by the first extensive scenes of soldiers laying into people at random: the violence quite literally bursts into the cinematic world when one soldier chases a student into the theatre where Min-u, Chin-u and Shin-ae sit amid a happy crowd watching an old-fashioned comic melodrama. There is an irruption of unprovoked viciousness on the street outside, of heads clubbed again and again, of blood splattering a film poster; for two minutes the genre soft-focus is wrenched around to look at a chaotic vision of hell on ordinary city streets and alleys.

These two sequences prepare for the killings on 21 May. A crowd has assembled upon learning that the military, at this point forced back to Province Hall, are preparing to retreat from Kwangju. When the national anthem begins playing from a speaker on top of the hall, the citizens stop their taunts and jeering and reverentially place hands on hearts. The soldiers in front of the hall open fire. What follows is a sustained five or so minutes of distilled terror created by a remarkable combination of set-design, special effects, stunt work, acrobatic camera work, editing, and every other craft in a very sophisticated industry's repertoire. Amid the whizzing bullets and exploding blood-squibs, Min-u searches for his brother. He is watching when Chin-u, trying to help a badly wounded man, is fatally shot himself. The film's father-figure, Pak Hŭng-su, rescues the two of them in a bullet-riddled truck; all arrive at the hospital where Shin-ae, a nurse, joins in the climatic scene of Chin-u's death.

The ability of *May 18* to deliver a visceral impact during the massacre before Province Hall takes the viewer out of the frame of reference of film as narration towards cinema's origins as spectacle—the train driving right off the screen at you.

The entire production focused a huge amount of effort and resources on achieving its hyper-realism. As director Kim has recalled, 'We spent KRW 3.0 billion just on the set. We made a 500 meter street with real asphalt, established 85% of the real provincial office, and had to make the fountain in front of the office as well as the nearby buildings … About 1,600 extras had to run away with the first gun shots' (*KFO* 23: 45). The impressive set, built outside central Kwangju, was later opened to the public.[9]

4.4 *Brotherhood*

During the above scene, amid the mini-pyrotechnics and panic, it may still be possible to experience an uncanny sense of déjà vu imparted by the conjunction of screen violence and the theme of two brothers, one desperately searching for the other in the middle of a frantic battle. We have been here before and, consciously or not, so have main story writer Pak Sang-yŏn and the young writers who provided the continuity scripts. Kang Che-gyu's *Taegŭkgi* (*Taegŭkgi hwinallimyŏ* 2004) was at the time of its release the most expensive production in Korean film history (US$12.8 million). It was also an even bigger hit than either *May 18* or *D-War* (see below) would be three years later. The first big-budget film the new Korean cinema had made about the Korean War, *Taegŭkgi* viewed the chaos and slaughter through two focal characters, an older working-class brother who sacrifices all for his younger sibling. The younger brother role was played by Wŏn Pin, then the sort of major trans-national star of TV drama and film that Yi Chun-gi is now. *Taegŭkgi* was inevitably compared to films such as *Saving Private Ryan* and Spielberg's TV production *Band of Brothers*, both for its narrative themes and the hyper-realism of battlefield effects. The techniques developed for the film are those transferred to the recreated streets of Kwangju by *May 18*.[10]

Critics might applaud *Taegŭkgi*'s attempt to make a major film about the war, but have serious reservations about the levelling effect of genre conventions. 'For much of *Taegŭkgi*'s extensive running time we are focused on the melodramatic discord that springs from the older brother's decision to sacrifice himself. This personal story dominates the film to the extent that, in some ways, the war is merely an

---

[9] According to Naver News, 13 September 2006. Online: http://news.naver.com/tv/read.php?mode=LSS2D&section_id=115&section_id2=291&office_id=130&article_id=0000011043&menu_id=115 (accessed May 2008).

[10] If *Taegukgi* translated themes and techniques from Hollywood battlefields, South Korean expertise has in turn been transferred to film-making outside the country. Feng Xiaogang's pioneering Chinese civil war blockbuster *Assembly* (2007) made use of South Korean technical staff; its scenes of urban warfare bear more than passing resemblance to those Kang Che-kyu created for his film.

elaborate backdrop. The film also makes little effort to say anything new about the conflict' (Paquet 2004). It is difficult to avoid similar conclusions about *May 18*, despite the very real shock delivered by the carefully constructed scenes of violence against the people of the city.

While genre-levelling may be inevitable in a large-scale production aimed at a mass audience, it can may have troubling results for the treatment of confrontation and political conflict. Consider the way the ROK military are depicted in the film. The name Chŏn Tu-hwan is written on protest placards and shouted in slogans, yet the film refrains from actually tracing authority back to its source in Seoul. Apart from retired officer Pak Hŭng-su and one of his old comrades, still serving with the occupying special forces, the soldiers and their officers seem two-dimensional villains. The character actor playing the commander of the special forces had a similar role near the end of *Taegŭkgi*. His commander scowls and growls at junior officers; when Pak Hŭng-su arrives at headquarters to beg him not to kill everyone in Kwangju, he dismisses him with disdain. If in *Taegŭkgi* 'North Korean soldiers are portrayed as crazed fanatics' (Paquet 2004), *May 18*'s villains are not portrayed with much complexity either. In contrast, we can point to *Bloody Sunday* as a film that avoids easy simplifications of responsibility for state-sanctioned violence. '*Bloody Sunday* does not rely upon a narrative humanistic framework which by pathologizing unsympathetic characters would displace the state's culpability in the event or reduce the complexity of historical injustices to the human foibles of a single character or group of characters' (Blaney 2007: 122).

That you could treat both sides of a conflict as bloody as Kwangju in less black-and-white fashion was demonstrated by the first major reconstruction of the Kwangju days: SBS's now classic 24-part TV drama *Sandglass* (*Morae shigye* 1995) devoted one full episode and portions of two others to events in Kwangju. The most sympathetic of the two male lead characters becomes a soldier in the conflict, the other a hoodlum who becomes caught up in the fighting. The technical level of realism available to a mid-1990s television production was limited. But the director-writer team of Kim Chong-hak and Song Chi-na managed to create a depiction of Kwangju as both human and political event that is still rivalled only by Chang Sŏn-u's film *Petal*.

If the officers and black berets are drawn in the stark outlines, what of the people they confront? 'If an intellectual is in a film,' director Kim Chi-hun has argued, 'he or she usually translates and presents direction. However, in this movie, there is no such intellectual. I thought that such a character was not needed in this film, as they get in the way of the real experiences of real people' (*KFO* 23: 45). In an eloquent review in the film journal *Cine 21*, Kim Hyae-ri noted how in the opening sections of *May 18*, Kwangju is depicted as a kind of 'cozy paradise'. Here, when new reports of a nationwide crackdown on dissent comes on the television screen, a minor character simply switches off the noisy broadcast. 'Considering the point in time that May of 1980 was, the citizens in the drama fail to make mention of politics to an almost unnatural degree. Yet a few days later, hearts rent by the bloody deaths, beside themselves at the inhumane cruelty, these people will take up arms' (Kim 2007). The Kwangju uprising could not have been directed by 'intellectuals' even if the people of Kwangju and/or its intellectuals had wanted to plan such an event. As has been well documented, most activists had been rounded up in police raids in the days and nights before 18 May (Lee 1999 [1985]: 40-41). Kwangju began in reaction to unprovoked attack, but that reaction increasingly took on the shape of a not unpredictable but still spontaneous insurrection with democratic goals more ambitious than many intellectuals may have dared to dream in 1980. The division of labour, and perhaps of intelligence and political commitment, which the young director takes for granted, may be one of the more unrealistic assumptions he made about what happened in May 1980 in the city of Kwangju.

5 CONCLUSION: PATRIOTIC MONSTROSITY

The new cinema of South Korea has looked back at the Kwangju uprising in the last few years and made films that do confirm the uprising—or, as the tamer official term puts it, the Kwangju Democratic People's Movement—as a central event on the long painful road to democratisation. *The Old Garden* and *May 18* are both reasonably well-made mainstream films. It is difficult to gauge, however, the significance of either film beyond the context of the film industry itself.

The release of *May 18* might have been expected to lead to a wider social and political discourse about the recent past and its continued significance, or, with Im Sang-su's film, its potentially negative legacies for contemporary South Korea. But it was another film that actually generated far more comment and debate well beyond the usual perimeters of the cinematic world.

The film that kept *May 18* from becoming the number one Korean film of the year was *D-War* (*Ti-Wŏ*), known on release in the US, and now in DVD format, as *Dragon Wars*. It is a strange mishmash of computer-generated monsters, American actors and Korean patriotism assembled by the enterprising Shim Hyŏng-rae.[11] Not so much a work or art or entertainment as a summertime happening, *D-War* persuaded 8.5 million viewers to sit and watch it on any of 689 screens, and soon developed a huge cyber-fan base. As Chŏng Han-sŏk put it, writing in the Korean Film Council annual report: '*D-War* had been in the spotlight even before its opening, due to the expectations for the film to become a Korean blockbuster' (*KC* 2007: 4).

Beyond the domestic market, the particular block director Shim intended to bust was the American cinema market. The former comic actor and tireless self-promoter put patriotism at the forefront of his long publicity campaign. This was the film that could beat the Americans at their own high-tech monsters and action game. As Shim declared to the *New York Times* (10 September 2007): 'The secret is to move beyond the melodrama that characterizes so many Korean films ... They [Korean film-makers] don't understand that to be commercial in the U.S., you need great action and effects.' To the Korean version of this English-language film, Shim added both Korean subtitles and a pitch to the audience at the end of the film. To the strains of the Seattle Symphony Orchestra's rendition of *Arirang*, a message appears among the scrolling credits, urging viewers to support the film as an expression of Korean pride. Many did. As the same *New York Times* article reported, 'A number of netizens supporting *D-War* were somewhat unforgiving of those who had criticized the film, and frequently leveled attacks on them that bordered on cyber terror.'

Maybe it is the sign of a fairly healthy democracy that a film on such a potentially divisive topic as *May 18* can now be made, released and seen by millions of South Koreans without creating much of a stir.

---

[11] For examples of a few of the more reasoned critical responses to the film, see Hartzell 2007 and Nam 2007. For a taste of the controversy surrounding the battle between critics and fans, try 'Critic Jin, Film Fans Duel over "D-War"', in: *The Korea Times* 15 August 2007. Online: http://www.koreatimes.co.kr/www/news/special/2008/05/178_8411.html (accessed May 2008). The controversy over the film and its laboured appeals to nationalism are given prominence in the Korean Film Council's annual report: see *KC* 2007: 4.

That the new Korean film industry has changed hugely since the 1990s and the daring required then to make a film such as Chang Sŏn-u's *Petal* is without doubt; whether this industry still has a significant place for an auteur-director such as Im Sang-su is not clear. But the success of *D-War,* on the heels on last year's top film, Pong Chun-ho's much better crafted monster film *The Host*, suggests that South Korean audiences are very likely to continue to be offered more by way of monsters and spectacle than film as historical and social reflection in any foreseeable future.

Acknowledgements: Cambridge graduate student Jeon Yong-woo generously provided help with DVD extras, Korean web resources and his own interpretations of the films discussed in this essay. Cambridge colleague Peter Kornicki showed generosity and patience in reading Korean-language reviews with me.

REFERENCES

Films: DVD/VHS

Bloody Sunday, dir. Paul Greengrass, Optimum Home Entertainment, 2008

Hwaryŏhan hyuga (*May 18*), dir. Kim Chi-hun, Limited special edition, CJ Entertainment, 2007

Kkonnip (*Petal*), dir. Chang Sŏn-u, Daewoo Corporation, 1996

Morae Shigye (*Sandglass*), dir. Kim Chong-hak, YA Entertainment, 1995

Oraedoen chŏngwŏn (*The Old Garden*), dir. Im Sang-su, Sidus CNI, 2007 (French version: *Le Vieux jardin*, Wild Side Video, 2008)

Summer Palace, dir. Luo Ye, Palm Pictures, 2006

Printed and online sources

Baker, Don (2003), 'Victims and Heroes: Competing Visions of May 18', in: Shin, Gi-wook and Hwang, Kyung Moon (2003), pp. 87-107

Blaney, Aileen (2007), 'Remembering Historical Trauma in Paul Greengrass's Bloody Sunday', in: *History & Memory*, 19 (2), Fall/Winter, pp. 113-138

Bordwell, David (2008), 'The Art Cinema as a Mode of Film Practice' [1979], in: David Bordwell, *Poetics of Cinema*, New York and London: Routledge, pp. 151-69

Ch'oe Yun, trans. Bruce Fulton and Ju-Chan Fulton (1997/8), 'There a Petal Silently Falls', in: *Korea Journal*, Winter 1997, pp. 221-38; Spring 1998, pp. 356-92 [First published in *Munhak-kwa sahoe*, Summer 1988]

Ch'oe Yun, trans. Patrick Maurus (2000), *Là-bas sans bruit tombe un pétale*, Paris: Babel

Cumings, Bruce (1997), *Korea's Place in the Sun: A Modern History*, New York and London: WW Norton & Co.

Han Sun-hee (2007), 'Size is the Problem'. Online: *KFO* 23, pp. 10-11

Hartzell, Adam (2007), 'Review of D-War'. Online: http://www.koreanfilm.org/kfilm07.html#d-war (accessed April 2008)

Hughes, Theodore (2007), 'Korean Memories of the Vietnam and Korean Wars: A Counter-History', in: *Japan Focus*. Online: http://japanfocus.org/products/details/2406 (accessed May 2008)

Huh, Moonyung, and Jung Ji-youn, trans. Colin A. Mouat (2008), *Im Sang-soo*, Korean Film Directors, Seoul: Korean Film Council

Hwang Sŏk-yŏng, trans. Jeong Eun-jin et Jacques Batillot (2005), *Le Vieux jardin*, Paris: Zulma [*Oraedoen chŏngwŏn* (2000), Seoul: Ch'angbi Publishers]

Im Sang-su (2005), 'Im Sang-soo Talks (The Old Garden)'. Online: http://twitchfilm.net/archives/004519.html (accessed May 2008)

KC 2007 (*Korean Cinema 2007*), available from the Korean Film Council. Online: http://www.koreanfilm.or.kr/KOFIC/Channel?task=kofic.user.eng.d_publication (accessed May 2007)

KFO 23 (*Korean Film Observatory* No. 23), available from the Korean Film Council. Online: http://www.koreanfilm.or.kr/index.jsp (accessed May 2008)

Kim Hyae-ri (2007), 'Kiok hajago marhanŭn Kwangju yŏnghwa *Hwaryŏhan hyuga*' [A Kwangju film that says let us remember: *An Elegant Vacation* (*May 18*)], in: *Cine 21* (25 July 2007). Online: http://www.cine21.com/Article/article_view.php?mm=002001001&article_id=47605 (accessed May 2008)

Lee Jai-eui, trans. Kap Su Seol and Nick Mamatas (1999 [1985]), *Kwangju Diary: Beyond Death, Beyond the Darkness of the Age*, UCLA Asian Pacific Monograph Series, Los Angeles CA: University of California

Lewis, Linda (2002), *Laying Claim to the Memory of May: A Look Back at the 1980 Kwangju Uprising*, Honolulu: University of Hawai'i Press

Morris, Mark (2008), 'Melodrama, Exorcism, Mimicry: Japan and the Colonial Past in the New Korean Cinema', in: Darren Aoki, Chris Berry, and Nicola Liscutin (eds), *Cultural Studies and Cultural Industries in Northeast Asia: What a Difference a Region Makes*, Hong Kong: University of Hong Kong Press (forthcoming)

Nam Da-eun (2007), 'The Imbalance between Art and Entertainment'. Online: *KFO* 23, pp. 29-31

Paquet, Darcy (2004), 'Review of *Taegukgi*'. Online: http://www.koreanfilm.org/kfilm04.html#taegukgi (accessed April 2008)

Paquet, Darcy (2007), '2007'. Online: http://www.koreanfilm.org/kfilm07.html (accessed April 2008)

Shin, Gi-Wook, and Hwang Kyung Moon (2003), *Contentious Kwangju: The May* 18 *Uprising in Korea's Past and Present*, Oxford: Rowan & Littlefield

Yi Yŏng-jin (2007), 'Sŏjŏnsiga pulkanŭnghan shidae-ŭi yŏnga *Oraedoen chŏngwŏn*' [Love poem for an era forbidden lyricism: *The Old Garden*], in: *Cine 21* (3 January 2007). Online: http://www.cine21.com/Article/article_view.php?mm=002001001&article_id=43801(accessed May 2008)

THE US-DPRK 1994 AGREED FRAMEWORK AND THE US ARMY'S RETURN TO NORTH KOREA[1]

C. Kenneth Quinones

ABSTRACT

The quest to regularize US-DPRK relations has proved extremely complex and time-consuming. Initially the effort, which dates from 1992, centered on the road map spelled out in the October 1994 bilateral Agreed Framework. While one of the goals of the accord was to halt North Korea's nuclear weapons program, this was actually one of five US prerequisites for the normalization of diplomatic and commercial relations with North Korea. One of the most successful undertakings in building co-operation and mutual trust was the US Army-Korean People's Army Joint Recovery Operations of 1996-2005. The Bush administration of 1989-93 had made recovery of the remains of US military personnel missing in action from the Korean War one of its priorities for the normalization of relations. Earlier, the US Senate had established its Select Committee on prisoners of war and missing in action to promote the effort regarding those missing in all wars. This paper reviews the history of the US Army's effort in North Korea between 1996 and 2005, and assesses its diplomatic, political and military consequences as they relate to the normalization of US-DPRK relations.

1 FINDING CORPORAL LEBOEUF

It took the United States (US) government 46 years to find Corporal Lawrence LeBoeuf. On a hot and humid day late in July 1996, an ageing North Korean farmer led a small group of North Korean and American soldiers across a lush green mountain ridge to a shallow grave southwest of Unsan, in North P'yŏngan province of the Democratic People's Republic of Korea (DPRK). A century earlier an

[1] This study is based on unclassified records collected by the author and his personal recollections. An East-West Center (Honolulu) POSCO grant made the study possible.

American company had won exclusive rights to mine the still productive gold mine at Unsan. Sixty years later, on a November morning in 1950 some 20 miles south of the China-DPRK border, bugles blared as thousands of Chinese People's Volunteers rushed up the ridge toward advance elements of the US Eighth Army. The corporal was one of some 800 American soldiers who died in the ensuing battle.

The farmer, a teenager in 1950, followed his father's instructions and buried LeBoeuf in his fox hole where he had died. We collected the corporal's remains, including his blond hair, confirmed his identification, and later his family was notified in Brooklyn, New York.

The search for Corporal LeBoeuf and his fellow soldiers achieved impressive results between 1996 and May 2005, but then the US Secretary of Defense Donald Rumsfeld abruptly and unilaterally ended the effort. Presented here are merely the endeavor's beginning and more apparent accomplishments. Eventually, it must be hoped, a fuller account will materialize.

2 Erasing the Past

Finding Corporal LeBoeuf was part of a complex US-DPRK effort to erase the legacy of mutual hatred and mistrust lingering from the Korean War (1950-53), with the aim of normalizing relations. The October 1994 bilateral Agreed Framework, the two nations' first diplomatic agreement, aspired to do much more than halt North Korea's nuclear weapons program. Most students of the 1994 Agreed Framework have focused on the negotiations that produced the accord and the subsequent international effort to build two nuclear reactors in North Korea. In actual fact, ending North Korea's nuclear programs was but one of five prerequisites for achieving normal relations. This focus and the passage of time have dimmed memories that the accord served primarily as a road map for achieving the normalization of US-DPRK relations.

When the agreement was being formulated, both sides recognized that successful implementation required more than words on paper. Unlike agreements between the US and other former enemies, Americans and North Koreans shared nothing but a legacy of killing and quarreling. The authors of the framework knew that building trust and fostering co-operation were imperative for the success of the accord and to sustain peace on the Korean peninsula. They built into it a series of 'simultaneous steps' and confidence-building programs designed to achieve these purposes.

This study aims to begin broadening our perspective of the Agreed Framework beyond its nuclear aspects and to clarify its ultimate goal: normal relations between the US and the DPRK.

3 Setting the Stage for the Agreed Framework

Prior to the Agreed Framework negotiations, the sole regular channel of bilateral communication from 1951 to 1992 had been the Military Armistice Commission (MAC) created by the Korean War armistice of 1953. Meetings of the MAC convened in P'anmunjŏm, a village in the Demilitarized Zone that became the de facto border between North and South Korea. There representatives of the United Nations Command (UNC), mostly US military personnel, frequently clashed with their counterparts from the North Korean People's Army (KPA). These meetings were not negotiating sessions, nor did they make any effort to end the Korean War. Rather they continued it by using words and propaganda.

Real diplomatic communication between the US and the DPRK commenced after 1988 when what was called the 'Beijing channel' opened. It facilitated limited bilateral diplomatic communication in the hope of resolving problems before they escalated into confrontation. But it was not until January 1992 that diplomats from the two sides finally sat face to face to discuss their nations' differences. This meeting on 22 January 1992 in New York City brought together ranking officials from both sides for a single day to exchange views on what each side wanted the other to do before bilateral relations could be normalized.

The US listed five preconditions for the normalization of relations. The DPRK should:

- end the nuclear program,
- continue the South-North Korea dialogue,
- facilitate the recovery of American military remains from the Korean War,
- cease the export of ballistic missiles,
- renounce publicly reliance on international terrorism.

All but the export of ballistic missiles became core elements of the Agreed Framework.

3.1 *US-DPRK negotiations 1993-1994*

A second major step toward improved relations followed when diplomats again met in New York in June 1993 to negotiate a halt to North Korea's threatened withdrawal from the Treaty on the Non-proliferation of Nuclear Weapons (NPT). Evidence collected by the International Atomic Energy Agency (IAEA) during its first inspection of the Yŏngbyŏn nuclear research center in June 1992 and US satellite photographs taken in August 1992 had strongly indicated that North Korea was attempting to hide the truth about its earlier plutonium production. At issue were North Korea's compliance with its promises under the NPT, its pledges under the Joint South-North Korea Declaration on the De-nuclearization of the Korean Peninsula (December 1992) and its ability to build a plutonium nuclear bomb.

Persistent diplomacy failed to induce North Korean co-operation. The IAEA, responsible for implementation of the NPT, at the end of February 1993 determined that the DPRK must submit to a 'special' inspection of its nuclear facilities. On 11 March, North Korea declared its intention to withdraw from the NPT at the end of the mandatory 90-day waiting period. A crisis ensued until North Korea agreed to engage in negotiations with the US. These yielded the June agreement that 'suspended' the DPRK's withdrawal from the NPT and enabled the negotiations to continue, culminating in two important developments: the first joint statement and the establishment of the 'New York' channel.

The 11 June 1993 US-DPRK Joint Statement formed the foundation of the Agreed Framework. It committed both sides to exchanging concessions of equivalent value. North Korea agreed to 'suspend' its withdrawal from the NPT and to maintain 'full scope nuclear safeguards' under IAEA monitoring. The US on its side promised not to use or threaten to use armed force against the DPRK. At the same time, the New York channel was opened to facilitate direct communication between the Department of State in Washington DC and the DPRK mission to the United Nations in New York. Originally it consisted of telephone and fax communication between the mission and the author, then North Korea affairs officer in the State Department's Office of Korea Affairs.

A third significant step came on 24 August 1993, when US Air Force Major General Nels Running, representing the United Nations (UN), and his North Korean counterpart, Major General Ri Dok Gyu, representing the KPA, signed the Agreement on Remains-related Matters (see below, Section 6). The fourth major step materialized in February 1994 when Thomas Hubbard, deputy assistant secretary of state, and Ho Jong, the DPRK's deputy permanent representative to the UN, reached the Agreed Conclusions. These formalized the process of 'simultaneous steps' by both sides when implementing their bilateral agreements. The process required both sides to act at the same time when exchanging concessions of equivalent value. The aim was to gradually build trust and confidence. For North Korea, 'simultaneous steps' remain a fundamental principle regarding its relationship with the US. The latter, however, assigned waning significance to the concept after the Clinton administration left office in January 2001.

These four elements initiated the process of creating trust and cooperation. Also established prior to signing of the Agreed Framework was both sides' commitment to allowing the State Department and the North Korean Ministry of Foreign Affairs (MFA) to play the lead roles in bilateral communication and the improvement of relations. Soon elements of the US Department of Defense and the KPA would take issue with this premise.

4 Implementing the Agreed Framework

Once the Agreed Framework had been finalized in October 1994, implementation began hesitantly with a series of simultaneous steps:

- The DPRK froze all activity at its Yŏngbyŏn nuclear research center;
- it allowed US nuclear experts to visit the center and to negotiate an accord to facilitate the placement of 8,000 nuclear spent fuel rods in long-term storage under IAEA monitoring;
- the US was to ship 50,000 metric tons of heavy fuel oil to North Korea as compensation for the latter shutting down the five-megawatt nuclear reactor at Yŏngbyŏn;

- the US undertook to host negotiations about opening diplomatic liaison offices in each other's capital;
- the US undertook to begin phasing out selected economic sanctions on North Korea;
- the UNC and the KPA undertook to negotiate an agreement to facilitate the recovery of the remains of American soldiers missing in action in the Korean War.

Robert Gallucci, the then US chief negotiator and assistant secretary of state for politico-military affairs assumed responsibility for overall co-ordination of the US effort and formed teams to implement various aspects of the agreement. The Arms Control and Disarmament Agency (ACDA) and the Department of Energy were to oversee the spent fuel project at Yŏngbyŏn. The State Department's Korea desk was to handle the liaison office issue. Implementation of the 24 August 1993 accord on recovery of the missing in action (MIA) was to be in the hands of the Defense Department's Prisoners of War (POW) and Missing in Action Office (DPMO), the UNC, and the US Army Central Identification Laboratory in Hawaii (CILHI).

From the beginning, the DPRK jumped ahead of the US when it came to carrying out 'simultaneous steps'. Within two weeks of the signing of the Agreed Framework, the US spent fuel team was able to visit Yŏngbyŏn, confirm that the nuclear reactor had been shut down, and negotiate the outline for an agreement on storage of the 8,000 spent fuel rods. Meanwhile, the IAEA resumed monitoring activities at the center.

The US, however, struggled with funding shortages and bureaucratic turf battles. This delayed for almost one year initiation of the spent fuel storage operation and prevented regular deliveries of heavy fuel oil for two years. The spent fuel project proved much more difficult to carry out than anticipated, but the lack of funds also impeded progress and it was not completed until late 1997.

North Korean confidence in US commitment to the Agreed Framework further eroded when the US failed to supply the heavy fuel oil on a timely and regular basis. From the beginning, the US was unable to fulfill its promises in this regard. Although the US formed the Korean Peninsula Energy Development Organization (KEDO) in March 1995 to provide the fuel oil and to construct the two nuclear reactors promised to the DPRK in the Agreed Framework, the State Department had responsibility for collecting funds for KEDO and its heavy fuel oil shipments. The lack of money for the purchases and shipments seriously impeded the program until South Korea assumed responsibility for KEDO funding in 1998.

Liaison office negotiations began on a positive note early in December 1994, but soon encountered debilitating problems. Both sides hammered out an agreement in principle. When the US insisted that its diplomats should travel between Seoul and Pyongyang via P'anmunjŏm, the MFA could only promise to do its best to convince the North Korean army to allow this. On 17 December 1994, the day of the MFA delegation's return to Pyongyang, a US Army helicopter pilot strayed repeatedly into North Korean air space. Lacking means of communication with the US army, the KPA shot down the helicopter, killing its pilot and capturing the passenger. Deputy Assistant Secretary Thomas Hubbard traveled to Pyongyang to resolve the incident and signed a written apology. The incident stymied progress on opening liaison offices. Late in 1995 it was agreed that the Swedish embassy in Pyongyang would represent the US, while the DPRK Mission to the UN would serve as North Korea's liaison office.

Nor did the phasing out of sanctions improve the situation. The US Department of Treasury hesitated for several weeks before beginning to phase out selected sanctions as promised in the Agreed Framework. Finally it authorized Americans to make telephone calls to North Korea and to use credit cards issued on US banks in Pyongyang. The North was not impressed.

Meanwhile, US-DPRK negotiations dragged on about the type of nuclear reactors to be built in North Korea. When the Agreed Framework reached its first anniversary, North Korea had much more to brag about than the US regarding implementation of the accord. Rather than pulling back, the MFA intensified efforts to impress the US Congress with its 'sincere' attitude, possibly hoping to compel the US government to catch up. Such thinking might also explain why the MFA became increasingly involved with the missing in action issue and began to press the army to accommodate US congressional concerns in this regard.

5 Historical context of the MIA remains issue

When the Korean War ended, the remains of 8,100 American soldiers had yet to be accounted for. The 1953 armistice required all parties 'to cooperate in the search for, recovery, and return of remains.' Between 1954 and 1991, about 1,000 MIA remains were recovered in South Korea. North Korea during the same period returned about 1,934 sets of remains through the Military Armistice Commission at P'anmunjŏm. This left an estimated 5,000 to 6,000 American remains still in the North. The remains-related agreement of August 1993 between the UNC and the KPA (see Sections 3.1 and 6) aspired to facilitate the recovery of these remains, but continuing tense relations between the UNC and the North Korean army retarded implementation.

One irritant was North Korea's circumvention during the 1980s of the UNC. North Korean authorities repeatedly engaged private US citizens, veterans groups and members of Congress on the remains issue. The Republic of Korea (ROK) suspected, and the US ambassador in Seoul agreed, that North Korea's overtures via unofficial channels were aiming to use the remains issue to manipulate the US into direct talks with the DPRK without either South Korean or UNC participation. The UNC also worried that the KPA was attempting to undermine its role as the primary channel for implementation of the armistice. Subsequently the US authorities barred their officials from meeting North Koreans other than at P'anmunjŏm. Late in 1986, the KPA accepted 'on a humanitarian basis' information from the UNC about US military remains and a month later proposed joint US Army-KPA recovery teams to locate MIA remains. The Department of Defense chose not to respond.

5.1 *Senate Select Committee on POW/MIA Affairs*

It is important to place the DPRK's overtures in the context of US-Vietnamese relations during the 1980s. The Vietnam War also had produced hatred between the US and Vietnam. But the American families of US missing in action from Vietnam, supported by American Vietnam War veterans, pressed their government to intensify the search for missing military personnel , believing that some might be alive in the jungles and prisons of Southeast Asia. Lending further impetus to this was President George Bush's assignment of top priority to the recovery of all US MIAs.

The Senate Select Committee on Prisoners of War and Missing in Action Affairs emerged under the co-chairmanship of Senator Bob Smith (Republican) and Senator John Kerry (Democrat). The committee prodded Defense to initiate joint recovery operations (JRO) staffed by members of the US and Vietnamese armies to recover US remains in Vietnam. These recovery operations commenced long before the two enemies regularized their relations, but their success contributed to the relatively rapid normalization of US-Vietnamese relations in 1995.

In 1987, the DPRK asked the Soviet embassy in Washington to invite select US congressmen to a meeting in New York to discuss the MIA issue. Nothing came of the overture until January 1990, when Ho Jong, North Korea's deputy permanent representative to the UN, met Sonny Montgomery, chairman of the House Veterans Affairs Committee, in New York to discuss the repatriation of remains. Five months later, in May 1990, the KPA handed five sets of remains to the congressman at a UNC- organized ceremony at P'anmunjŏm. For a while, Ho Jong became the main point of contact between the US Congress and the DPRK government.

Senator Bob Smith had the Vietnam joint recovery operations in mind when he met Ho Jong in New York in February 1991. He indicated to Ho that his government should avoid trying to imitate Vietnam by using the recovery of remains as a device to entice the US into normalizing relations with the North. Senator Smith next met a DPRK delegation at P'anmunjŏm in June 1991, which included Kang Sok Ju, the North Korean first vice-minister of foreign affairs, who later became the DPRK's chief negotiator in the US-DPRK nuclear talks from 1993 to 1994. After a private meeting between Smith and Kang, DPRK officials gave the senator eleven sets of remains. Smith's priority was to press for information about any living Americans, prisoners of war or otherwise, in North Korea. Kang, while promising to look into the matter, seemed intent upon bypassing the MAC and working directly with the US Congress, but Smith avoided making any commitment to Kang. North Korean officials also continued to insist there were no living American missing in action or prisoners of war in North Korea.

During 1992, the KPA re-engaged the MAC on the remains issue by expressing interest in concluding another agreement, but rejected a US proposal for joint recovery operations. Instead the KPA for the first time asserted a claim for compensation of expenses connected to its prior unilateral recovery and repatriation of US remains. This shifted the focus from recovery and return to money, a move that stymied progress until August 1993.

5.2 *Senator Smith goes to Pyongyang*

Senator Smith led the first US congressional delegation to Pyongyang from 19 to 21 December 1992. It was the first visit by a senator and a US diplomat (the author) to North Korea. Also accompanying them were a US marine congressional liaison officer and a member of the senator's staff. Initially, Lawrence Eagleburger, acting secretary of state, fearing that a US diplomat's presence in the delegation might arouse suspicions in the ROK that the US was making a fundamental shift in its North Korea policy, opposed such diplomatic participation. At the time South Koreans were electing a new president. But Brent Scowcroft, chief national security adviser, supported the senator's request, and the author traveled to Pyongyang.

It was dark and cold when the delegation reached Pyongyang by plane from Beijing. We were taken to an MFA guest house, where we learned that our luggage was still in China and no flights would arrive from Beijing until the day of our departure. We also learned that 'China had stopped oil shipments'. This meant there was no heat or hot water in our quarters. Tired, cold, hungry and unwashed, we retired for the night.

On Sunday, 20 December, after a cold breakfast, we began discussions with MFA officials. Bob Smith and Kang Sok Ju cordially exchanged views. Smith asked repeatedly whether there were any living American prisoners in North Korea and inquired about the extent of Chinese handling of UN POWs during the Korean War and similar questions. He stressed that his primary purpose was to ensure that the DPRK appreciated the Americans' intense desire for a full accounting of all US military personnel missing in action in the Korean War. North Korea's cooperation in this regard could improve the atmosphere between the two nations. He explained that he had neither the authority nor the desire to negotiate anything and urged the DPRK to conclude a new agreement with the UNC regarding compensation for MIA recovery-related expenses. He further urged the KPA in the future to preserve the context of sites where remains were discovered to improve prospects for identification. Toward this end, he proposed that North Korea give the US government access to documents and artifacts concerning the handling of prisoners of war during the war.

The North Korean side promised to provide access to archives, but urged that first bilateral technical talks be convened to sort out specifics. On China, the US side was advised to raise with Chinese authorities their control over UN POWs after their military intervened in the fall of 1950. The North Koreans claimed that some photographs of American POW camps had been taken in northeast China during the war. They confirmed what Smith had learned earlier in Moscow—26 US Army and 15 Air Force personnel were sent to the Soviet Union for interrogation. The North Koreans claimed that these prisoners had returned to camps in China and North Korea.

Monday morning, 21 December, began on a positive note. We paid a courtesy call on the chairman of the Supreme People's Assembly, Yang Hyon Sop, a relative by marriage of Kim Il Sung. A tour of the enormous Mansudae Supreme People's Assembly Hall followed. Afterwards, to our amazement, we headed to the war museum. There we even explored the basement and photographed a floor-to-ceiling collage of pictures that depicted hundreds of American POWs being marched to prison camps. Piled on the floor in front of the display were hundreds of American rifles, helmets, uniforms, personal belongings and regimental battle flags. The display was designed to convince North Koreans that their army had defeated the United States 'imperialist' army.

Senator Smith impressed the North Koreans with his earnestness, patience, candor and adroit handling of sensitive issues. The visit succeeded beyond expectations. Only the UNC in Seoul was uncomfortable because the delegation's success posed a threat to its continuing management of the MIA issue. Thereafter, DPMO and State would play the lead role in handling the issue.

6 UNC-KPA TALKS RESUME

The UNC and KPA signed a new Agreement on Remains-related Matters on 24 August 1993. It supplemented and expanded upon the more general terms of the Korean War armistice regarding this issue. Both sides affirmed their willingness to co-operate in 'locating, exhuming, repatriating and identifying remains of UNC personnel north of the MDL [Military Demarcation Line].' For the first time the US military agreed to 'render support' to the North Korean army's efforts and to form a working group of technical specialists and observers to settle the specifics of recovery and identification procedures.

No sooner had the agreement been signed than progress ceased. The KPA interpreted 'render support' to mean that the UNC owed it

US$3 million to compensate for costs associated with the remains repatriated between 1990 and 1993. This impasse persisted until the spring of 1996. In September 1994, CILHI sought to break it by inviting a KPA delegation to Hawaii for talks, but the invitation was declined.

6.1 *Return to the Pyongyang War Museum*

Meanwhile, the Agreed Framework had been signed in October 1994 and its implementation initiated. My stint as the State Department liaison between the US spent fuel team and the North Korean General Bureau of Atomic Energy required my living several months at Yŏngbyŏn during 1995. Thus in October 1995 I again visited the Korean War museum in Pyongyang, where I photographed the military identification cards of five American airmen whose B-29 bomber had been shot down near Pyongyang.

Back in Washington, the photographs of the ID cards confirmed that they belonged to five previously unaccounted for military personnel. DPMO then asked me to contact the DPRK mission to the UN. With State's approval, I informed Han Song Ryol, minister at the DPRK's New York mission, of the US government's interest in obtaining more information about the five airmen. Shortly thereafter Kim Byong Hong, director of the North Korean Institute for Disarmament and Peace, hinted during a New York visit that the impasse over compensation might end if it was discussed through a civilian rather than a military channel. Han contacted David Brown, director of the State Department's Office of Korea Affairs, to tell him that 'Kim Byong Hong is the person in the MFA responsible for the remains issue.' Han inquired if the September 1994 CILHI invitation was still available. Brown asked DPMO about this and a new invitation was promptly issued for seven DPRK officials to visit CILHI to resume talks.

6.2 *Aloha Hawaii*

US and North Korean authorities agreed to convene talks in Honolulu from 10 to 12 January 1996, but stormy weather delayed the start until 12 January. The US Army did its best to impress the DPRK delegation, the first time KPA members had visited the US. On 12 January the two delegations headed to Hickam Air Force Base near Pearl Harbor. The chief delegates were General James W. Wold (retired) of the US Army, who was assistant secretary of defense for POW/MIA affairs, and Senior Colonel Pak Rim Su of the KPA's P'anmunjŏm mission. The KPA gave me a copy of their talking points to ensure that their position was clearly understood. Pak declared that the DPRK had already fulfilled its requirements under the Korean War armistice regarding the issue of prisoners of war and missing in action. But since North Korea considered the issue a humanitarian one, it had continued discussions with the UNC. He concluded that the negotiations at P'anmunjŏm had become 'a spinning wheel talk only to come to a deadlock.'

In classic KPA negotiating style, Pak declared that the US position remained unacceptable. He claimed that 'our soldiers are strongly protesting against the US remains recovery, enraged by the continuous hostile policy of the US against our country. Since the US is making a preparation for a military adventure against us, we cannot but take counter-measures to cope with it' (a reference to the annual spring US-South Korea joint military exercise Team Spirit.) Pak continued that '... if the remains issue can be solved smoothly, the hostility and belligerence should be removed' between our two countries and added '... and the hostile policy of the US against us should be removed.' To drive his point home, Pak reiterated: 'Only when the US promise to remove hostile policy and take practical measures complying with the spirit of the [1994] DPRK-US framework agreement, can our people and army men believe it.' His comments continue to echo twelve years later at all US-North Korea talks.

Senior Colonel Pak then raised compensation. He asserted that '... priority should be given to the discussion of the issue of compensation for the labour [*sic*] work, material, equipment and facilities used up and damaged in searching for, disinterring and identifying the US remains.' (It may be noted that none of the remains returned up to that point could be identified because no information had been supplied about where they had been found or any other details. Furthermore, some of the remains had been mixed together, making it impossible to separate them by individual.)

The US delegation had come prepared to reach quick agreement on the compensation issue in the hope of moving to an agreement on joint recovery operations. According to DPMO's draft agreement dated 14

January 1996, the UNC would agree to reimburse the DPRK US $2 million, and 1 February 1996 in P'anmunjŏm had been selected as the date and place for payment. But the KPA demanded US$3 million, a sum which DPMO rejected. Clearly the KPA was in control of the North Korean delegation, and MFA officials were primarily observers. The talks quickly came to resemble the verbal dueling that characterized MAC meetings at P'anmunjŏm rather than the diplomatic negotiations that had produced the Agreed Framework. By the afternoon of the first day, the talks reached an impasse when Pak rejected the idea of joint recovery operations pending agreement on compensation.

That evening I sat with Ja Song Nam,[2] head of the MFA politico-military affairs section. I had met him at the time of Senator Bob Smith's visit to Pyongyang. At the Honolulu talks, Ja sought to find common ground so that the talks might end on a positive note. He intended to formulate a joint statement that would list areas of agreement and disagreement to be addressed at future talks, but its discussion was deferred until after both delegations had toured CILHI. When the talks resumed, the atmosphere quickly turned sour. Pak pressed for more compensation. For him and his KPA colleagues, the goal was victory, not compromise and co-operation. This exhausted the patience of the Defense Department delegates. Early the next morning the KPA delegation was sent to the airport for an early return to Pyongyang. Clearly the KPA had mistakenly assumed that the US was so eager to resume the repatriation effort that it would accommodate all of the North Korean wishes. Later Defense released a neutrally worded press release that concluded: 'The talks failed to resolve any of the problems that have blocked progress on this important humanitarian issue.' On 20 January, once the DPRK delegation had reached Pyongyang, the MFA released a rather harshly worded statement that read in part, 'DPRK-US talks on the remains of GIs were held in Hawaii at the proposal of the US from 11-14 January. ... a

[2] In December 1994, Ja had almost died when an army car rushing him to P'anmunjŏm crashed near Kaesŏng. The MFA had dispatched him to P'anmunjŏm to confirm that the helicopter incident (see Section 4) had been resolved and that the KPA should release the detained US pilot and his dead companion's remains. Along the way, an elderly Korean woman abruptly appeared on the highway in front of the speeding car, causing the car to crash. Two army officers died and Ja and the driver were seriously injured. Despite several broken bones and serious cuts, Ja continued his journey in another car to deliver the North Korean orders. Only then did he go to the hospital. In 2006, after service in New York, Ja became the DPRK ambassador to the United Kingdom.

complete agreement could not be reached owning to the unreasonable stand of the US side.'

6.3 *Return to the negotiating table*

At first glance the MFA statement was disheartening. It suggested that the impasse would persist, but there was a subtle reason for optimism. Until then the KPA had played the lead role on the remains issue but the MFA had issued the statement. This suggested that the MFA might take over from the army. Confirmation of this came three weeks later when Han Song Ryol on 13 February 1996 in an oral message to the State Department's Korea desk explained his government was prepared to resume the remains negotiations in late February or early March in P'anmunjŏm. Han also expressed confidence that major outstanding issues, i.e. compensation and recovery operations, could be resolved.

At the time the MFA had Kim Jong Il's confidence. Distanced from its long-time allies China and Russia, North Korea in 1996 appeared on the brink of economic and even political collapse. Its economy was bankrupt, its foreign trade had evaporated and its people were suffering famine.

Kim Jong Il, it could be argued, saw successful implementation of the Agreed Framework as imperative for his regime's survival and thus was eager to project a co-operative attitude toward the US. This was indicated when he personally hosted a dinner to honor the DPRK negotiating team and promoted its members. Subsequently they complained about but demonstrated patience with the erratic deliveries of heavy fuel oil, the stymied opening of liaison offices, and tardy US initiation of the spent nuclear fuel project. The KPA, however, had persisted in its traditional belligerent attitude toward the US government. Possibly to soften the North's image and to project a more co-operative face to the US Congress and Department of Defense, the MFA assumed primary responsibility for the MIA negotiations. This suggests that Kim Jong Il decided to relieve the KPA of this task, a decision neither the ministry nor the army had the authority to make.

6.4 *The New York agreement*

On 1 March 1996, the State Department responded positively to the North's overture to resume the remains talks. Instead of meeting in P'anmunjŏm, the Korea desk at State and the DPMO concurred on reconvening in New York in late April. The MFA agreed in principle, but Senior Colonel Pak insisted on meeting his UNC counterpart Colonel Ormes on 20 March in P'anmunjŏm. Again, Pak's foremost concern was compensation. Ormes deflected Pak's repeated demands that the compensation issue be resolved before the proposed April talks. Pak finally accepted the fact that the KPA could not get any money until formal talks reconvened in New York.

Pak's efforts convinced US officials that the MFA and the KPA were pursuing separate goals. The army's objective was to get US dollars, but the MFA was more interested in building positive relations and political capital with the US. Sensitivity to these divergent goals helped ensure success for the US at the New York talks. Nevertheless, some in the US government remained convinced that the North Koreans were trying to manipulate US negotiators by playing a game of 'good cop, bad cop'. All the while, Defense and State kept the ROK government informed about the negotiations on the remains of missing personnel. They emphasized that the issue was a humanitarian, not a bilateral political matter. While the US was glad to keep the ROK fully informed, it emphasized that South Korean involvement was unnecessary and undesired.

On 24 April, I contacted a senior DPRK diplomat in New York about his country's response to the US invitation to reconvene MIA talks in New York, then scheduled for early May. My contact told me that the KPA was reluctant to accept the US invitation and suggested that the US propose new dates for the talks. He said the KPA believed it was gaining nothing from its co-operation. The same official indicated that his government was ready to approve compensation worth US$2 million and suggested that the US be prepared to make the payment when the talks resumed in New York. As for the US primary concern—joint recovery operations—the diplomat said his government accepted the proposal in principle but specifics would have to be worked out in technical talks. On 29 April, Han informed State that his government would resume the MIA remains talks in New York on 4 May 1996 and provided the names of the DPRK delegates. Kim Byong Hong, not Senior Colonel Pak would head the delegation.

The talks convened on 4 May. From the start they did not go well. Compensation immediately emerged as the problem. Kim Byong Hong repeated the North Korean demand for US$3 million and General Wold countered with US$1 million. After several exchanges, Richard Christenson, State deputy director for Korea affairs, reiterated Wold's position and urged the DPRK to demonstrate 'sincerity'. This visibly displeased Kim. Toward the end of the morning session, Wold doubled the US offer to US$2 million but Kim still expressed dissatisfaction. The session ended inconclusively.

At dinner that evening, Kim Byong Hong, who was suffering from a cold and jet lag, complained that the US offer of US$2 million was unacceptable but reiterated his government's readiness to move forward on the MIA issue. Pak Sok Gyun, deputy director of the MFA's North American division, complained that the rhetoric had become unnecessarily heated, a reference to Christenson's comment that discussion of the Agreed Framework was unwarranted and that the DPRK should demonstrate sincerity. Pak reiterated that the DPRK had already demonstrated its sincerity regarding the Agreed Framework and resolution of the missing in action issue. Kim followed up on Pak's comments, saying he had come to negotiate with Wold and 'no one else'. This too was a clear reference to Christenson's frequent interjections during the morning session. Kim concurred with Pak's earlier assessment that the KPA saw the US commitment to the Agreed Framework as being 'empty since it had given nothing except the symbolic gesture of lifting of sanctions.' He pointed out that KEDO, not the US government, was providing heavy fuel oil.

The talks resumed on Monday morning after the DPRK delegation had recovered and also had received additional instructions from Pyongyang. Christenson had returned to Washington. Although the 6 May discussions again proved inconclusive, the DPRK appeared to be probing the US side's resolve regarding its US$2 million offer. Once convinced that the US would not give more, the DPRK accepted the offer. Kim then agreed in principle to the holding of joint recovery operations by the US Army and the KPA. That evening the UNC/MAC representatives expressed displeasure with DPMO's handling of the negotiations. Wold, however, had the support of the White House and the Defense and State departments and overruled UNC's objections.

On the morning of 9 May 1996, Wold and Kim signed the New York Agreement on USA-DPRK Remains Talks. It reads as follows:

1. The US side expresses appreciation to the DPRK side for its past sincere efforts in recovering and returning 162 sets of US servicemen's remains. The US side will pay the DPRK side two million US dollars during the week of 20 May at Panmunjom for the costs associated with labor, materials, equipment and facilities used by the DPRK.
2. Both sides agreed to a working level meeting during the first half of June at a place to be determined. At this meeting, they will discuss the specific timing, sites, personnel and all other necessary requirements, including any reimbursement for expenses in support of these joint recovery operations. Both sides expect this technical meeting will result in joint recovery operations this year.
3. Both sides express their belief that this agreement in New York City will contribute to the improvement of US-DPRK relations.

James W. Wold (signed) Head of the US delegation Deputy Assistant Secretary of Defense for POW/MIA Affairs	Kim Byong Hong (signed) Head of the DPRK delegation Director, Ministry of Foreign Affairs

(Written note: Both sides agreed this compensation would not serve as a precedent for any future compensation.)

6.5 *Paying compensation*

Payment of the US$2 million was set for 20 May in P'anmunjŏm, but the transaction proved far more complex than anyone could have imagined. Furthermore, the amount excited claims among the program's critics that the US government had 'bought' the remains of missing personnel from the KPA to the benefit of Kim Jong Il's regime. Actually the principle of compensation followed the precedent set by the US MIA recovery effort in Vietnam. That program provided the Vietnamese government agreed-upon reimbursement for specific expenses such as a laborer's daily salary, compensation for farmland or forest disturbed during excavation, the cost of transporting personnel, food, and supporting equipment to and from recovery sites, and other expenses.

In the case of North Korea, it was impossible to specify compensation for expenses connected to the remains returned during 1990-93. Instead, DPMO preferred to settle the matter with a single, lump-sum payment. The Vietnam JRO schedule of reimbursement would be applied to all future operations in North Korea, a matter to be determined at future technical talks. Although groundless, critics' claims that the KPA was paid for remains persisted and gradually eroded public support for the US Army-KPA joint operations

6.6 *Congressman Richardson's visit*

One of the more bizarre incidents involving the MIA recovery effort occurred during US Congressman Bill Richardson's second visit to North Korea. Richardson,[3] a Democrat and personal friend of President Clinton, had first visited Pyongyang in December 1994 during the US-KPA helicopter incident (see Section 4 above). He attempted unsuccessfully to obtain the release of the surviving American pilot and his deceased companion. He next visited Pyongyang in May 1996 shortly after the New York MIA agreement had been signed. Alan Liotta, deputy head of DPMO, and Richard Christenson, deputy head at the State Department's Korea desk, accompanied him. Again the Congressman's assertive tendencies, already apparent on his first visit, almost sparked a bilateral incident.

Liotta had briefed the congressman about the New York accord before the visit and while in Pyongyang settled with the MFA the dates and place for technical talks on the US Army-KPA joint recovery operations. At some point, while Liotta was resting, Richardson proposed to MFA officials that the DPRK accept food aid as compensation for the repatriation of future MIA remains. When Liotta learned this, he pointed out that this would be inconsistent with the 9 May New York Agreement and established DPMO policy. Christenson sought the view of the National Security Council (NSC) via telephone about the congressman's offer, but the NSC rejected it and apparently reminded the congressman that US law bars members of Congress from negotiating on behalf of the US government.

Richardson withdrew his offer, but not without consequences. His departure from Pyongyang was delayed for several hours while the KPA tried to convince him to win US approval of his food aid offer. The KPA finally relented and Richardson belatedly departed. DPMO did not again seek the advice or assistance of Congressman Richardson and Richard Christenson.

---

[3] Richardson later served in Clinton's cabinet as secretary of energy and ambassador to the UN.

7 Joint US Army-KPA recovery operations

Technical talks to establish procedures for the first operation commenced near Pyongyang on 8 June 1996. North Korean army experts accompanied by MFA officials met their American counterparts Colonel Bill Jordan, Captain Mario Garcia, Sergeant Frank Tauanuu (all of CILHI), together with Lieutenant Colonel Martin Wisda of DPMO and the author from the State Department.

When Senior Colonel Pak joined the talks, progress slowed. His aim was to squeeze the US for as much money as possible for each category of compensation. Patience soon dissipated. At 3am the MFA intervened and an agreement was hammered out. Discussion of specific compensation amounts was deferred until the operation had commenced.

Ten US personnel were authorized to enter North Korea to conduct JRO #1. Eight CILHI experts would live and work at the JRO work site near Unsan, about 150 miles north of Pyongyang near the DPRK-China border. Two US personnel, Wisda and the author, would provide liaison between the JRO field team, the North Korean MFA and the US government while residing at the Koryo Hotel in Pyongyang. Upwards of 90 KPA soldiers would provide security and labor while the US side would supply sufficient food, equipment and vehicles to support all JRO members living in the field for 20 days.

7.1 *Logistical problems*

Two developments complicated logistical support. The schedule for the joint recovery operation required that all US personnel, equipment and food arrive in North Korea by 9 July, just three weeks after the agreement had been reached. In addition, the Defense Attaché at the US Beijing Embassy disallowed any support from his office to the operation.

DPMO turned to me for assistance. Only one US company then had legal permission to do business with the DPRK. Daniel Murphy, a retired US Navy admiral and former CIA deputy director, had established Nikko of New Jersey in 1989 to export up to one billion US dollars' worth of goods to meet 'basic human needs' to North Korea using a US government license issued by the Department of Commerce. He teamed up with a Korean-American rice dealer and together they exported several millions of dollars' worth of grain to North Korea between 1990 and 1993. When North Korea defaulted on payment, Murphy sold his half of the company to his partner who formed a new company called B&B. B&B retained the license which enabled it to do business with North Korea. CILHI had no recourse but to rely on B&B, which had a branch office in Beijing, to provide logistical support for the first joint recovery operation.

B&B purchased eight Jeep Cherokees, three cargo trucks, a micro bus, tents and other camping equipment and food. Air Koryo was contracted to transport the equipment and food from Beijing to Pyongyang. Each of three flights cost the standard international fee of US $30,000, paid in advance.

7.2 *JRO advance team*

The JRO advance team consisted of Major Cohen of DPMO, Sergeant Tauanuu of CILHI and myself. We reached Pyongyang on 4 July. There a KPA officer accosted us in the airport parking lot, where he labeled us representatives of a 'hostile military force', which required that we be placed in detention. Instead of being sent to the Koryo Hotel, we were temporarily housed in Kobongsan Guest House outside Pyongyang. We then endured three days of harassment at the hands of this intensely anti-American official. He denied all our requests, including permission to make telephone calls. After repeated confrontations, I told him that unless he allowed me to visit the MFA, North Korea's Olympic Team would not be able to obtain visas to attend the 1996 Olympiad in Atlanta in Georgia. When I showed him the letter I had from the US Embassy in Beijing that invited North Korea's Olympic contestants to apply for visas, he directed that I be driven to the MFA. No sooner had I told my diplomatic counterpart of our plight than he arranged for us to be moved to the Koryo Hotel and thereafter we met daily with Mr. Ja from the MFA.

The first cargo flight arrived at 1:30am on 8 July. Our KPA hosts guided us to the Soviet-built IL-76 jet as it parked. The opening of the large rear doors revealed much more than the JRO cargo. Two Isuzu cargo trucks (each filled with bottled water purchased in China) and a Jeep Cherokee were slowly backed out of the airplane. A cargo pallet filled with CILHI equipment followed. Then emerged four huge tires, a US-made Hewlett-Packard computer server and other communication equipment, all addressed to the DPRK Ministry of Telecommunication, plus cases of European wine and liquor. We had been told that taking pictures was permitted, but when Tauanuu photographed the cargo, a KPA officer seized his camera. A few minutes later, however, it was returned, the offending KPA officer disappeared and another officer commended the sergeant's restraint. The cargo was stored in nearby warehouses pending customs clearance. Two KPA officers spent the night with the cargo in the mosquito-infested and sweltering warehouses.

Two more cargo flights arrived early on 9 July with seven Jeep Cherokees, tents, small generators, propane gas stoves and related equipment plus a ton of rice and a variety of condiments and fresh vegetables. The sight of the Jeeps angered Senior Colonel Pak, and a KPA officer tried to pry the Jeep symbol from one vehicle. Pak claimed the KPA would be embarrassed to drive Jeeps while the UN World Food Program used much more expensive Toyota Land Cruisers. His grumbling ended after it was explained that the US-designed jeeps had been purchased to minimize possible criticism from the US Congress.

The absence of US Army 'meals ready to eat' became a much more contentious issue. Colonel Jordan had promised at the technical talks to supply sufficient such meals for 90 persons for 20 days, but then CILHI decided against this. Colonel Pak accused CILHI of 'insincerity' and of failing to keep its promises. Resolution finally came after DPMO authorized the provision of sufficient money to the KPA to purchase beef and other fresh food for the operation's North Korean army members.

As soon as customs officials had cleared the JRO team's gear, it was loaded in the trucks and driven north to the JRO site by KPA drivers. The trip took nearly six hours over first an expressway and then very rough, unpaved roads. Upon arrival, Major Joyner, team leader of the US JRO, received the following written statement:

> Warning Notes for the Personnel of the US Side
>
> 1. Recovery works of the remains shall be stopped immediately and all the personnel of the US side be withdrawn from recovery site in case that they make or take disgraceful remarks and acts against the Great Leader [Kim Il Sung] and our respected Supreme Commander [Kim Jong Il], or make statements slandering our socialist system and that they take pictures and make video tapes recording the ob-

jects which has nothing to do with the recovery work of the remains without our permission.

2. The personnel of the U.S. side is not allowed to go out of this area [camp and working site] or go to a village in the vicinity and meet soldiers and people.
3. The personnel of the U.S. side shall use telephone in Hyangsan Hotel [*Comment*: more than a two-hour trip over rough dirt roads] when they need to have telephone communication with their personnel staying in Pyongyang and use of any communication instrument is not allowed.
4. Those who violate these rules shall be punished according to the law of our country.

Only once during the nine years of the joint recovery operations was a US JRO member expelled from the DPRK for verbally confronting a KPA officer in front of KPA enlisted men. Armed KPA guards, rain, heat and humidity together with isolation made for miserable living conditions at the JRO camp. A small amount of water was provided each day for washing, but no bathing facilities were available. The KPA soldiers ate freshly cooked meals twice a day but the Americans survived on 'meals ready to eat' and canned food that they had brought with them from Hawaii. Everyone drank bottled water brought from China.

7.3 *JRO liaison team*

Meanwhile Lieutenant Colonel Wisda and I lived at the Koryo Hotel. Every other day we traveled to the JRO site because there was no other means of communication. We took with us what fresh food we could purchase. At the site, we reviewed the situation with the JRO team leader. If an issue could not be resolved quickly at the site, I would visit the MFA the next day in Pyongyang to discuss the matter with an MFA counterpart. This proved mutually beneficial because it minimized the risk of confrontation at the site while facilitating smooth co-operation for both sides.

In Pyongyang, the liaison team worked with the MFA to establish a medical evacuation plan from the JRO site to Pyongyang, surveyed medical facilities in Pyongyang, and negotiated successfully an air evacuation route by US Air Force aircraft from Pyongyang to Japan. We also traveled to P'anmunjŏm to arrange for the repatriation of Corporal LeBoeuf's remains to the UNC on 29 July.

7.4 *A bitter-sweet end*

Unfortunately, the first joint recovery operation ended on a negative note. Senior Colonel Pak continued to press for maximum compensation despite having agreed to accept fixed sums for specific expenses. The last day of the JRO's stay in Pyongyang ended with the KPA officers demanding enormous sums of money, which the US side rejected. When the KPA persisted in its claims the following morning, the entire US group boarded their vehicles and headed for the airport and their flight to Beijing. Stunned, the KPA assumed that the MFA would bar our departure. When this failed to happen, a North Korean army colonel rushed to the airport and demanded payment. Since all of the Americans had processed through immigration when he arrived, he could not reach them. I was directed to tell the KPA officer that he could either accept payment as determined according to the agreed guidelines, or get nothing. When he reluctantly agreed to the offered amount, I paid him and had him sign a receipt confirming that he had received full payment. The US team then departed. Colonel Pak was furious but helpless. The MFA must have facilitated our departure.

8 The JRO Endeavor in its Political and Historical Context

Relatively speaking, the first joint recovery operation went fairly smoothly. There were numerous minor confrontations, disagreements and misunderstandings, but each was resolved through patient dialogue, several with the MFA's help. After all, this was the first time in history that members of the two still hostile armies had worked together. It had taken years for politicians, private veterans organizations, soldiers and diplomats from the US, North Korea and South Korea to overcome a half-century of intense hatred, distrust and superpower rivalry to initiate the US Army-KPA joint recovery operations. Inaugurated in July 1996, the JROs continued until May 2005.

The JROs proved more successful in terms of their duration and the extent of US-North Korea co-operation than anyone could have foreseen. Literally hundreds of soldiers from two hostile armies experienced working together. Thousands of ordinary North Korean citizens in Pyongyang and the countryside saw American soldiers riding with and working with members of the KPA. Hundreds of North Korean airline stewardesses, customs officials, drivers, hotel clerks, waiters and waitresses, cleaning personnel, museum guides and farmers witnessed the peaceful return of the American army to North Korea.

During the near decade of co-operation, no American soldier in North Korea experienced any willful harm at the hands of North Koreans or committed any serious offense against a North Korean or the government. Despite tense, difficult and highly regulated living conditions, all American soldiers in the JRO program conducted themselves in a manner that belied the highly distorted image of American soldiers and citizens that the DPRK government had projected to the North Korean people for almost half a century.

The operations ultimately located and returned to the US the remains of nearly 500 American soldiers missing in North Korea since the Korean War and which now await identification at the US Army's Central Identification Laboratory in Hawaii.

Another largely ignored benefit was the ability of the US Army to survey what was happening in much of North Korea. During the subsequent spring, summer and fall operations, American military personnel were permitted to travel far beyond Pyongyang and pass through most of North Korea's provinces, including areas closed to UN and foreign humanitarian organizations. During these trips it was possible to determine normal and abnormal patterns of activity. The KPA actually assisted in this regard by allowing the American soldiers increasing access to wider areas for their travel to former battle fields. Never before had the US military been able to assess so accurately conditions in North Korea, evaluate its political intentions, and witness the levels of economic and military activity.

The North Korean MFA considered the presence of American soldiers an informal but effective guarantee that the US would not attack while recovery teams were present. This acquired increasing importance after President Bush declared in 2002 his strategy of pre-emptive strike against any nation he felt threatened US security and after he pronounced North Korea to be a member of the 'axis of evil'.

A decade of joint effort is too brief to erase a half-century of animosity between two nations, two governments and two armies. Sadly, the greater the JROs' success, the more resolute became their opponents in the US administration to end them. From the very beginning, ranking US officers in the UNC saw the operations as undermining their authority and that of the MAC in its oversight of the Korean War armistice. Some South Korean politicians and political pundits claimed that the program's compensation of expenses sustained the

North Korean dictatorship at a time when it appeared near collapse. Even some members of American humanitarian organizations shared such views.

Overlooked was the reality that the US Army had peacefully returned to North Korea and had worked without incident with its arch-enemy. This accomplishment came when the US government was wrestling diplomatically with North Korea to end its nuclear weapons and ballistic missile programs, and South-North Korean hostility often flared to the brink of war. Indirectly, the joint recovery operations gave cooler heads in each government reason to resolve differences through dialogue rather than confrontation.

The JRO success began in 1996 and 1997 just as official North Korean confidence in the US government's ability to implement the 1994 Agreed Framework was waning. Many in the US administration sought to separate the JRO effort from the Agreed Framework, insisting it was 'humanitarian' and unrelated to the politically oriented Agreed Framework. But the DPRK never accepted this. It insisted that the two elements were 'simultaneous steps' linked to the primary goal of achieving normal bilateral US-DPRK relations. After all, this interpretation was consistent with the preconditions that the US government had set forth at the January 1992 bilateral talks.

North Korea insisted that its co-operation with the recovery operations obliged the US to respond in kind by intensifying efforts to more effectively implement the Agreed Framework. Specifically this meant, between 1996 and 1998, regular deliveries of heavy fuel oil and intensified efforts to begin building the two nuclear light water reactors promised in the Agreed Framework. In fact, effective implementation of both elements began in 1998 only after the South Korean government took over responsibility for funding and managing KEDO. By then North Korean critics of the Agreed Framework formed a potent chorus that challenged US credibility regarding implementation of the accord. As evidence, they pointed to the growing number of congressmen who attacked the Agreed Framework as an example of 'appeasement' and as supporting a totalitarian regime insensitive to human rights. Congress gradually approved measures that restricted the US government's ability to effectively implement the agreement. When the Bush administration entered the White House in 2001, it moved to either re-negotiate or to discard the Agreed Framework.

Ultimately critics of both the Agreed Framework and the joint recovery operations achieved their goal. In 2002, the Bush administration discarded the Agreed Framework, claiming that the DPRK had failed to fulfill its commitments. At the end of May 2005, US Secretary of Defense Donald Rumsfeld, citing unspecified threats to US military personnel involved with the JROs in North Korea, ordered a unilateral halt to them. US Secretary of State Rice promptly proclaimed that she, not Rumsfeld, oversaw US policy toward North Korea; but the damage had been done. The KPA immediately declared that co-operation had ended and was unlikely to resume. Ever since, not a single member of the US military has been able to work in North Korea or to engage their North Korean counterparts in rational dialogue. And the US military is once again blind to what is happening inside North Korea.

Meanwhile, the memories of co-operation are fading, while the remains of Corporal LeBoeuf's fellow soldiers await recovery and return to their homeland.

List of Abbreviations

ACDA	Arms Control and Disarmament Agency
CILHI	Central Identification Laboratory, Hawaii (US Army)
CODEL	Congressional delegation
DPMO	Department of Defense Prisoners of War and Missing in Action Office
EAP/K	State Department Bureau of East Asia and Pacific Affairs, Office of Korea Affairs
IAEA	International Atomic Energy Agency
JRO	Joint recovery operation
KEDO	Korean Peninsula Energy Development Organization
KPA	Korean People's Army (DPRK)
MAC	Military Armistice Commission
MFA	Ministry of Foreign Affairs (DPRK)
MIA	Missing in action
NPT	Treaty on the Non-proliferation of Nuclear Weapons
NSC	National Security Council (USA)
POW	Prisoner of war
PRC	People's Republic of China
UN	United Nations
UNC	United Nations Command

REFERENCES

Published sources

Galucci, Robert, Daniel Poneman and Joel Wit (2003), *Going Critical: The First North Korean Nuclear Crisis*, Washington DC: Brookings Institute

Korean Central News Agency (1999), 'Selected Disarmament Policy [*sic*] of DPRK (1971-1996)', in: *People's Korea* website. Online: www.korea-np.co.jp/pk

Oberdorfer, Donald, (1997), *The Two Koreas: A Contemporary History*, Reading MA: Addison-Wesley

Paik Sun Yup, (1992), *From Pusan to Panmunjom*, New York: Brassey's

Ridgeway, Matthew B.(1967), *The Korean War*, Garden City NY: Doubleday

Sigal, Leon (1998), *Disarming Strangers: Nuclear Diplomacy with North Korea,* Princeton NJ: Princeton University Press

Unpublished official sources

1992 congressional delegation led by Senator Smith

16 December, EAP/K press guidance, 'CODEL Smith'

22 December, US Senate Select Committee on POW/MIA Affairs, press release, 'Senator Smith Discusses Historic Visit to Asia Concerning American POWs from the Korean and Vietnam Conflicts',

1993 January, DPMO, 'CODEL Smith US-PRC POW/MIA Talks in Beijing July 1992 and January 1993'

12 February, C. Kenneth Quinones, CODEL Smith EAP/K memorandum

24 August, 'Agreement on Remains-related Matters'

1996 US-DPRK remains negotiations

5 January, DPMO draft press release, 'U.S.-North Korea Meet in Honolulu'

5 January, DPMO press release, 'U.S.-North Korea Meet on POW/MIA Issues'

10 January, DPMO, 'US draft agreement'

12 January, KPA, 'Talking Points for Hawaii Talks'

14 January, DPMO press release, 'U.S.-North Korea Unable to Resolve Key Issues on Korean War Remains'

14 January, DPMO, Draft memo of agreement on US-DPRK POW/MIA discussions

20 January, Foreign Broadcast Information Service report, 'MFA Statement–DPRK Official Calls U.S. Stand at Remains Talks "Unreasonable"'

1 March, Oral message to DPRK UN Mission Counselor Han Song-ryol

15 March, Oral message to DPRK UN Mission Counselor Han Song-ryol

22 March, memorandum from Secretary, UNC/MAC to Joint Staff Washington/J5, 'UNC-KPA Meeting 20 March 1996'

18 April, DPMO, memorandum for the record, 'Pre-brief of ROK DATT on Upcoming Remains Talks with DPRK Delegation'

24 April, DPMO, memorandum for the record, 'Remains Talks with North Koreans'

29 April, DPRK UN Mission, official correspondence, 'Letter to EAP/K on Remains Talks'

1 May, DPMO, 'US and DPRK Delegations to 4-7 May New York Talks'

3 May, DPMO, memorandum, 'Talking Points: Remains Talks with North Koreans, 4-6 1996'
4 May, C. Kenneth Quinones, 'Notes on US-DPRK MIA Talks, May 4, 1996'
7 May, DPMO press release, 'US-North Korea to Cooperate on Korean War Remains Issues'
9 May, DPMO, 'New York Agreement on USA-DPRK Remains Talks'
12 May, DPMO, Department of Defense, 'Travel Orders for Quinones'
25 May, DPRK UN Mission, official correspondence, 'Letter to EAP/K David Brown on Remains Talks'
25 May, DPMO Note to DPRK UN Mission, 'Subject: Venue/Arrangements for Korean War Remains Working-level Talks'

1996 JRO #1
22 June, Quinones, memorandum to Han Song-ryol, 'US Joint Recovery Operation Team'
5 July, Quinones, fax to EAP/K, 'JRO Advance Team Arrives Pyongyang'
7 July, Quinones, fax to EAP/K, 'All Equipment Arrives'
7 July, DPMO memorandum, 'List of JRO Advance Team's Concerns'
8-30 July, Quinones, hand-written diary
8 July, Quinones, fax to EAP/K, 'Situation Report'
8 July, Quinones, fax to B&B/Beijing, 'Propane Gas Delivery'
10 July, Quinones, fax to EAP/K, 'JRO Team Arrives Pyongyang'
12 July, Quinones, fax to US Embassy Beijing, 'Request for Assistance'
15 July, Quinones, fax to EAP/K, 'Visit to JRO Site'
15 July, 'Activity Schedule for JRO Liaison Team, July 15-30'
19 July, Quinones, fax to EAP/K, 'JRO Liaison Visit to Panmunjom'
21 July, DPMO, letter to Senior Colonel Pak, 'Congratulations'
24 July, 'JRO Team Leader Situation Report'
25 July, Senior Col Pak Rim-su, 'Letter to Col Ashton Ormes'
25 July, Senior Col Pak Rim-su, 'Letter to DPMO Deputy Director'
25 July, Quinones, fax to US Embassy Beijing, Major Rounds, 'Request for Assistance'
25 July, Quinones, fax to EAP/K, 'US Remains Recovered'
25 July, Quinones, fax to US Spent Fuel Team, 'Inability to Meet in Pyongyang'
26 July, Quinones, fax to EAP/K, 'DPRK MFA Concerns Regarding US Policy'
20 July, US Embassy Seoul, 'Appointment Schedule for Ken Quinones Seoul Consultations July 30 to August 1'
18 August, Senior Colonel Pak, letter to DPMO, 'KPA Concerns and Future JROs'
19 August, Quinones, memorandum to EAP/K, 'DPRK Notice to US JRO Team'
4 October, EAP/K, 'Approved DPMO Report on JRO #1'
Undated DPRK Memorandum, 'Talking Points Regarding Calculation of Reimbursement of Expenses in Connection with JROs'

1997 Department of State, Office of Korea Affairs, unclassified information memorandum, *ca* 1997, 'U.S. Korean War Remains Recovery Issue: Diplomatic History (1985-1996)'

Press sources

1992 12 December, Korean Central News Agency (KCNA), Pyongyang, 'U.S. Senator Arrives'

18 December, Reuter, 'U.S. Sets First Visit to North Korea Since War'

18 December, Yonhap news agency, 'U.S. Senator Reportedly to Visit Pyongyang'

20 December, KCNA, Pyongyang, 'Discussions between Kang Sok-ju, Vice Chairman of the Foreign Affairs Committee of the Supreme People's Assembly and U.S. Senator Robert Smith'

20 December, KCNA, Pyongyang, 'Courtesy Call on Yang Hyong-sop, chairman of the Supreme People's Assembly'

21 December, KCNA, Pyongyang, 'Chairman Yang and Vice Chairman Kang have talks with U.S. Senator Robert Smith'

21 December, KCNA, Pyongyang, 'U.S. Senator Robert Smith and his entourage depart'

24 December, Carleton R. Bryant, 'News of POWs Buoys Relatives 40 Years Later', in: *Washington Times*

1996 15 January, Tim Weiner, 'U.S. at Least Breaks the Ice With North Korea on MIA's', in: *New York Times*, p. A9

31 July, Kwang Doo-hyung, 'U.S. Ready to Supply Information on S. Korean MIA, POWs in N. Korea', in: *Korea Herald*

9 September, Nicholas D. Kristof, 'New Account Adds to the Mystery About the Fate of American P.O.W.'s in North Korea', in: *New York Times*, pp. 10-11

BENCHMARKS OF ECONOMIC REFORM IN NORTH KOREA

Patrick McEachern[1]

ABSTRACT

North Korea's economic reform is central to debates concerning the future of that state. Reform optimists claim gradual reform promotes a peaceful and sustainable transformation, while pessimists question whether the country is pursuing reform and whether reform could change the regime. This article shows the difficulty in taking stock in reform efforts by reference to the China model. Instead, it mediates between these views by briefly sketching the general economic forces that could compel post-Communist political transformation. It then places North Korea's economic changes to date within this context. I conclude that given this perspective, North Korea's economic actions to date reside only in the least salient area of reform and are not outside of the state's control. I suggest specific areas to watch that would signal important changes in economic forces that could unravel the state.

1 INTRODUCTION

Economic reform in the Democratic People's Republic of Korea (DPRK) is central to debates concerning the future of that state. Reform optimists claim gradual reform promotes a peaceful and sustainable transformation of the regime and its external policy. Pessimists question whether the DPRK is pursuing reform—explicitly or inadvertently—and whether it could change the regime. North Korea has made significant progress in liberalizing prices and rationalizing exchange rates, some progress in reducing budget deficits, fostering credit and legalizing private enterprises, and little progress in ending

[1] For helpful comments, the author wishes to thank Bill Clark, Wonik Kim, Yong Wook Lee, the *Korea Yearbook* editors, and the participants of the Symposium on Guideposts for North Korea's Radical Economic Change, February 8–9, 2007. The views expressed in this article are those of the author and do not necessarily reflect those of the U.S. Department of State or the U.S. Government.

discrimination against private enterprise and in establishing property rights. But how does one evaluate these changes? How significant are North Korean economic decisions to date?

Theory implicitly or explicitly guides this discussion. Which economic changes are most important to force political change? Theory helps distinguish between relevant economic factors and forces from reporting everything that looks like an element of a market economy. This article briefly sketches theoretical expectations of post-Communist economic changes to highlight the importance of North Korean economic changes to date. It then places North Korean economic policy in this context. Put differently, it compares North Korean actions to not just a single country's economic transition (e.g. China's) but compares them to the common characteristics of all previous post-Communist economic reforms.

This approach has its built-in critics. There is an intuitive appeal to compare North Korea to China. Single-country examples are most comprehensible and concrete, but this comparison has been overused. China provides a normative model for the DPRK but leaves little guidance on how far along North Korea is on a transition track. This article offers an alternative metric by which to judge the pace and direction of North Korea's economic changes. These changes can be placed within a framework that provides a means to judge the significance of the state's economic changes to date. I conclude by noting how this framework can direct our attention to specific areas to watch for politically meaningful economic changes in the North.

2 Changing the Socialist System

2.1 *Cross-national model*

János Kornai (1992, 1995) explains how a classical socialist system functions and reveals the structural factors that alter the system. Reform measures must affect either the bureaucracy's policy co-ordination or large-scale property relations. The most significant stage—affecting the political structure—is sufficiently radical that Kornai labels it revolution, not reform. States can jump directly to the most central revolutionary actions, as Hungary did in 1956, or slowly progress through increasingly more salient reform measures. Table 1 ranks reform measures from the most superficial actions befitting the label 'reform' to the most revolutionary.

Table 1 Stages of economic reform

I. Bureaucratic policy coordination
- Price reforms
- Market socialism

II. Large-scale property rights
- Self-management
- Revival of private sector

III. Political structure
- Political liberalization

Source: Kornai 1992.

The first group of changes reflects changes in the mode of policy co-ordination. First, the introduction of some price reforms such as removing subsidies and allowing the market to determine values in limited circumstances undermines the bureaucracy's policy co-ordination role. The state attempts to raise revenue and increase efficiency with markets at the expense of strict administrative control. As will be demonstrated, prices that reflect market values are a prerequisite for each of the following reforms, except political liberalization.

Under the second, more significant move towards market co-ordination is the creation of 'market socialism'. This describes the economic situation when public ownership still dominates the economy, but market co-ordination becomes at least as important as the plan in allocating resources. Markets become a means of accounting for the value of goods. Critically, consumers, rather than the state, assign values to goods. Price liberalization is a prerequisite, because prices must be free to fluctuate with supply and demand in order for the market to serve this accounting function. If the state sets all or most prices, there can be little to no meaningful market. While monopolies remain in many instances, firms begin to compete with one another by offering lower prices and/or higher-quality goods and services. At this stage leaders may attempt to keep socialist politics and rhetoric but increasingly move away from socialist economics.

Property relations represent the most radical form of economic change possible prior to revolution. The first stage, self-management, removes much of the centralized control over modes of production and alters public management. Workers select their firms' leadership and collectively keep the firms' revenue (after costs and consistently-applied taxes). This creates a profit motive for workers in industry. Self-management represents a more radical departure from socialist economics but not a complete step away from socialist politics. Leaders can still argue this move is in line with socialist ideals of a stateless, democratic organization. The average workers select the leadership of the firm, not exploitive capitalists. Nevertheless, the move reduces paternalism in major business organizations. It recognizes an important, real role for workers to take responsibility for their own fortunes.

The second, deeper application of property relations is a revival of the private sector. At this stage of reform, the private sector economy and public enterprise operate in the same national market. An individual can not only keep some of a higher proportion of profit by working more, but he or she can enjoy capital returns. The state allows citizens to employ others, own part of a company, and profit from bank interest, bonds and real estate investments. Furthermore, the state's resources, such as sowing machines and transportation in agriculture, are available to individuals. While the authorities may have looked the other way at prior stages of economic reform when farmers sold part of their excess production in markets, at this stage the farmer can use or lease state resources to produce much more efficiently and on a much larger scale. This stage is radical and requires a key change in the prevailing socialist ideology.

China's family responsibility system exemplifies this type of change in property relations. In 1978, co-operatives accounted for 98 percent of agricultural production and individuals did not officially register any commercial agricultural production. By 1987, co-operatives produced 39 percent of agricultural products and individuals 57 percent. Chinese peasants could utilize state resources such as tractors and trucks to transfer their produce to market. This stage marks an explosion of the scale of market-based activities.

Finally, reform approaches revolution when economic changes alter the political structure and foster significant liberalization. These changes affect the political structure or official ideology and change the way the state operates.

This model is useful not only for what it includes, but for what it excludes. For example, there is no discussion of trade or international opening. These factors figure prominently in the reform optimists' contention. Some argue that efforts to reform the economy, open up to the outside world, and even normalize relations with its neighbors and the United States are part of a coherent package for North Korea, which stands to gain tremendous economic and political rewards for such a decision.

While important in their own right, trade and international opening are at best indicators of reform and opening, not early causes of it. To the reform optimists, these reflect at some level a political decision to change. However, it begs the question what compels North Korea's leadership to pursue trade or international opening when these same incentives have been offered for many years. This article focuses on the underlying social and economic pressures that encourage the state to change—to pursue policies that may eventually include more significant trade liberalization and international opening. It discusses how these can become forces on their own and compel political change. While efforts like price reforms are themselves political decisions as well, I show how they are linked to these underlying social and economic forces that the state cannot turn on and off at will.

2.2 *The China model*

China's broad economic success, political continuity, and influence in North Korea make it an attractive model for North Korean efforts to enhance its economic standing. Before showing how North Korean reform efforts stack up against the pattern just outlined, it is important to discuss this competing set of metrics by which to judge North Korea's reform progress.

The Chinese economic reform is an appealing normative model for the North Koreans. China is closer to North Korea geographically and culturally than the former socialist states. The Chinese economic transformation has brought tremendous, sustained economic growth while maintaining political stability. A similar model seems to have had similar benefits in Vietnam as well. China has a great deal of influence in North Korea and has actively advocated its development path to the North Koreans. Advocates of the China model contend that North Korea can benefit from following the same path and moderate its domestic and foreign policies in the process.

While China provides a good normative model, this should not be confused with an analytical model. We should not judge North

Korea's progress on the basis of China's specific actions. North Korean efforts that diverge from the China model are not necessarily counter-reform. Without comparison, one cannot determine which of China's actions were necessary components of its economic success and which were superfluous. China and North Korea do not need to follow exactly the same path in order to reach the same end. Evaluating other reform experiences as well helps bridge the gap between China's specific path and a greater range of actions that promote economic reform.

Likewise, all of the required components of China's reform are not necessarily important for a different country. China and North Korea have different starting points and economic composition, making any one-country model inherently limited to judge the state of North Korea's economic changes. While the China model seemed to work for Vietnam, North Korea's economy is substantively different from that of both of these states. At the most basic level, approximately 70 percent of China and Vietnam's labor forces worked in agriculture, making the introduction of property rights a very distinct process from the industrial Soviet bloc. China and Vietnam did not need to worry about dividing up the nation's industrial wealth with various industrial privatization schemes. Instead, agricultural policy changes proved most important. North Korea is an industrial state; less than one-third of its gross domestic product (GDP) is attributed to agriculture. Putting geography and culture aside for the moment, the economic challenges facing North Korea more closely resemble those confronting the former Soviet bloc than China or Vietnam.

Compounding the economic sector problem, North Korea's population and geography are substantially different than China's. North Korea has 1.8 percent of China's population and 1.25 percent of its landmass. This makes centralized economic control easier in North Korea and the isolation of Special Economic Zones (SEZs) more difficult (Åslund 2004).[2] This is important for understanding the political effects of North Korea's following the China model. If SEZs are more difficult to isolate from the rest of society, the DPRK has more reason to feel threatened by capitalist ideas seeping into the rest of the country. This makes SEZs more significant in North Korea than in China

[2] Of course, Vietnam also was only a fraction of the size of China in terms of population (6.4 percent of China) and landmass (3.4 percent of China), yet that country followed the Chinese model quite closely.

in general, but also means the state is more likely to restrict their activities.

Furthermore, the Chinese were exhausted from the Great Leap Forward (1958-60) and the Cultural Revolution (1966-76) in a way that has not manifested itself politically in North Korea despite the famine in the 1990s (Frank 2005: 285). Chinese élites and the masses alike suffered the peaks of revolutionary fervor during the Great Leap Forward and the Cultural Revolution and were ready for exploring an alternative. The North Korean famine is likely to have affected a portion of the state's élites and masses in the same way, but it does not appear that a similar groundswell of support has shifted in the same way. In sum, China in 1978 is more different from North Korea in 2008 than proponents of the China model often indicate.

2.3 *Other single-country models*

Single-country models from other post-Communist transitions of industrialized states are less encouraging. While they share methodological challenges with the China model and other difficulties in comparison, they remind the analyst that permanently stalled reform is a real possibility (Hellman 1998). North Korea's economic actions have been compared to Evsei Liberman's effort to introduce performance incentives and monetized accounting under the 'New Economic System' in the Soviet Union of the 1960s. These reforms were limited and did not prompt political change (Seliger 2005). Likewise, Albania shared many elements with North Korea, including very limited private ownership, distorted prices and exchange rates, fiscal crisis, a highly national socialist dictatorship, and poverty. Still, Albania did not embark on transition until the Communist bloc started to fall apart (Åslund 2004). North Korea weathered that collapse. If North Korea is on the same path as Albania, it is unclear where that path leads.

Single-country models have a difficult time detailing which conditions foster the desired changes. The question should not be how similar North Korea's economic decisions in recent years are to China's or the Soviet Union's reform paths. Rather it should be whether North Korea's economic policies are fostering real change—economic and political—in the state. For this task, comparing North Korea's actions to cross-nationally derived theory is our best option.

3 Taking stock: are North Korea's economic changes significant?

The remainder of this article assesses the state of North Korean actions in light of Kornai's theoretical guidance. The most identifiable economic changes have been concentrated in the first stage of undermining bureaucratic policy co-ordination: price reforms. While price reforms are easily identified, they are not the only economic changes the state has undertaken. North Korea has made some efforts to allow the market to allocate resources between large-scale enterprises, but the state retains a dominant role in this more salient stage of bureaucratic policy co-ordination. Efforts to establish large-scale property rights in terms of self-managing enterprises or the revival of the private sector are limited and fall far short of 'deep and permanent' measures. Finally, the state has not been fundamentally reoriented by sudden and widespread revolution.

3.1 *Bureaucratic policy co-ordination*

3.1.1 *Price reforms*

The 1 July 2002 price liberalization is the best documented and least disputed aspect of North Korea's economic actions. Prior to 2002, significant gaps between official and black market prices created arbitrage opportunities. Some individuals who could afford to pay off corrupt officials developed greater independence from the state. Possible concern with the development of these alternative power sources and an ostensible concern about the overall state of the economy culminated in the 1 July measures. The North Korean authorities had to weigh the inflation risks of closing the gap between black market and official rates against the cost of closing markets by brute force, which could spark another food crisis (Lim 2005: 6-7).

North Korea chose the market route over the administrative one. The state monetized transactions and prices skyrocketed. Prices rose on average 25-fold (Kim and Choi 2005: 7). Rice prices, originally set in 1946 and left unchanged for 56 years, jumped 550-fold by administrative decree (Table 2) (You 2004: 106). The state moderated price hikes somewhat. State prices were nominal prior to 1 July, but one could buy only a limited amount of rations from the state. To survive, North Koreans had to buy the remainder of their food on black markets. When the state restructured prices to more closely match black market prices, it imposed price ceilings on essential goods such as rice and oil. They reset prices every ten days based on supply and demand (Lee and Yoon 2004: 57).

Table 2 Prices of basic goods before and after 1 July 2002

	Rice (state)	Rice (market)	Corn (state)	Corn (market)	Electricity	Bus ride
Old price	0.08 won	60-70 won	0.49 won	25-30 won	0.035 won	0.1 won
New price	44 won	220-250 won	20 won	150-180 won	1.8 won	2 won
Price change factor	550	~4	40.82	~6	51.43	20
Purchasing power change for ordinary workers	0.033	4.5	0.445	3	0.353	0.909
Purchasing power change for prioritized professions	0.1	13.5	1.34	9	1.06	2.73

Source: Frank 2005: 296-7, 300.

By definition, North Korea experienced inflation with the rising prices. To partially offset the effect of higher prices, the state as employer raised wages. Inflation affected segments of society differently. Ordinary workers received an 18-fold rise, while skilled laborers enjoyed rises as high as 54-fold. More productive workers would also enjoy new performance pay (Lim 2005: 10-11; Kim and Choi 2005: 7). The reforms also favored new entrepreneurs who could supplement their incomes in the increasingly tolerated general markets. Former black market traders who saved their money in North Korean won lost out as the currency lost 95 percent of its domestic value (Frank 2005: 299; Noland 2003: 52). Those on a fixed income, such as pensioners, the unemployed and the disabled, generally could not engage in the market activity necessary to supplement their income; as the socialist food sector shrank, they found themselves in the most precarious economic situation that threatened their basic ability to survive.

North Korea also reformed the price of its currency. With the 1 July reforms, the authorities legalized the direct conversion of foreign currency into North Korean currency (Lee and Yoon 2004: 54). The following month, they raised the exchange rate to bring it closer to the market rate, producing a 70-fold currency devaluation (Kim and Choi 2005: 7-15; Carlin and Wit 2006: 31). North Korea had long maintained a symbolic official exchange rate with the US dollar of 2.16:1, celebrating Kim Jong Il's birthday on 16 February. However, the official exchange rate valued each dollar at 150 won by December 2002 and at 170 won by December 2004. By 2006, the official exchange valued each dollar slightly less at 141 won, while the black market rate valued each dollar at 2,500-3,000 won (CIA World Factbook 2007).

3.1.2 *Market socialism*

Discussions of North Korea's markets usually focus on the retail sector. Individuals increasingly use general markets. While this exposes a large number of North Koreans to entrepreneurship, business-to-business transactions and credit growth are more economically significant. Consumer goods are only the last transaction of a small segment of output. Many industries, most notably the privileged defense and heavy industries, have nothing to do with this retail market. Even those firms that are engaged in producing consumer goods at some stage of the production chain may only produce intermediate goods as an input for other enterprises. They do not interact with the ground-level enterprising merchant. Even the final product may be exported abroad or distributed through public channels instead of being sold in local markets. General markets are an important development, but they represent a small percentage of total transactions and do not suggest that firm-to-firm exchanges are also guided by market principles.

There has been some move to account for business-to-business trade through market mechanisms. Since 1964, North Korea's State Planning Committee emphasized 'unified and detailed planning' including regulating operations between state-owned enterprises involving both production quotas and planning procedure. It aimed to balance supply and demand through bureaucratic means but could not account for the flow of resources. The problem of tracking a large number of resources was compounded by data distortions. Enterprise managers and bureaucrats had an incentive to produce false reports, inflating production numbers. Kim Il Sung first recognized this problem in the early 1970s and the state introduced independent accounting measures and granted some managerial discretion in December 1984. Nevertheless, the efforts had limited impact. The state continued to insist on centralized control of accounting and to judge enterprises by quantity of production. Shortages further prevented managers from providing incentives to workers. In short, bureaucratic co-ordination of business-to-business transactions remained (Kim Sung Chull 2003: 15-17).

After 2002, North Korea moved seriously to monetize transactions to enhance economic efficiency. The April 2002 Finance Act sought to produce an 'increase in net profit' from state- owned enterprises, which called on managers to 'focus on generating profits'. Likewise, the March 2003 Accounting Act sought to bring about a 'reduction of the prime cost' of state-owned enterprises. The director of North Korea's State Price Discrimination Bureau, Kang Gyeong Soon, said at the time that '80% of the standard wage will be guaranteed if 80% of the plan is achieved, and 200% of the wages will be guaranteed if 200% of the plan is achieved' (Kim and Choi 2005: 15-30). Yet there is no bankruptcy mechanism or social safety net in place. Unprofitable enterprises cannot close their doors or stop paying employees, so proclamations that subsidies have ended may be overstated. Managers instead are expected to succeed, and the state, implicitly, is likely to continue to subsidize non-performing enterprises (Noland 2003: 47).

The price reforms allowed the market to value goods more effectively. The state allowed firms to trade a portion of their production with other firms, introducing an important market for raw materials and intermediate goods (Kim Il-gi 2007). The state moreover publicly emphasized profit over quantity and granted enterprise managers more discretion (Kwon 2006). Still, marketization remains partial. The state has eliminated neither planning nor political guidance. One observer noted: 'The market function seen in the North after July 1, 2002 measures outdoes the government's planning function' (Suh 2005: 21), although precise data on the extent of marketization versus planning in practice is not available.

Relations between enterprises and market-based credit sources are a critical component in replacing bureaucratic co-ordination with market co-ordination. North Korea's financial sector remains highly statist. Enterprises seeking credit must turn to the Central Bank (Mun 2006). They cannot borrow from one another directly or from individuals. Individuals cannot own partial shares in industry, buy meaningful bonds, or earn interest on bank accounts. Credit has grown only from foreign sources. The DPRK has intensified its effort to gain hard currency through a number of projects, including establishing SEZs, attracting foreign capital to profitable joint ventures, and lowering taxes and easing insurance rules for foreign investors. North Korea established the Rajin-Sonbong free trade zone in the remote northeast corner of the country in December 1991, developed the Kaesŏng Industrial Complex with South Korean capital and management, has shown tentative commitment to Sinuiju on the Chinese border, and has also earned foreign currency with the Mt Kŭmgang tourism project.

The state has reduced taxes to make its labor competitive with neighboring countries. Corporate income tax was set at 10-25 percent as opposed to 30-35 percent in Southeast Asia; transactional taxes at 1-15 percent as opposed to 30-60 percent in Southeast Asia; electricity charges were set at US$67 per 1,000 kWh as opposed to US$80-120 in neighboring countries; and water charges at US$38 per 100 m^3 as opposed to US$120-130 in neighboring countries (Kim and Choi 2005: 41-2).

The SEZs and attempts to make foreign investment conditions more favorable in North Korea are a start, but they are still quite limited. Trade shares comprised approximately 12 percent of North Korea's GDP in 2000 (Noland 2000: 61). Establishing domestic credit institutions would be a significant step towards market socialism and particularly worthy of note. North Korea has made some major, albeit partial, moves towards market socialism.

3.2 *Large-scale property rights*

The classic socialist system recognizes small-scale property rights. The state does not own everything, but it does own all the major means of production. Allowing individuals to own small garden plots or provide services for a fee, for example, is well within the socialist ideal type and does not undermine the system. Limited forms of private property are recognized in North Korean law. The Compensation Act and a constitutional amendment, the Inheritance Act, both passed in September 1998, affect small-scale North Korean owners. The Compensation Act generally 'stipulates the protection of property rights', while the Inheritance Act allows personal property such as houses, automobiles and savings to be transferred to heirs (Lim 2005:

10; Kim and Choi 2005: 12-13). Privately owned small restaurants, retail stores, casinos,[3] street entrepreneurs, private tutoring and small-plot farming (Michell 1998; Lee and Yoon 2004; Seliger 2006) have little economic impact, although one may debate their symbolic importance. Large-scale property rights mean either moves towards self-management or a more widespread revival of the private sector.

3.2.1 *Self-management*

The North Korean state has grappled with different strategies to improve enterprise efficiency for decades. Prior to the wage and price reforms of 1 July 2002, its economic policy documents cited a need for evaluating enterprises on the basis of profitability and more decentralized authority. Two years after the price reforms made market-based accounting possible, the state granted a new generation of managers more autonomy in managing enterprises. Central authorities restricted their own input in business decisions to political guidance (Choi 2005). This move allowed managers to share profits with workers, spend profits on worker welfare, or reinvest in the firm. The decision remained with the appointed manager.

However, workers do not elect their manager, one of Kornai's key points. Workers do not have a say in how profits are distributed. North Korea maintains a paternalistic system even among the changed enterprise management structure. The move decentralized authority but did not reform public management in a way that introduced a limited conception of property into these enterprises. Individual workers may receive more compensation in some form, but they do not have control over their own financial destiny in the way that property ownership allows.

3.2.2 *Revival of the private sector*

Traditional property rights are limited for North Korean citizens, but they do enjoy certain usage rights—particularly in the area of rural land development. In de Soto's definition (2000: 209-21), traditional property rights are transferable and secured by a legal system. They force owners to be accountable for how their property is utilized. They

[3] *Ed*. North Koreans are not permitted to gamble, and access to the country's few casinos is restricted to foreigners.

also allow owners to leverage their assets productively and give rise to credit. Owned assets are more than one's access to physical assets; owners can produce surplus value by merging, dividing or investing property. In short, only the owners are the capitalists, and the most significant moves toward capitalism require owners.

The DPRK introduced the work squad system pilot program to some co-operatives in 1996 to allow farmers to legally keep a portion of their excess production (Kim Young-yoon 2006), yet by 2004 the program remained restricted to two provinces (Kwon 2006). Outside the pilot program provinces, farmers use their own assets, capital, and raw materials—regardless of state or personal ownership—to produce (Kim Sung-chull 2003: 22). They attempt to sell only quota-levels of production to the state at its low prices. Likewise, other entrepreneurs outside the agricultural sector attempt to keep their own wares. Whatever the entrepreneurs can keep, he or she can sell for private gain in intermittently tolerated markets.

The state has oscillated in its policy on allowing or restricting market activity. On 5 May 2003, Cabinet Resolutions 24 and 27 officially recognized markets and established new markets, with a goal of 300 markets nationwide (Lim 2005: 12). However, by October 2005, the authorities had decided to reintroduce the Public Distribution System (PDS). Since the PDS and private farmers interested in selling agricultural surplus in markets compete with one another for the same production, North Korea took limited steps to close markets.

The inconsistency in applying property rights distorts the entrepreneurs' incentive structure. If the state is going to confiscate all production and shut down general markets in order to distribute goods publicly, then the market incentive diminishes. Entrepreneurs are unsure if they have any reason to work harder this year to produce more, especially when the production cycle takes several months as in agriculture. In short, the state has not recognized in practice firm, consistent property rights.

Foreigners have fared better. Ironically, they can leverage property in a state concerned about foreign capitalist exploitation while its own citizens largely cannot. The North Korean government encourages some foreign investment, including joint ventures and foreign ownership. A series of laws such as the Foreign Investment Law and the Contractual Joint Venture Law provide a means for foreign capital to seek profit legally. North Korean law even allows for the arbitration of business disputes. The law provides foreigners more latitude than potential domestic entrepreneurs. Foreign firms have something that potential domestic entrepreneurs do not: access to large capital outlays outside the regime's control.

North Korea has established joint ventures with Russian and Chinese partners to build shopping malls, department stores and mining operations. North Korea has also had a wavering commitment to large-scale joint ventures with foreign partners on projects such as the trans-Korean railroad, port developments and special economic zones. In addition, the North Korean government has authorized joint legal consulting offices with British, Singaporean and Italian firms in Pyongyang (Kim and Choi 2005: 41). Nevertheless, most foreign firms remain wary of doing business in the North, reducing the effect of these formal property rights institutions. While several foreign projects are large by North Korean standards, they are still few in number.

The country has not created an environment attractive to a large number of foreign investors. Despite legal pronouncements that the government will protect property rights, foreign firms may judge the risk overwhelms the prospect of returns. For example, China suspended shipping goods into North Korea by rail in 2007, because too many of the rail cars never came back. The Chinese apparently suspected that the North Koreans used the rail cars for their own domestic transport or sold the rail cars back to them as scrap metal (Fifield and McGregor 2007). In an environment where the basic mode of transport cannot be guaranteed, it is little surprise that foreign investors worry about their property not being respected.

If the role of traditional property rights is to progress beyond the symbolic effect of the state recognizing a private sphere, then property rights must be utilized in practice and businesses must be confident in their application. Ownership rights have been restricted to foreigners, and these laws do not suggest extension to domestic entrepreneurs. Indeed, one may speculate that the regime may be more comfortable politically with private wealth accumulating outside of its borders. Private wealth accumulation by its own citizens risks developing alternative power centers that owe their power only in part to the government. Whatever the reason, the effect remains the same. North Korea lacks a national private sector.

4 Conclusions

The Chinese government and three successive South Korean administrations have placed economic reform in North Korea at the top of their foreign policy strategy towards that state. If economic reform is to proceed, certain political benefits could follow. They contend that the DPRK's intention to pursue economic reform is not at the heart of the question. Policies that stimulate economic reform take on a life of their own outside of the North's complete control (Lee and Yoon 2004). Reform gives increasingly powerful individuals financial stakes in the system; these stakes help perpetuate and deepen reform (Snyder 2000). Further, creating various interests within society and inadvertently empowering those interests provides the basis of plurality. Threatening the homogenous North Korean system lays the groundwork for eventual transformation.

One should not confuse economic inducements and economic reform. Reducing tensions is generally good for international business. In 2000, Pyongyang established diplomatic relations with 14 of the then 15 European Union member states, Kim Jong Il and Kim Dae-jung held an inter-Korean summit, and North Korea and Russia signed a new friendship and cooperation treaty (Frank 2005). The DPRK pursued bilateral negotiations with Japan until early 2006. Japan held out the primary carrot of normalization of diplomatic relations, which were likely to come with significant financial reparations for the colonial period, as normalization with South Korea had brought in 1965. Kim hosted Prime Minister Koizumi in Pyongyang in 2002 and 2004 to seriously pursue these economic benefits.

These economic inducements certainly sweeten the pot for North Korea's leadership to select a reform path. But the offer has been on the table for years, and the state has not eagerly jumped at it. One can hope that North Korea will recognize the benefits of a changed strategy or one can evaluate the factors that may change the regime's outlook towards the offer. This article attempts to sketch out those economic and social forces within the state that compel the leadership to re-evaluate that offer. I have evaluated the state of the social and economic forces that the DPRK cannot turn on and off at will that could potentially unravel the existing order.

This research leads me to conclude that North Korea's limited reform actions to date do not portend meaningful political change. Instead, these data support Nicholas Eberstadt's measured conclusion that 'the reform package … remonetized a limited portion of the DPRK domestic economy … It does not, to begin, represent an unambiguous move toward market principles … Nor do they have any obvious or direct bearing on the prospects for a shift to China-style or Vietnam-style export-led growth' (Eberstadt 2004). Past efforts at reform such as the joint ventures law of 1984 and the Rajin-Sonbong economic zone project in 1991 did not produce political opening (Ahn et al. 2004). North Korea may decide to pursue a path towards economic reform, but its actions to date have not put this in process. The decision is still firmly one for the central government to make without pressures from internal social and economic forces to compel regime transformation.

REFERENCES

Ahn, Choong-yong, Nicholas Eberstadt and Lee Young-sun (2004), 'Introduction and Overview', in: Ahn Choong-yong, Nicholas Eberstadt and Lee Young-sun (eds), *A New International Engagement Framework for North Korea? Contending Perspectives,* Washington DC: Korea Economic Institute, pp. 3-14

Åslund, Anders (2004), 'Prospects and Preconditions for Market Economic Transformation in North Korea', in: Ahn Choong-yong, Nicholas Eberstadt and Lee Young-sun (eds), *A New International Engagement Framework for North Korea? Contending Perspectives*, Washington DC: Korea Economic Institute, pp. 175-95

Carlin, Robert, and Joel Wit (2006), *North Korean Reform*, Adelphi Papers 382, London: International Institute for Strategic Studies

Choi, Soo-young (2005), 'Changing Aspects of the North Korean Economy Following the July 1, 2002 Measures', in: *Vantage Point*, 28 (7), pp. 44-54

CIA World Factbook (2007), 'Korea, North: Economy'. Online: http://www.cia.gov/library/publications/the-world-factbook/geos/kn.html#Econ (accessed 1 December 2007)

de Soto, Hernando (2000), *The Mystery of Capital: Why Capitalism Triumphs in the West and Fails Everywhere Else*, New York: Basic Book

Eberstadt, Nicholas (2004), 'North Korea's Survival Game: Understanding the Recent Past, Thinking about the Future', in: Ahn Choong-yong, Nicholas Eberstadt and Lee Young-sun (eds), *A New International Engagement Framework for North Korea? Contending Perspectives*, Washington DC: Korea Economic Institute, pp. 63-88

Fifield, Anna, and Richard McGregor (2007), 'China Halts Rail Freight to North Korea', in: *Financial Times*, 19 October 2007, p. 4

Frank, Ruediger (2005), 'Economic Reforms in North Korea (1998-2004): Systemic Restrictions, Quantitative Analysis, Ideological Background', in: *Journal of the Asia Pacific Economy*, 10 (3), pp. 278- 311

Hellman, Joel (1998), 'Winners Take All: The Politics of Partial Reform in Postcommunist Transitions', in: *World Politics*, 50 (2), pp. 203-34

Kim, Il-gi (2007), 'The Substance and Characteristics of Reform and Opening-up in North Korea', in: *Vantage Point*, 30 (4), pp. 42-53

Kim, Sung-chull (2003), 'Fluctuating Institutions of Economic Management in North Korea: Prospects for Local Enterprise Reform', in: *Journal of Communist Studies and Transition Politics*, 19 (1), pp. 10-34

Kim, Young-yoon (2006), 'North Korea's Economy in Fourth Year of the July 1 Reform Measures: Evaluation and Prospects', in: *Vantage Point*, 29 (10), pp. 48-59

Kim, Young-yoon and Soo-young Choi (2005), *Understanding North Korea's Economic Reforms*, Seoul: Center for the North Korean Economy, Korea Institute for National Unification

Kornai, János (1992), *The Socialist System: The Political Economy of Communism*, Princeton, NJ: Princeton University Press

Kornai, János (1995), *Highways and Byways: Studies on Reform and Post-Communist Transition*, Cambridge MA: MIT Press

Kwon, Young-kyong (2006), 'An Analysis of Trends in North Korea's Economic Reform in Recent Years', in: *Vantage Point*, 29 (2), pp. 44-55

Lee, Young-sun and Yoon Deok-ryong (2004), 'The Structure of North Korea's Political Economy: Change and Effects', in: Ahn Choong-yong, Nicholas Eberstadt and Lee Young-sun (eds), *A New International Engagement Framework for*

North Korea? Contending Perspectives, Washington DC: Korea Economic Institute, pp. 45-61

Lim, Wonhyuk (2005), 'North Korea's Economic Futures: Internal and External Dimensions', Center for Northeast Asian Policy Studies Paper. Online: http://www.brookings.edu/fp/cnaps/events/lim_20051102.pdf (accessed 15 September 2006)

Michell, Anthony (1998), 'The Current North Korean Economy', in: Marcus Noland (ed.), *Economic Integration of the Korean Peninsula*, Washington DC: Institute for International Economics, pp. 137-63

Mun, Sung-min (2006), 'Changing Aspects of the International Financial System in North Korea', in: *Vantage Point*, 29 (3), pp. 43-55

Noland, Marcus (2000), *Avoiding the Apocalypse: The Future of the Two Koreas*, Washington DC: Institute for International Economics

Noland, Marcus (2003), *Korea After Kim Jong-Il*, Washington DC: Institute for International Economics

Seliger, Bernhard (2005), 'The July 2002 Reforms in North Korea: Liberman-Style Reforms of Road to Transformation?', in: *North Korean Review*, 1 (2), pp. 22-36

Seliger, Bernhard (2006), 'North Korea's Economy at a Crossroads', in: KEIA (ed.), *Korea's Economy 2006,* pp. 62-71. Online: http://www.keia.org/Publications/KoreasEconomy/2006/06Seliger.pdf (accessed 1 November 2006)

Snyder, Scott (2000), 'North Korea's Challenge of Regime Survival: Internal Problems and Implication for the Future', in: *Pacific Affairs*, 73 (4), pp. 517-33

Suh, Jae-jean (2005), 'Analysis of Changes in N. Korea after Economic Difficulties', in: *Vantage Point*, 28 (2), pp. 20-24

You, Xie Hi (2004), 'On the Prospects for Reforming and Opening Up North Korea', in: *Far Eastern Affairs*, 32 (2), pp. 102-07

TRENDS AND PROSPECTS OF INTER-KOREAN ECONOMIC CO-OPERATION

Kyung Tae Lee
Hyung-Gon Jeong[1]

ABSTRACT

During the nearly 20 years since 1989, the inter-Korean economic co-operation project has not only expanded in scale, but has also maintained itself through systems related to the project, in particular, the Kaesŏng Industrial Complex and Mt Kŭmgang tourism. However, many business companies are still sceptical about advancing into the North, citing problems such as the North's actions in restricting visits, ignorance of the market economy, lack of willingness to reform and open up, and lack of related infrastructure. Against that, the South-North summit talks held in 2007 were intended to settle many of these problems and provide an opportunity to expand inter-Korean economic co-operation. With these conditions in mind, five requirements need to be met for co-operation to progress effectively: there needs to be a premise for a settlement of the North Korean nuclear issue centring on the Six Party Talks; co-operation should progress strategically on the basis of an order of priorities centred on economic criteria; government initiative should be converted to private initiative; the notion of support should give way to one of co-operation; and progress should be phased in accordance with the principles of selection and concentration.

1 INTRODUCTION

With the Special Declaration for National Existence, Unification and Prosperity, the '7.7' or 7 July 1988 declaration,[2] the government of the

---

[1] The views expressed by both authors in this article represent their personal opinions and should not necessarily be taken as reflecting the views of the Korea International Trade Association or the Korea Institute for International Economic Policy.

[2] Declaration made by President Roh Tae-woo on 7 July 1988. Since the spring of that year, debates on the unification of North and South Korea had spread, centring on

Republic of Korea (ROK—South Korea) proclaimed it would 'break down barriers dividing the South and the North and carry out exchanges in all fields'. Inter-Korean economic co-operation development was to provide the foundation for carrying this out. The declaration announced a new era for the nation's existence and prosperity by virtue of achieving a social, cultural, economic and political community where all the national constituents should participate according to the principles of autonomy, peace, democracy and welfare. It suggested detailed programmes for the execution of such plans: firstly, opening doors for mutual exchanges between the South and the North and free visits between the two parts of the peninsula by those exiled from their homeland; secondly, exchange of letters between dispersed families and strong support for mutual visits; thirdly, an opening for inter-Korean trade; fourthly, approval of trade in non-military commodities between the ROK's allies and the Democratic People's Republic of Korea (DPRK—North Korea); fifthly, forgoing attritional and confrontational diplomacy in favour of mutual co-operation between the representatives of South and North; and sixthly, improvement of relations between the North and the ROK's allies on the one hand, and between the socialist nations and South Korea on the other hand. Consequently, for the first time trade between the South and the North was actualised to show US$18 million in 1989. Thereafter, with the announcement of 'revitalizing measures for inter-Korean economic cooperation'[3] declared in November 1994, a new turning point was reached, and the Mutual Declaration of 15 June 2000 created a

citizens' groups and student associations. Moreover, President Roh announced a 'six-stage North Korean policy', incorporating an open-door policy towards the DPRK, China, and Russia. At the same time, the movement for unification was becoming more heated as insistence on '6-10 South and North Student Association talks' caused collisions between students and the police force. Roh's announcement catalysed the South-North dialogue, led to preliminary talks for South-North National Assembly talks and South-North high-level talks and initiated promotion of the Northern Policy, which advocated forming economic exchanges and friendly relations with the socialist bloc.

[3] After the Geneva agreement in October 1994 on an Agreed Framework between the DPRK and the United States (US), the North's nuclear issue was for the time being resolved. In November of that same year, the ROK government announced operations for revitalisation of North and South economic co-operation with the aim of encouraging such co-operation. The actions envisaged mainly involved, firstly, the approval of mutual visits by North and South business representatives, such as a South Korean businessmen's visit to the North; secondly, the approval of provision of equipment supplies for processing brought-in materials and visits by South Korean technicians to the North; and thirdly, the demonstration of economic co-operation projects by way of showing an example.

momentum for widening and revitalising inter-Korean economic activity on a full scale. Economic activity has exhibited both qualitative and quantitative results for the most part, but there are as well a number of problems to solve for improvement of the co-operative environment. This investigation seeks to analyse the results and problems in economic co-operation up to the present and to suggest plans for revitalising this co-operation in the future.

2 Trends in Inter-Korean Economic Co-operation

2.1 *Trade*

From 1991 to late 2007, trade between the ROK and the DPRK totalled US$9.16 billion. In the year 2007, it amounted to US$1.798 billion. The volume of trade increased by approximately 16 times since 1991, when it stood at US$111 million (T'ongilbu 2008a) (see Figure 1). In addition, the number of trade items increased 14.9 times from 57 to 853 and the number of businesses increased 7.6 times from 56 to 425 (see Figure 2). Trade between South and North Korea increased at an annual average of 25.5 percent over the five years from 2003 to 2007. In particular, over the same period exports from South to North Korea increased at an annual average of 24.1 percent and imports from North to South Korea increased at an annual average of 27.5 percent (Han'guk Muyŏk Hyŏphoe 2008). South Korea has become the North's second trade partner, with the South occupying 37.8 percent of North Korea's foreign trade at the end of 2007 as the trade between South and North Korea has increased (Han'guk Muyŏk T'uja Chinhŭng Kongsa 2008). China, being North Korea's first trade partner, occupied 41.7 percent of North Korea's foreign trade at the end of 2007.

The trade between South and North Korea shows an expansion quantitatively after the summit talks in June 2000. However, qualitatively speaking, the trade between the two still shows some weaknesses, such as a preponderance of imports. Still, 'non-transactional trade', involving such support items as food loans and fertiliser and goods for joint business like equipment and railroad materials, occupies a large share in transactions. The 'true transactional trade' is more in the form of imports from the North than exports to the North. Im-port items are mostly agricultural, forestry and marine products, with textiles from brought-in materials processed on commission occupying 70 to 80 percent (Han'guk Muyŏk Hyŏphoe 2008).

Figure 1 Size of trade

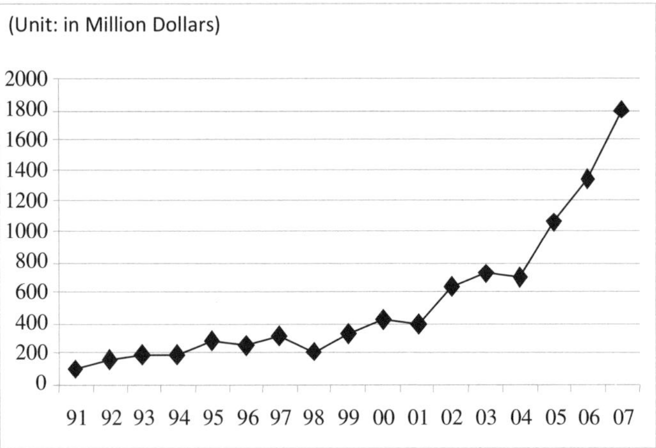

Source: Ministry of Unification (2008), *Annual Trends in Trade between South and North Korea,* Seoul: MOU.

Figure 2 Trade enterprise & items

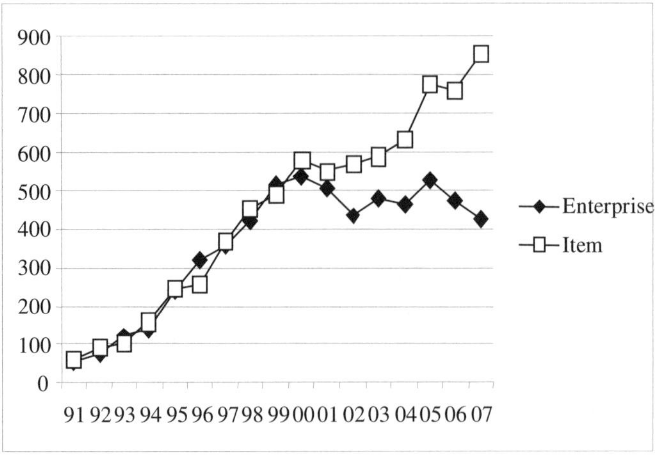

Source: Ministry of Unification (2008), *Annual Trends in Trade between South and North Korea,* Seoul: MOU.

Table 1 Changes in volume of imports and exports (Units: in thousand US dollars, %)

	2000	2001	2002	2003	2004	2005	2006	2007
Imports	152,373 (49.4)	176,170 (25.3)	271,575 (54.2)	289,252 (6.5)	258,039 (-10.8)	340,281 (31.9)	519,539 (52.6)	765,346 (47.3)
Exports	272,775 (28.8)	226,787 (-16.9)	370,155 (63.2)	434,965 (17.5)	439,001 (0.9)	715,472 (63.0)	830,200 (16.0)	1,032,550 (24.3)
Total	425,148 (27.5)	402,957 (-5.2)	641,730 (59.3)	724,217 (12.9)	697,040 (-3.8)	1,055,753 (51.5)	1,349,739 (27.8)	1,797,896 (33.2)
Revenue & expenditure	120,402	50,617	98,580	145,713	180,962	375,191	310,661	267,204

Note: ( ) indicates the rate of increase compared to previous year.
Source: Korea International Trade Association (2008), *Trends in trade between South and North Korea for year 2007*, Seoul: KITA.

Table 2 Changes in scales of trade for commercial and non-commercial businesses (Units: in million US dollars, %)

	2000	2001	2002	2003	2004	2005	2006	2007
Commercial transactions	256 (60)	244 (61)	355 (55)	425 (59)	437 (63)	690 (65)	928 (68)	1,431 (80)
Non-commercial transactions	169 (40)	159 (39)	287 (45)	299 (41)	260 (37)	366 (35)	421 (32)	366 (20)
Total	425 (100)	403 (100)	642 (100)	724 (100)	697 (100)	1,056 (100)	1,349 (100)	1,797 (100)

Note: ( ) indicates the weighting in the amount of trade between South and North Korea.
Source: Korea International Trade Association (2008), *Trends in trade between South and North Korea for year 2007*, Seoul: KITA.

As shown in Table 2, commercial transactions occupied 80 percent of trade in 2007, which is the highest record since the 2000s. Joint businesses such as general trade and processing of brought-in materials increased their share in commercial trade, and the one-sided trade is diminishing. Table 3 shows that Kaesŏng Industrial Complex is becoming significant in commercial transactions in South-North trade.

Table 3 Trends in commercial transactions by type (Unit: in million US dollars)

	2000	2001	2002	2003	2004	2005	2006	2007
General trade	111	111	171	223	171	210	341	461
Trade in processing on commission	129	125	171	185	176	210	253	329
Kaesŏng Industrial Complex	0	0	0	0	42	177	299	440
Others	16	8	13	17	48	93	35	201
Total	256	244	355	425	437	690	928	1,431

Source: Korea International Trade Association (2008), *Trends in trade between South and North Korea for year 2007*, Seoul: KITA.

Following the recovery in the relationship between the two parties in 2005 and after the North's return to the Six Party Talks in late October 2006, trade between South and North Korea showed an increasing rate (reflected in the above tables), as both South and North approached trade from a materialistic point of view and looked to an increase in exports as a means of supporting the recovering relationship. Both parties co-operated not only through their practical decision to deal separately with the nuclear issue and political and military issues, but also by expanding support through fertilisers .

Commercial trade shows a high increasing rate, with growth consequent upon the development of the Kaesŏng Industrial Complex and an expansion in Mt Kŭmgang tourism. The Kaesŏng Industrial Complex construction project agreed upon during the Kim Dae-jung administration started work in June 2003 and reached its model stage in June 2004. In May 2007, the first stage of the main complex was completed and as of March 2008, approximately 25,000 North Korean workers are working in 65 businesses. The complex's accumulated yield amounts to US$201 million (T'ongilbu 2008b). Mt Kŭmgang tourism began to stabilise with the opening of overland tourism in September 2003, and by September 2007 a total of 1.6 million tourists had visited after the opening of the Inner Kŭmgang route in May

2007. After the establishment of the road connection in December 2005 and the operation of the showcase railway in May 2007, a daily average of approximately 1,700 people and 360 vehicles have been going through the border (Ministry of Unification 2007).

Nonetheless, trade is still weak between the two parties, despite an increase and a movement towards overall systematisation in economic co-operation. It is expected that such systematisation will settle the uncertainty surrounding investment in North Korea through the inter-Korean summit and prime ministerial meetings. However, the speed of any improvement is something to watch, since a new government has been established in the South and the North Korean nuclear issue is at a deadlock.

2.2 *Investment*

South Korean business interest in direct investment on North Korea was expressed in a total of 109 cases (T'ongilbu 2007a) from the year 1994 to April 2007, but actual investment in process merely involved ten businesses such as Pyongwha Automobile Corporation, Green Cross, Taechang, Woori Bank and Kukyang Marine Corporation. (Business related to Mt Kŭmgang tourism and the Kaesŏng Industrial Complex is excluded from these figures.) The main investment businesses like Hyundai Asan invested US$303.16 million, Pyonghwa invested US$56.54 million, Taechang US$9.8 million, and Woori Bank US$5 million. Investment in North Korea increased with the initiation of measures for the revitalisation of economic co-operation in 1994 and 1998. In particular, the number of investment approvals grew rapidly after movement on the development of the Kaesŏng Industrial Complex (T'ongilbu 2007b).

3 Issues in Inter-Korean Economic Co-operation

3.1 *Political aspects*

South Korea's economic co-operation with the North has so far proceeded without any systematic and strategic models to guide it. Co-operation has been partly preceded by North Korea's unilateral demands. There is, therefore, a strategic need to lead inter-Korean economic co-operation through a systematic formation, with the process for unification or for North Korea's economic development kept in mind. In particular, even though it may take some time, the South needs to show a strategic position that counter-moves strongly on North Korea's excessive demands, in order to establish an orderly form of co-operation.

In addition, since South Korean governmental support presently lacks guidance on the advance of business into the North, there are many companies that move forward with business with the North with vague expectations and without understanding the reality of the economic co-operation between the two parties. Businesses wishing to enter the North Korean market need sufficient information on entry into that market, but the South Korean government fails to offer a support system to provide the information. There have been cases where companies fell by the way through meeting with inappropriate brokers. It is necessary, therefore, for the government to establish organisations that can provide various services to businesses wishing to enter the North Korean market, such as making sufficient information available.

Moreover, the South Korean government's interest in businesses wishing to enter markets in areas such as Pyongyang and Namp'o is negligible, while most of its attention is directed towards developments in the Kaesŏng Industrial Complex and Mt Kŭmgang tourism. So far as regulations regarding inter-Korean co-operation are concerned, the required documents for South Koreans to register for approval of contact with North Koreans are complex and demand a lengthy period of time (15 days). In particular, the North insists on submission of an invitation when registering for approval for a visit to the North, a procedure that takes from two weeks to two months.

3.2 *Issues related to South Korean business*

Cases have arisen where South Korean companies have invested in the North in a haphazard manner without considering the conditions for undertaking business within North Korea and the ability to provide sufficient funds. A typical example is the case of Daewoo Inc. (see box), which in January 1999 had to suspend its activity because of deepening financial difficulties created by North Korea's insistence on being sole operator of the business; this despite the company being the first to establish a North-South joint venture in Namp'o and investing US$5.12 million. Furthermore, there are cases where companies impair the trust between South and North and disturb the orderly flow of economic co-operation between the two parties by operating with inappropriate intentions, such as engaging in speculative business and morally suspect conduct involving 'forgery of country of origin'.

Daewoo Inc.'s investment in North Korea

After the settlement of US-DPRK negotiations regarding North Korea's nuclear programme in October 1994 and the South Korean government's loosening of controls, Kim Woo-choong, chairman of Daewoo Inc., visited Namp'o in January 1995 and made concrete agreements to establish a light industry plant. In May 1995, Daewoo received project approval from the Ministry of National Unification, and in April 1996, Minjok Sanŏp Ch'onghoesa [General Corporation] was established as a joint investment company between Daewoo Inc. and the North's Samch'ŏlli Ch'onghoesa. Minjok Sanŏp Ch'onghoesa was the first North-South joint investment company. The investment ratio was 50:50, with Daewoo investing a total of US$5.12 million in cash, and the North investing in land, building and the cost of labour during the time of preparation.

3.3 *North Korean issues*

As of present, the majority of problems regarding economic co-operation between the two parties lie on the North Korean side. First of all, the DPRK restricts visits by South Koreans to the North and contacts with North Korean people. In addition, the DPRK's lack of knowledge of international commercial transactions and the market economy and lack of will in reforming and opening its market has led to many errors in actual business proceedings with North Korea. Any reform and opening on the part of the North would give some guarantee for economic activities by South Korean businessmen through an understanding of the free economy system and from accepting international customs. This might mean that businessmen from the South would be able to visit business sites freely and that technicians might have assurances that they could stay for a certain period of time to maintain quality control. Furthermore, private companies with the capability to make independent decisions might appear in the North. Economic reform and opening on the part of the DPRK is thus a premise for the revitalisation of inter-Korean economic co-operation.

However, the actuality is that North Korea casts economic co-operation in a supporting role, not as the means for creating mutual gains, let alone reform and opening. This dependence on the South is an obstacle to improvement and growth in South-North economic co-operation. Stable and continuous business proceedings are further set back by delays in follow-up measures to provide a systematic framework, such as publication of a written agreement between the South and North. Initial investors, moreover, feel the burden of a lack of infrastructure in physical distribution, exacerbated by restrictions in overland transportation and a poor social overhead capital environment, and by high distribution costs. For these reasons, despite other advantages accruing from South-North economic co-operation, many capable companies are sceptical about entering the North Korean market, and activities for co-operation are being delayed through a stagnation in private sector investment.

4 Outlook for Inter-Korean Economic Co-operation and Requirements for the Future

4.1 *Outlook for economic co-operation*

After agreement in the second South-North summit talks in October 2007 on establishing various economic co-operation programmes, co-operation has benefited from the opportunity to revitalise itself. The second summit talks focused on the issues of transit, communication and customs clearance, which have been obstacles to economic co-operation between the two parties, and agreed to quickly complete the provision of an overall system of guarantees. These actions can be viewed as allowing economic co-operation to take a further step forward. Moreover, the two parties agreed to foster 'a special area for peaceful cooperation in the West Sea', which permits an opportunity for a virtuous circle of economy and peace to establish itself by approaching military issues such as the Northern Limit Line from the perspective of common economic interests. Against the background of such agreements, renovation and common use of the Kaesŏng-Sinŭiju railway and the Kaesŏng-Pyongyang expressway would make possible the provision of an infrastructure for inter-Korean economic co-operation and connections for inter-continental railways. In particular, an agreement to raise the level of contact at economic co-operation meetings from that of deputy minister to the level of minister, if fully executed, should enhance the scope and momentum of North-South co-operation in the future.

However, such signs of revitalisation after second summit meeting face a new situation with the administration of Lee Myung-bak, inaugurated in 2008. Lee's North Korea policy, entitled 'Denuclearisation, Reform and Opening, 3000', promises to help raise per capita income in the DPRK to US$3,000 only if the North decides to abandon its nuclear programme and open its market. However, since it is difficult for the North to commit to such action, the signs for future South-North economic co-operation do not seem favorable. Since the Lee Myung-bak administration is according higher priority to an international effort to resolve the nuclear crisis than the previous administration, there is a high possibility of a link being made between economic co-operation and resolution of the nuclear question. Future inter-Korean economic co-operation would seem, therefore, to depend on attitudes towards resolving the nuclear issue. Scepticism about success in this area is spreading, since the high expectations of solving the North's nuclear question after the 13 February 2007 agreement have diminished now that the situation is in deadlock a year after the agreement. Despite that, during the year following the agreement, the DPRK abandoned its nuclear facilities and made much progress in disabling them. Moreover, much of that disabling work had never been attempted but has now come into force. The trust between North Korea and the United States, established through negotiations to resolve the Banco Delta Asia issue is valued as an important asset in establishing future denuclearisation. However, even though the deadline for the second phase specified in the 3 October 2007 agreement has passed, a breakthrough of the stalemate has hardly been achieved, with the US and North Korea confronting each other over the uranium enrichment programme and North Korea's suspected co-operation with Syria. Attention to the North's nuclear programme is not at full pitch, since the Bush administration's term of office ends within the year, South Korea's new government is at the stage of seeking a direction for its North Korea policy, and China is focused on preparing for the Olympics. There is therefore a high possibility that South-North economic co-operation will make slow progress if this kind of situation continues, despite co-operation in various ventures agreed upon in the second South-North Korean summit talks.

4.2 *Requirements for economic co-operation*

4.2.1 *Improvement in security conditions*

It is difficult to guarantee the future relationship between South and North Korea, even though a wide and varied range of agreements emerged from the 2007 summit talks and succeeding talks. The problem lies in the variables existing outside the economy in the relationship between the two parties. The DPRK's nuclear programme is, in particular, the key element deciding the possibility of future success for inter-Korean co-operation. If denuclearisation progresses without any problems, the relationship between the two parties will also move forward as agreed upon. However, if the rate of denuclearisation is slower than expected or is ruptured, there is a possibility of a brake being put on that relationship. Since Lee Myung-bak's administration views resolution of the North Korean nuclear issue and the reform and opening of the North's economy as a premise for South-North co-operation, a link will certainly be made between the DPRK-US relationship and resolution of the nuclear crisis, and between the North's motivation for opening up and economic co-operation.

Summing up the present situation, there is a high possibility that inter-Korean economic co-operation will stay at its current level if there is no progress over the North Korean nuclear question. There is a need for a creative solution to overcome the present situation in order to improve the security situation on the Korean peninsula as well as economic co-operation, especially since there is no progress in the Six Party Talks. To change the situation, the ROK, the US and Japan need, first of all, to take the initiative and bring in North Korea to become part of the dialogue. It is very ineffective to wait, putting North Korea outside the talks. North Korea is at an advantage in that South Korea, the US and Japan have time constraints which the North, not bound by the requirements of an elective, presidential system, does not. Moreover, the three countries may find themselves pressured to hurry for internal political reasons if North Korea carries another unexpected act such as the previous nuclear test, to attract attention. The best policy and solution for the present situation is to improve the atmosphere for North Korean economic co-operation and to continue to work to remove nuclear temptations for the DPRK of any kind.

4.2.2 *Systematic approach to South-North economic co-operation*

First of all, there is a need to stick to a systematic and strategic approach to inter-Korean economic co-operation. The business activities agreed upon in the 2007 summit talks are mostly ideas for economic co-operation that the ROK government had planned for a long time. This indicates that, unlike the co-operation between the two parties in the past, this is an agreement led by the South. However, there is no order of priority and in some instances the question arises whether the agreed-upon volume of business can be realised. There is, therefore, a need to consider the order of priority for those factors it is possible to realise at the present stage and to check the overall agreement. There is a need to decide on a reasonable business scale by rationally analysing the surrounding factors of the South-North relationship, such as a rapid improvement in relations between the DPRK and the US, and by evaluating the project feasibility, economic feasibility, and possibility for resource mobilisation of each business. Furthermore, it is necessary to separate privately promoted projects from government-promoted projects by the nature of the business, and when the government needs to take part in the process, it must decide whether it will be a formal loan or gratuitous aid. In the case of gratuitous aid, the government needs to seek what kind of return service it will ask of the North.

4.2.3 *A turnabout in economic sense*

South-North economic co-operation needs to switch to an economic mode. In the past when the two parties faced political conflicts, co-operation acted as a tool to alleviate the tension between the two. However, the relationship between the two parties has now developed tremendously, so there need not be a political and military restraint on the improvement in economic relations between the two. In the past, with economic co-operative business activities promoted through political negotiations, the authorities in the North revealed their dependence on the South by viewing economic co-operation as a form of support rather than a tool for mutual profit creation. Such an attitude acts as a big obstacle to quality improvement and growth in co-operation. Therefore, even though it takes time to negotiate with the North, the South needs to show a strategic attitude that logically counter-moves on the North's excessive demands in order to establish an orderly economic co-operation built on 'economic sense'. Even investment in the North should first consider the possibility of retrieval. In other words, the government should place public funds in businesses with a potential for returns that are having difficulties with early, large-scale input, so that they can gradually retrieve the investment.

4.2.4 *A turnabout from government initiative to private initiative*

The ROK government's role is to develop an environment and infrastructure for economic co-operation and to focus on leading open competition regarding co-operation between the two parties. The government should also exclude excessive support and initiate support for companies high in public character, while other individual businesses should be supported by non-governmental initiatives. The reality is that companies participating in economic co-operation are depending too much on funds earmarked for such co-operation, and individual businesses that are planning to enter the arena are demanding economic co-operation support funds for basic facilities. The funds for economic co-operation are thought of as a free lunch by South Korean companies and the DPRK authorities alike. The South Korean government needs to seek an appropriate economic co-operation policy to change such perceptions. Investment should now be based on the high possibility of growth and economic validity. Therefore, businesses investing in the North should consider their own risk-bearing factors and stick to the principles of the market economy. The government, moreover, should where possible support projects related to infrastructure-building but otherwise pass projects to private businesses, suggesting principles and conditions in clear terms.

4.2.5 *A switch of concept from support to co-operation*

North Korea should no longer be thought of as a subject for unification, but as a partner with which South Korea can develop and live together through co-operation. As economic co-operation development proceeds, the government applies the principle of common prosperity and life, but this is based more on the construction of infrastructure and a systematic approach to changing and developing the North's economy for unification, rather than purely on a co-operative relationship. Since co-operation is maturing in quality, it should work solely for the mutual gain of the two parties and exclude any other special understanding. It should be approached by the avenue of mutual gain instead of unilateral support and should establish a systematic approach by building an economically effective division of labour between the South and the North.

4.2.6 *Promotion of economic co-operation on principles of selection and focus*

The economic co-operation project between the two parties should proceed with a strategy of selection, focus and expansion in the interests of efficiency. First of all, the selection of which companies should engage with the North should be examined with consideration of the ripple effect on the South's economy and the effect on development for the North's economy. The process should work in phases, following an order of priority already decided upon and with the effect on already existing businesses and mutual connections taken into consideration. Proceedings should aim to build a cluster by considering a given industry's links with the South's industry, and direct the selection and focus of economic co-operation projects towards the support of necessary social overhead capital. Moreover, the government should focus its support for promising businesses and areas already selected by expanding and exploiting the creation of an industrial base and collaborative strength. Even in the case of China, the developmental strategy has been to expand through developing areas centred on the east coast, with the western part of China still remaining in the backward area of the country. Following such principles, it would be appropriate for the North to expand in areas from Sinŭiju to Hamhŭng and from Wŏnsan to Ch'ŏngjin and Rajin, while co-operation is centred upon Pyongyang, Namp'o, Kaesŏng and Mt Kŭmgang. The west coast and the Hamhŭng area are light industry areas and can be developed for small- and medium-sized businesses, while Ch'ŏngjin and Wŏnsan are heavy chemical and manufacturing industry areas and can be developed for large-sized businesses. It is thus necessary to ensure the development of light industry on the western seaboard and heavy chemical industry on the eastern.

References

Han'guk Muyŏk Hyŏphoe [Korea International Trade Association] (2008), *2007 nyŏn nambuk kyoyŏk tonghyang* [Trends in trade between South and North Korea for year 2007], Seoul: KITA

Han'guk Muyŏk T'uja Chinhŭng Kongsa [Korea Trade Investment Promotion Agency] (2008), *2007 nyŏn pukhanŭi taewoe muyŏk tonghyang* [North Korean trends in foreign trade for year 2007], Seoul: KOTRA

T'ongilbu [Ministry of Unification] (2007a), *Wŏlgan nambuk kyoryu hyŏmnyŏk tonghyang, che 190 ho* [Trends in monthly inter-Korean exchange and co-operation, Report no. 190], Seoul: Ministry of Unification

T'ongilbu [Ministry of Unification] (2007b), *Wŏlgan nambuk kyoryu hyŏmnyŏk tonghyang, che 198 ho* [Trends in monthly inter-Korean exchange and co-operation, Report no. 198], Seoul: Ministry of Unification

Ministry of Unification (2007), *2007 South-North Korean Summit and inter-Korean Economic Cooperation*, Seoul: Ministry of Unification

T'ongilbu [Ministry of Unification] (2008a), *Nambuk kyŏngje hyŏmnyŏk tonghyang* [Trends in inter-Korean economic co-operation], Seoul: Ministry of Unification

T'ongilbu [Ministry of Unification] (2008b), *Kaesŏng kongdan saengsanaek mit' pukhan kŭlloja hyŏnhwang, t'ongilbu homp'eiji t'onggye* [Status of turnout and North Korean labourers in Kaesŏng Industrial Complex, Statistics from the Ministry of Unification]. Online: www.unikorea.go.kr

ABOUT THE AUTHORS AND EDITORS

Rüdiger Frank
is Professor of East Asian Economy and Society at the University of Vienna. He holds a M.A. in Korean Studies, Economics and International Relations from Humboldt University of Berlin and a Ph.D. in Economics from Mercator University Duisburg. He held Visiting Professorships at Columbia University New York and Korea University Seoul. He is a Council member of the Association for Korean Studies in Europe, Vice Speaker of the Vienna School of Governance, founding member of the Europe-Asia Working Group of the European Association of Development Research and Training Institutes. His first five-month visit to North Korea took place in 1991. His major research fields are socialist transformation in Asia and Europe (with a focus on North Korea) and state-business relations (with a focus on South Korea). See www.koreanstudies.de/frank.
Email: ruediger.frank@univie.ac.at

James E. Hoare
Ph.D., retired from the British Diplomatic Service in 2003. His last appointment was as British Chargé d'Affaires and Consul General in Pyongyang. He now writes and broadcasts about East Asia. Among his recent publications are *A Political and Economic Dictionary of East Asia* (Routledge, 2005) and *North Korea in the 21st Century: An Interpretative Guide* (Global Oriental 2005), both written with his wife, Susan Pares. He is a Research Associate of the School of Oriental and African Studies, London, and Consultant on Security in East Asia, David Davies Memorial Institute of International Studies, Aberystwyth. He lives in London.
Email: jim@jhoare10.fsnet.co.uk

Hyung-Gon Jeong
is currently research fellow at the Center for Northeast Asian Economic Cooperation of the Korea Institute for International Economic Policy (KIEP). He was director-general of the Office of Policy Co-

ordination of the National Security Council in the Office of the President, July-December 2005, and director-general of the Office of Strategy Planning of the National Security Council in the Office of the President, June 2003-June 2005. He has also served as an adjunct professor of economics at Yonsei University, Seoul. Dr Jeong received his Ph.D. in economics at the University of Cologne, Germany. He is the author of 'The Determinants of Economic Growth of Transition Economics: Economic Reform vs. Initial Conditions' (*International Economic Journal*, 20 (2), June 2006) and *From East Asian FTAs to an EAFTA* (2006).
Email: hgjeong@kiep.go.kr

Youngmi Kim
holds a Ph.D. in Politics, is a Leverhulme Trust Early Career Fellow at the University of Edinburgh, UK, and also lectures at University College Dublin, Ireland. She completed her Ph.D. on 'Minority coalition government and governability in South Korea: The case of the Kim Dae-jung administration (1998-2003)' at the University of Sheffield in 2007. Her publications include 'Explaining minority coalition government and governability in South Korea: A review essay' (*Korea Observer*, 39 (1), 2008) and 'Coalition theories and the dynamics of coalition party politics in Japan and Korea' (*Papers of the British Association for Korean Studies*, 10, 2005).
Email: youngmi.kim@ed.ac.uk

Patrick Köllner
is Acting Director of the Institute of Asian Studies, GIGA German Institute of Global and Area Studies. He holds a Ph.D. and a Habilitation in political science. Between 1996 and 2006 he was sole editor of the German-language Korea Yearbook. His research focuses on Japanese and Korean politics and political parties more generally. Recent publications include a country study on South and North Korea (*Südkorea und Nordkorea*, co-edited with Thomas Kern, Campus 2005), a comparative volume on factionalism in political parties (*Innerparteiliche Machtgruppen*, co-edited with Matthias Basedau and Gero Erdmann, Campus 2006), and a monograph on the organisation of Japanese political parties (*Die Organisation japanischer Parteien*, GIGA Institute of Asian Studies 2006).
Email: koellner@giga-hamburg.de

Kyung Tae Lee
is currently president of the Korea International Trade Association (KITA) and was president of the Korea Institute for International Economic Policy (KIEP) between 2005 and 2008. He was ambassador of the Permanent Delegation of the ROK to the OECD, 2001-04, and chair of the APEC Economic Committee, 2005-06. Lee obtained a Ph.D. degree in economics at George Washington University in 1983, and is the author of *Is APEC Moving Towards the Bogor Goal?* (2001), *China's Integration with the World Economy: Repercussions of China's Accession to the WTO* (2001), *Korea's Foreign Trade Strategy in the New Millennium* (2003), and *Korea's Economic Strategy in the Globalization Era* (2003).
Email: ktlee123@kita.net

Alon Levkowitz
Ph.D., was a visiting scholar at the Institute of Asian Research, University of British Columbia, until July 2008. He teaches East Asian International Relations at Hebrew University of Jerusalem and Tel Aviv University. His research focuses on Korean security and international relations. His articles have appeared in *Defense and Peace Economics*, *Harvard Asia Quarterly*, *International Relations of the Asia-Pacific*, *Iran Pulse*, and *North Korean Review*.
Email: levko@smile.net.il

Peter Mayer
is Professor for International Economics at the University of Applied Sciences in Osnabrück/Germany. After receiving his doctorate degree from Johann-Wolfgang Goethe University in Frankfurt, he worked for a German non-governmental organisation in Ghana and South Korea. He served for four years as Vice-President for International Affairs of the University of Applied Sciences Osnabrück. He is a member of the accreditation committee for private universities of the German Science Council, and is in charge of a training programme for deans from Asia and Africa run by the German Academic Exchange Service and the German Rectors' Conference. His research interests are higher education management and quality management in higher education. He has published a number of articles about economic transformation in South Korea and higher education management.
Email: mayer@wi.fh-osnabrueck.de

Patrick McEachern
is a Foreign Service Officer and doctoral candidate in Political Science at Louisiana State University. He was an analyst in the Northeast Asia Division of the State Department's Bureau of Intelligence and Research from 2005 to 2006, focusing on North Korea. His publications include 'Interest Groups in North Korean Politics', *Journal of East Asian Studies* 8 (2), 2008, and 'North Korea's Policy Process: Assessing Institutional Preferences', forthcoming in *Asian Survey*. He is now researching a dissertation tentatively entitled 'Inside the Red Box: Understanding North Korea's Policy Process'.
Email: pmceac1@lsu.edu

Mark Morris
Ph.D., is University Lecturer in Japanese Cultural History at the University of Cambridge and a Fellow of Trinity College. His main teaching and research interests concern Japanese modern fiction and film, and Korean film. Work in progress includes a study of South and North Korean film which locates films and film genres in their social and historical contexts and also in a more general, comparative film-historical context.
Email: mrm1000@cam.ac.uk

Susan Pares
has worked in Research Department of the Foreign and Commonwealth Office and, since 1987, as an editor and writer in East Asian subjects. She edited *Asian Affairs*, 1997-2001, and between 2000 and 2007 the *Papers of the British Association for Korean Studies*. She served in the British Embassy in Beijing, 1975-76 and accompanied her husband, James Hoare, on postings to Seoul (1981-85), Beijing (1988-91) and Pyongyang (2001-02). They are co-authors of several books dealing with East Asian and specifically Korean affairs. The most recent is *North Korea in the 21st Century: An Interpretative Guide* (Global Oriental 2005).
Email: spares@myway.com

C. Kenneth Quinones
is currently Dean for Research Evaluation and Professor of Korean Studies at Akita International University in Japan. After retiring from the U.S. Foreign Service in 1997, he arranged US-North Korea educational and agricultural exchanges for US NGOs. Since 2001 he

has concentrated on writing and commenting about US relations with Northeast Asia, particularly the Korean Peninsula. Since 2000 he has published three books: *The North Korea Nuclear Crisis – Off the Record Memories* (translated into Korean and Japanese in 2000), *Beyond Diplomacy: Implementation of the Agreed Framework* (published in Japanese in 2003), and *The Complete Idiot's Guide to Understanding North Korea* (published in English by Penguin Publishers' Alpha Books in 2004). Dr. Quinones holds a Ph.D. in History and East Asian Languages from Harvard University.
Email: ckquinones@aiu.ac.jp

John Swenson-Wright
received an MA in International Relations from Johns Hopkins University and a D.Phil. in International Relations from St Antony's College, University of Oxford. He is Senior Lecturer in Modern Japanese Studies (Politics and International Relations) at the Faculty of Asian and Middle Eastern Studies, University of Cambridge, and fellow of Darwin College, Cambridge. He is the author of *Unequal Allies?: United States Security and Alliance Policy Toward Japan, 1945-1960* (2005), an edited translation of the memoirs of Wakaizumi Kei, *The Best Course Available* (2002), dealing with the post-1945 reversion of Okinawa to Japan, and recently has published, together with Andrew Bell and Karin Tyberg, *Evidence* (2008), an edited series of articles from the Darwin lecture series. He is an Associate Fellow at The Royal Institute of International Affairs (Chatham House), where he convenes a regular discussion group on contemporary Korea. He is currently working on a monograph on Japan's 20th and 21st century relations with the Korean peninsula.
Email: jhs22@cam.ac.uk

MAP OF THE KOREAN PENINSULA

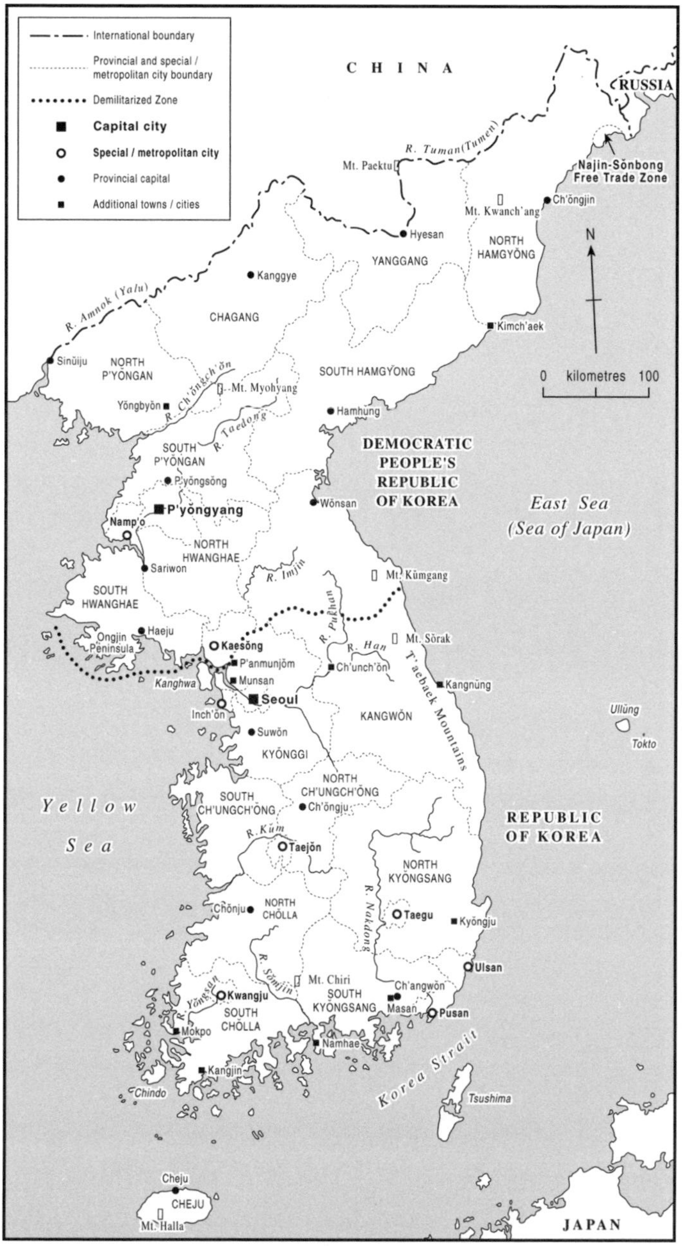

Design and Imaging Unit, Durham University.